A Traveller's History of London

To Katrine Prince, Helen Tozer, Lindsay Macleod,
Philip Gelling, John Makey and to the members of
'The Blue Badge' Guides Course of 1990–91

THE AUTHOR   Richard Tames read history at Cambridge and took his Master's degree at the University of London, where he worked for over 15 years and was three times a Teacher Fellow. He now lectures for the London programmes of Syracuse University and the American University and is a London Tourist Board registered 'Blue Badge' guide. He is the author of *American Walks in London, Bloomsbury Past, Soho Past, The City of London Past, Clerkenwell & Finsbury Past, Earl's Court & Brompton Past* and *Southwark Past.*

SERIES EDITOR   Professor Denis Judd is a graduate of Oxford, a Fellow of the Royal Historical Society and Professor of History at the University of North London. He has published over 20 books including the biographies of Joseph Chamberlain, Prince Philip, George VI and Alison Uttley, historical and military subjects, stories for children and two novels. His most recent book is the highly praised *Empire: The British Imperial Experience from 1765 to the Present.* He has reviewed and written extensively in the national press and in journals and is an advisor to the BBC *History* Magazine.

Other Titles in the Series

Some critical comment on The Traveller's Histories

'Ideal before-you-go reading'
The Daily Telegraph

'An excellent series of brief histories'
New York Times

REVIEWS OF INDIVIDUAL TITLES

A TRAVELLER'S HISTORY OF JAPAN

'It succeeds admirably in its goal of making the present country comprehensible through a narrative of the past, with asides on everything from bonsai to zazen, in a brisk, highly readable style ... you could read it on the flight over, if you skip the movie.'
The Washington Post

A TRAVELLER'S HISTORY OF FRANCE

'Undoubtedly the best way to prepare for a trip to France is to bone up on some history. *The Traveller's History of France* by Robert Cole is concise and gives the essential facts in a very readable form.'
The Independent

A TRAVELLER'S HISTORY OF CHINA

'The author manages to get 2 million years into 300 pages. An excellent addition to a series which is already invaluable, whether you are travelling or not.'
The Guardian

A TRAVELLER'S HISTORY OF INDIA

'For anyone ... planning a trip to India, the latest in the excellent *Traveller's History* series ... provides a useful grounding for those whose curiosity exceeds the time available for research.'
The London Evening Standard

A TRAVELLER'S HISTORY OF ITALY

'If you can't tell your Asti from your Alba *A Traveller's History of Italy* makes ideal reading, putting names and places ... into proper perspective'
The Daily Telegraph

A Traveller's History of London

FOURTH EDITION

RICHARD TAMES

Series Editor   DENIS JUDD
Line Drawings   JOHN HOSTE

CASSELL&CO
A WINDRUSH PRESS BOOK

Contents

Preface

This is the best book that I have so far read on London. It is comprehensive, intelligent, informative, well structured, beautifully written and, above all, extremely useful. Not merely will visitors to the capital find it an indispensible aid in discovering the city, with all its varied and complex pleasures, but I suspect that the great majority of Londoners would benefit enormously from reading it too.

London has great potency both as a symbol and as a physical entity. All over the world the word has resonance and meaning. The symbolism is predictably diverse. The name can conjure up images of stately, splendid, often royal, ceremonial: the changing of the guard, the trooping of the colour, visits of heads of overseas governments, as well as the occasional coronation and funeral procession. London is, above all, a capital city. Once it stood for an Empire which comprised a quarter of the human race; now, rather like Vienna, it is a great heart beating within a shrunken body politic. London still equals power and wealth and privilege, and is as much resented as admired for these perceived qualities. Britain's other capital cities, Edinburgh and Cardiff, see themselves as rivals; uncrowned provincial capitals, Manchester, Leeds, Birmingham, Bristol and the rest, emphasise their civic and cultural accomplishments in London's shadow. London is where it all 'happens'. Its air of easy superiority provokes irritation and a sense of inadequacy in equal measure.

For all of these reasons, London, and Londoners, are the recipients of some dislike. Marauding Northern football fans, 'Up for the Cup', abuse both its thoroughfares and its citizenry; on days like these the streets of London are paved with empty lager cans rather than with gold. For some years the supporters of Scotland's international football team were denied tickets to the biannual encounter with the team of the 'auld enemy' at Wembley on account of the havoc they created. North of Watford, Londoners are often written off as cold, unneighbourly, snobbish individuals, typified by the 'yuppie' with his (or her) filofax and Thatcherite tendencies. At the root of this discord is, inevitably a brew of envy, a history of provincial dispossession, the class system, and a tangle of myth and reality.

For the foreign visitor, London can seem too large, too difficult to know, let alone love. It is the biggest conurbation in Europe, and its size is daunting. To feed the pigeons in Trafalgar Square is one thing, to appreciate the difference between Southall and Sydenham, Willesden and Wandsworth, Chelsea and Catford is another thing altogether. Even if one is told that London is merely a collection of 'villages', the distance between them can seem enormous, rather like venturing into the urban equivalent of the Russian steppes. Moreover, the 'natives', though invariably friendly when asked for directions, have little skill with foreign languages, and the local, Cockney dialect may prove to be an impenetrable verbal thicket.

But London is also one of the most wonderful cities in the world. Its history alone would repay a lifetime of study and appreciation, from Roman Londinium, to the Jewish East End and the heroic soaking up of unprecedented nightly punishment during the Blitz of World War Two. Because, with very rare exceptions, systematic town planning has never been a British forte, you can also stumble upon ravishing architectural or semi-rural beauty merely by walking round a corner. The variety of visual treats that London can offer is matched by the astounding range of cultural experiences that are there for the taking. From the Royal Shakespeare Company's performances at the Barbican to the buskers of Covent Garden, from the classical music of the Festival Hall to the light comedies of the West End theatres, the visitor, given only a reasonable amount of stamina and cash, can gorge on a city culture unsurpassed in the rest of the world.

Above all, London is a generous city: generous in size and space and in its philosophy. It has been a haven, over the centuries, for refugees and exiles of all sorts. In this sense it has been the final bastion of freedom in countless causes. It is, therefore, essentially a tolerant city. Some areas of traditional immigrant settlement experience predictable displays of prejudice, but the visitor will be left alone to wander wherever he or she wishes. Even political passions seem muted in the capital: violent demonstrations are almost unknown, and, at the height of the Cold War, Karl Marx lay tranquilly at rest in Highgate cemetery, his grave unmolested. Modern feminist writers have also remarked on the anonymous safety that women generally feel in London, compared, say, with New York and other more turbulent cities. The individual may feel lost in London, even lonely, but hardly ever unsafe.

The publication of this fine addition to the literature on London will only enhance the attractions and enduring appeal of one of the world's greatest monuments to human endeavour and achievement. Richard Tames's authoritative and fascinating book will enrich all who read it.

Denis Judd
London, 1992

The Lloyds' building

Clearing-House of the World

London is not, and never has been, an English city. London is, and always has been, an international city, living by trade, thronged with visitors, home to a never-ending stream of migrants from every region of the British Isles, of Europe and of the continents beyond. In 1904, when it was the heart of the greatest empire in history, Joseph Chamberlain summarised it in a sentence – clearing-house of the world. The tidal Thames has ever been its lifeline, linking it to the oceans which have created its wealth and shaped its destiny, a relationship brilliantly evoked in the opening passages of Conrad's *Heart of Darkness* and epitomised with crisp brevity in Nelson's salty dictum that 'the City of London ... exists by victories at sea.' Globetrotter Freya Stark, an intrepid voyager in the wastelands of the Arab world, once confessed that:

> ... a walk on the City pavements is one of the most romantic things in the world; the austere and unpretentious doors – the River Plate Company, or Burma Oil, or affairs in Argentina or Ecuador or Hudson's Bay – they jostle each other and lead away to strange places, and create a feeling of being all over the world at once....

London was founded by Romans – most of whom were probably Italianised Gauls from northern France. The English – the Anglo-Saxons – took centuries to accept and accommodate themselves to the city which was to figure so largely in the literature to which their language gave birth, in the works of Chaucer, of Shakespeare, of Dickens, Londoners all by birth or by adoption.

The Mansion-House of Liberty

Ever since Alfred the Great refortified the city over a thousand years ago every century has brought its infusion of newcomers, whether as traders, craftsmen, artists or refugees. John Milton called London the 'mansion-house of liberty' and so it has proved for generations. Karl Marx found shelter here from a failed revolution in Germany, as did Mazzini from Italy, Kossuth from Hungary and Herzen from Russia. Contingents were raised here to fight with Bolivar, with Byron, with Garibaldi and in the Spanish civil war.

Few readers, perhaps, will be surprised to learn that there were over 100,000 Irish living in London a century ago; but there were 30,000 Germans as well. If a visitor nowadays passes an hour in a 'fitness centre' it might be appropriate to remember that it was German exiles who first brought the alien notion of a 'gymnasium' to London. Travel writer Jonathan Raban has predicted that 'when anything really important happens on some outcrop of the globe with an unpronounceable name it will show up a few months later on the Earl's Court Road.' And elsewhere. Tower Hamlets is well known for its Bangladeshi community, but there are Somalis and Kurds as well. At a single school, less than a mile from Marble Arch, over 60 different languages are spoken by the pupils whose Moroccan and Portuguese and Filipino parents change the sheets and serve the breakfasts of Japanese and Brazilian tourists in the nearby hotels. No wonder that 50 years ago H.V. Morton concluded that 'one of the charms of London is that there are no Londoners' – and he was writing a book called *In Search of Scotland*!

Novelist Evelyn Waugh was characteristically splenetic on the same subject: 'The English ... are already hard to find in London. No one lives there who is not paid to do so. You will find strange tongues on the streets; tourists in the hotels ... I believe that London society has ceased to exist; all hospitality now is commercial or official.'

'LONDON PRIDE'

London represents both the nation and a wider world in its very streets and buildings. If brick from the surrounding countryside has been its most common building material since the Great Fire of 1666 gutted the

City, there were precedents stretching back to Roman times for importing marble and other such extravagances from as far away as the Middle East. Nelson's column incorporates granite from both ends of the kingdom – Cornwall and the Highlands. It looks down on buildings whose façades have been quarried in Sweden and Italy and France and Norway. Tower Bridge may look so much a part of London's landscape that it could seem as though it grew from the very ground – but it is made of steel forged in Glasgow.

Noël Coward's sentimental hymn to the city under fire was entitled 'London Pride', a fitting title, for London's pride is one of its most enduring traditions. Three centuries ago Thomas Fuller boasted that it was: '. . . the second city in Christendom for greatness and the first for good government. There is no civilized part of the world but that it hath heard thereof, though many with this mistake, that they conceive London to be the country and England but the city therein.'

Writing at the beginning of Victoria's reign the Reverend Sydney Smith asserted, with more panache than elegance, that: '. . . the parallelogram between Oxford St., Piccadilly, Regent St. and Hyde Park, encloses more intelligence and human ability, to say nothing of wealth and beauty, than the world has ever collected in such a space before.'

'The Flower of Cities All'

London around 1500 was, in the eyes of the Scottish poet William Dunbar, 'the flower of cities all.' Travel agents are sometimes fond of adding that extra touch of pseudo-authenticity by quoting him in his original orthography (i.e. 'flour') which is closer to his pronunciation (i.e. 'flure') but this may well no doubt lead to understandable confusion among literal-minded tourists and those for whom English is a second language. As modern scholarship now seems to suggest that this oft-quoted line wasn't written by Dunbar anyway, perhaps we shall hear less of it in future. That said, let it be remembered that the compliment came from a Scotsman, whoever he was.

However proud they may be, Londoners have seldom claimed that their city is beautiful in the way that, say, Paris is. Indeed, they often seem to suggest that every change in its appearance is for the worse. Over half-a-century ago novelist E.M. Forster was decrying the debasement of Nash's Regent Street, which had occurred in his own lifetime:

> It was not great architecture, but it knew what it was doing, and where it was going; it was reasonable and refined. Of course, it had to be scrapped. Greed moulds the landscape of London.... If you want a muddle look around you as you walk from Piccadilly Circus to Oxford Circus. Here are monuments that do not adorn, features that feature nothing ... uniformity without harmony, bigness without size. Even when the shops are built at the same moment and by architects of equal fatuity, they manage to contradict one another. Here is the heart of the Empire, and the best it can do.

The judgments of aesthetes, however well-informed, are not necessarily those of time. One wrote scathingly of Piccadilly Circus as 'an impossible site on which to place any outcome of the human brain except possibly an underground lavatory.' That was Sir Alfred Gilbert and the outcome of his brain was London's first aluminium statue – Eros. It met with such a hostile reaction that its creator lived in self-imposed exile for 30 years after it was unveiled. Now it is one of London's best-loved, as well as best-known, landmarks.

Size and Population

At the beginning of the present century London was the largest city in the world. It no longer is so, but it is still by far the largest city in Britain, three times as populous as either of its nearest rivals, Birmingham and Glasgow. Around 1500 its population was a mere 75,000, but it was three times larger than its nearest rivals then, Norwich, Bristol and York. Generations of visitors have been overwhelmed by its immensity, its seemingly relentless capacity to devour everything around it. In *Humphrey Clinker* (1771) Smollett has Matthew Bramble exclaim: 'What I left open fields, producing hay and corn, I now find covered with streets and squares and palaces and churches ... Pimlico and Knightsbridge are now almost joined to Chelsea and Kensington, and if this infatuation continues for half-a-century, I suppose the whole county of Middlesex will be covered in brick.'

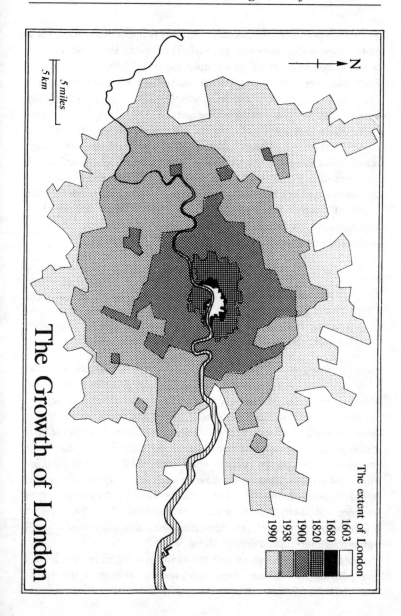

The Growth of London

The extent of London

1990
1938
1900
1820
1680
1603

5 miles
5 km

N

Twenty years later the dilettante Horace Walpole deplored the fact that: 'There will soon be one street from London to Brentford; ay, and from London to every village ten miles round! ... London is ... much fuller than ever I saw it. I have twice this spring been going to stop my coach in Piccadilly, to inquire what was the matter, thinking there was a mob – not at all; it was only passengers.'

American novelist Henry James, soon after arriving in London, confessed that he had been 'crushed under a sense of the mere magnitude of London – its inconceivable immensity. . . . The place sits on you, broods on you ... In fine it is anything but a cheerful or a charming city. Yet it is a very splendid one.' A decade later, although he could still concede that it was 'ugly, dusky, dreary, more destitute than any European city of graceful and decorative incident', he was more enthralled than intimidated by its 'agglomerated immensity':

> At any given point London looks huge; even in narrow corners you have a sense of its hugeness, and petty places acquire a certain interest from their being parts of so mighty a whole. Nowhere else is so much human life gathered together and nowhere does it press upon you with so many suggestions. These are not all of an exhilarating kind; far from it. But they are of every possible kind, and that is the interest of London.

Many visitors, as well as Londoners, have rejected the notion that London's vastness represents a dull, endless, repetitious uniformity. Rather, they claim, it must be understood as a series of villages. Stepney Green may not look much like a village green any more, enclosed with iron railings and hemmed in by tenement blocks; but approach it through Hayfield Passage and you can still see that it was one. Someone who has never actually been to Highgate or Dulwich may think of them just as suburbs but they still retain sufficient visual coherence and social continuity to qualify as authentic communities. As any long-term resident will hasten to reassure you, in many parts of London, while it might be overly romantic to characterise their area as a village it is still something more than a mere address.

London is home to about one Briton in every eight, but it is almost every Briton's second city. Newcastle, almost 300 miles to the north-east, can be reached by rail in just over two-and-a-half hours. Probably four-fifths of the nation can go to the capital and be back home the same day. If there are Britons who have never seen their capital it is because they have no wish to and not, as in so many larger countries, because it is, or seems, so far away.

The United States has Washington as its capital, New York as its financial centre, Los Angeles as the powerhouse of its popular culture and Chicago, perhaps, as the hub of its industrial heartland and network of communications. Britain has had London as all of these. Only in the last two centuries has the capital gradually relinquished its leading role in industry, only within the last generation has it ceased to be the greatest port. All other functions it retains and is, in addition, the nation's largest single centre for retailing, publishing, higher education, medicine, sport, art, theatre, music, tourism, scandal and crime. It always has been. Robert Southey, writing around 1800 in the guise of an imaginary Spanish traveller, Don Manuel Alvarez Espriella, declared London to be: 'The single spot whereon were crowded together more wealth, more splendour, more ingenuity, more worldly wisdom, and alas!, more worldly blindness, poverty, depravity, dishonesty, and wretchedness, than upon any other spot in the whole habitable earth.'

Literature and Illusion

London is, perhaps, the world's most written-about city. Its life and characters have inspired Britain's greatest dramatists and most prolific diarists. It has given birth in the imagination to such immortal characters as Fagin and Falstaff, Eliza Doolittle and Sherlock Holmes. It has actually given birth to Milton and Keats, Blake and Lamb, Browning and Forster. Henry James and Bret Harte and T.S. Eliot came from America to make it their home. Readers of *The Waste Land* will, in their imaginations, have crossed bustling London Bridge, tramped up noisy King William Street and stood wondering in the gloomy calm of St Mary Woolnoth. But the literary pilgrim is not invariably fulfilled by reality. In 1925 the Czech writer Karel Capek penned a brief but singularly morose account of one such futile odyssey:

> ... of course I went to look at Baker Street, but I came back terribly disappointed. There is not the slightest trace of Sherlock Holmes there: it is a

business thoroughfare of unexampled respectability, which serves no higher purpose than to lead to Regent's Park.... If we also briefly touch upon its underground railway station, we have exhausted everything, including our patience.

London is, as Jan Morris has observed with characteristic insight, 'more than any other city in Europe ... a show, living by bluff and display.' Nowadays Capek would not have been disappointed. A Sherlock Holmes museum has been fabricated in Baker Street to beguile the acolytes of the world's first super-sleuth and just off Northumberland Avenue a Victorian pub has been renamed in his honour and refitted to house a reconstruction of his famous study.

London has long been famed for the wealth of at least some of its inhabitants. When the Prussian Field Marshal Blücher was shown the capital from the vantage-point of St Paul's his soldierly reaction was concise – '_Was für plunder!_' (What a place to loot!). London still has some of the world's most highly-priced real-estate and is legendary for its skill in separating people from their money. As the writer William Shenstone noted mordantly two centuries ago 'nothing is certain in London but expense.' Perhaps. But London also offers the casual onlooker a hundred shows a day for free – a lunchtime concert of chamber music in a Wren church, street-jugglers at Covent Garden, the Changing of the Guard, the paintings hung along the railings of Green Park, the rather better paintings at the Tate or the National Gallery.

'A city no one ever knew'

Perhaps London's essence lies neither in its immensity nor its complexity, neither in its antiquity nor its modernity, but in the fact that having all these properties and dimensions, it can never be mastered. Novelist V.S. Naipaul described it as: '... a good place for getting lost in, a city no one ever knew, a city explored from the neutral heart outwards, until, after years, it defined itself into a jumble of clearings, separated by stretches of the unknown, through which the narrowest of paths had been cut.'

And he was only speaking about street-level. Anyone who fails to recognise that there is, in effect, another London under London has, quite literally, only a superficial knowledge. Behind the Mansion House nestles perhaps the most stunning of all Wren's church interiors, that of St Stephen Walbrook, first home of the Samaritans. Nearby still runs the River Walbrook, from which archaeologists have recovered skulls of the Roman period and the rubbish and lost property of the succeeding millennium.

Since the fifteenth century this 'lost river' has been covered over, but it still flows into the Thames, just as the Fleet runs under Farringdon Street and the West Bourne feeds the lakes in Hyde Park before gushing through a pipe which passes over the heads of passengers waiting for the next District line train at Sloane Square station. Every year 600,000 holes are dug in the surface of London's streets and squares. The site of Shakespeare's Globe Theatre and of Roman London's amphitheatre have only been rediscovered within the last few years. Who can tell what next year may unearth?

Whether a traveller arrives in London for the first or the hundredth time there will always be more to see, more to know. London can never be exhausted, never used up. Arrive knowing that, even if you have never been here before, this is your city. Depart and carry with you the certainty that, as Byron's biographer and friend Thomas Moore so neatly put it:

> Go where we may, rest where we will.
> Eternal London haunts us still.

CHAPTER ONE

Londinium and Lundenwic, 43–1066

Unusually for a great city London makes no claim to a precise foundation date, as Rome does – which is ironic, for it was Rome that founded London.

Hunter-gatherers were living in the Thames valley half-a-million years ago. It was well-wooded, had fertile soils and offered abundant water, not merely from the main river itself but also from its many tributaries. Isolated settlements existed on both sides of the river which, because it was roughly four metres shallower than it is today, could be crossed with relative ease. On the other hand, perhaps because it was twice as broad as it is today, it seems often to have served as a frontier between tribal groups, which may explain why the location where London now stands was not, until the Roman invasion, the site of any significant settlement. As a site for settlement London did, however, offer major attractions to an invader. In relation to the surrounding marshy region it stood elevated and well-drained, with surface soil suitable for brick-making and gravel deposits either side of the river capable of taking pilings for a bridge. Most important of all, the site marked the point nearest its mouth where the tidal Thames was sufficiently narrow to make bridge-building a practical proposition and sufficiently deep to provide anchorage for large ships. It also had the political advantage of lying near the borders of the territories of four powerful tribal groupings.

From Invasion to Disaster

The Roman invasion force which sailed from Boulogne under the command of Aulus Plautius consisted of four legions, supported by non-Roman auxiliaries, perhaps 40,000 men in all. The landing at Rutupiae (Richborough) at the eastern-most tip of Kent the invaders thrust westward, winning a decisive encounter at the River Medway and pushing on to cross the Thames, probably by means of a pontoon bridge, in the region which was to become London. (The actual crossing-point – or points – is a matter of scholarly dispute. Westminster or even Chelsea are other possibilities.) Here the expedition regrouped until it was joined by the Emperor Claudius in person.

Claudius, nominally at least, led the advance north-east across Essex which culminated in the capture of Camulodunum (Colchester) the most powerful tribal centre in lowland Britain. Having received the formal surrender of 11 British kings, the emperor then returned to Rome and a triumph, his entire involvement having lasted just 16 days. Crippled, stammering Claudius had secured the shaky beginnings of his reign by achieving what the legendary Caesar had shied away from – the conquest of Britain. Camulodunum, selected to serve as the provisional capital of the new province of Britannia, was to be adorned with a great temple to honour the conquering emperor. (Its remains can still be seen beneath the huge keep of Colchester Castle.)

Over the course of the next decade the pacification of lowland Britain proceeded methodically and was accompanied by the construction of strategic military routes. Those which linked Camulodunum with the Kent coast – and hence to Continental supply-bases – passed via the crossing-point over the Thames, which acquired a permanent bridge probably around or soon after AD 50. This became the focal point of a road system whose major arteries stretched south and west to the tribal capitals of Noviomagus (Chichester) and Calleva (Silchester) and north to Verulamium (St Albans).

TRIBAL POLITICS

The orderly progress of imposing Roman rule was savagely disrupted in AD 60 when the occupation forces grossly mishandled tribal politics, provoking a major uprising. Prasutagus, chief of the Iceni of Norfolk, and an ally of Rome, died bequeathing half his realm to his family and half to the emperor, hoping thus to secure official support for his dynasty's continued rule. Instead the Romans decided to take all, adding the humiliation of a flogging for his widow, Boudicca (Boadicea) and the rape of his daughters. The Iceni rose in revolt and, supported by the Trinovantes of Essex, marched on and sacked Camulodunum, where the hapless garrison made its last stand at the emperor's new temple. The Romans were taken completely off-balance, the army being scattered throughout Britain and the governor, Suetonius Paulinus, being away in far-distant Anglesey, off the coast of north Wales, crushing resistance in the Druids' sacred stronghold. At the head of his cavalry he reached Londinium before Boudicca's host but, recognising he had too few troops to hold an unfortified town, decided to evacuate all who were willing to abandon their property and belongings and 'sacrifice the single city of Londinium to save the province as a whole.'

Those who remained were massacred and Londinium was put to the torch, a fate attested by a layer of orange-red burnt clay and pottery shards uncovered by excavations in the area of Lombard Street, Gracechurch Street and Fenchurch Street. It is grimly appropriate that the name London may have come from a Celtic word meaning 'place of the fierce one.' Verulamium suffered the same fate as the other cities. Then came the final confrontation between Suetonius Paulinus and Boudicca, somewhere in the south Midlands. Although hopelessly outnumbered, the disciplined legions proved victorious. Boudicca committed suicide. A flamboyant statue of the rebel queen in a scythe-wheeled chariot, now stands at the northern end of Westminster Bridge.

From Recovery to Ruin

After the Boudiccan catastrophe a recovery programme was placed in the hands of a newly-appointed procurator (director of finances) Julius Alpinus Classicianus. A just and far-sighted administrator, he saw that Roman interests would be better served by conciliation than retribution. No doubt with an eye to future revenue he seems to have given priority to the reconstruction of business premises. Fragments of his dignified tomb (ignominiously recycled into a defensive bastion) were found in the Tower Hill area in 1852 and 1935 and can be seen in the British Museum. A copy is set into the wall of the Wakefield Gardens, just outside Tower Hill Underground station, to the east.

ROMAN LONDON

The Roman historian, Tacitus, whose father-in-law, Agricola, was governor of Britain (AD 77–83) noted that the original, pre-sacked London 'did not rank as a Roman settlement (*colonia*) but was an important centre for businessmen and merchandise.' The significance of its site within the overall pattern of Roman rule is confirmed by the fact that the city was quickly rebuilt and remained the seat of both procurator and governor, plus their supporting secretariat and garrison.

The nucleus of reborn London was around Cornhill, the highest point on the land immediately to the north of the bridge. Settlement to the west of the Walbrook was and remained much less dense. The most important building was the basilica and forum, which together combined the functions of townhall, lawcourts, meeting-place and shopping-mall and stood on a site over 150-metres square. The basilica had marble-surfaced walls 70-feet high and was bigger than that of any other city north of the Alps. The forum was four times as large as Trafalgar Square.

Down by the bank of the river stood the governor's palace, a sprawling complex of offices, reception halls and private apartments covering at least 13,000 square metres and with its own baths and a vast ornamental pool. As the governor usually spent the summer campaigning or inspecting the provinces it probably served as his winter headquarters. The site is now covered by Cannon Street station.

Public bath-houses were among the earliest urban conveniences to be constructed. One stood on what is now Upper Thames Street near the river and was fed by a natural spring. It was large and probably for general public use. Another on Cheapside was much smaller and possibly reserved for military use. Tacitus slyly informs us that Roman policy was to encourage the bathing habit among local Britons as part of a softening-up process which seduced their leaders to renounce resistance in favour of a luxurious enslavement.

The effective functioning of London as an administrative centre

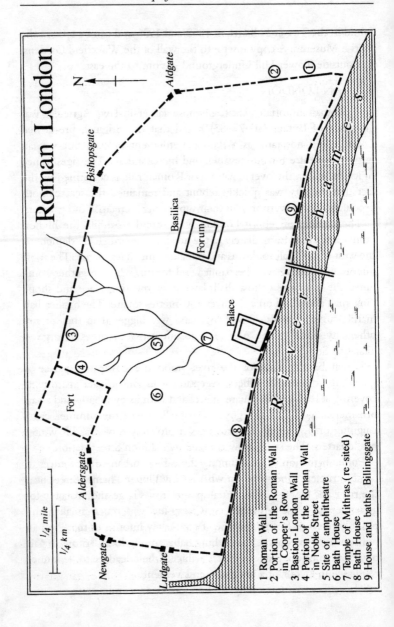

Roman London

N

Aldgate

Bishopsgate

Basilica

Forum

Palace

Fort

Aldersgate

Newgate

Ludgate

River Thames

¼ mile
¼ km

1 Roman Wall
2 Portion of the Roman Wall in Cooper's Row
3 Bastion-London Wall
4 Portion of the Roman Wall in Noble Street
5 Site of amphitheatre
6 Bath House
7 Temple of Mithras, (re-sited)
8 Bath House
9 House and baths, Billingsgate

required the revival of its commercial life, partly to raise revenue through taxing trade and partly to supply the comforts and conveniences which could not yet be manufactured locally. Port facilities were therefore rapidly upgraded and a large timber quay and stone storehouses were constructed around AD 80. Samian ware, a glossy, red ceramic was imported from Gaul (France) in bulk. Fine glass came from the Rhineland, Italy and as far away as Spain. Marble for tombs and prestigious buildings came from Gaul, Italy, Greece and Turkey. Large pottery amphorae were used to bring wine from Italy, dried fruit from Palestine and, from Spain, olive oil for cooking and lighting, and the fishsauce which added piquancy to many Roman recipes. Luxury goods included bronze tableware from Italy itself, emeralds from Egypt, amber from the Baltic and enamelled brooches from Belgium. Gradually local British manufactures replaced imports of pottery and tableware. Exports consisted of corn, hides, timber, jet, pewter, silver, slaves and much-prized hunting-dogs.

THE LONDON GARRISON

By about AD 100 the area between the river and the forum was densely packed with shops and other commercial buildings, with smart residences in the quieter parts away from the main streets. At the northwest corner of the city stood a fort. Its purpose was less defensive than residential, to provide separate accommodation in a proper military atmosphere, for the garrison of about 1,000 men, which performed ceremonial, security and administrative duties. It probably also served as a transit facility. Covering some five hectares (12 acres) it was only about a quarter of the size of a major frontier encampment like Chester, but it followed the standard rectangular pattern, with four gates, and walls of rubble and concrete faced with squared-off blocks of Kentish ragstone. A V-section ditch ran round the outside, with the spoil from the ditch being used to strengthen the inside of the wall. The remains of this wall, with foundations of a turret and the rounded south-west corner tower can be seen to the west of Noble Street today. The northern end of nearby Wood Street roughly follows the line of the road which once ran through the centre of the fort.

An artist's impression of a gateway to Roman London

AMPHITHEATRE

Another major military facility was the amphitheatre, uncovered near Guildhall as recently as 1988. This oval arena of packed sand had an under-floor drainage system and was regularly used as a drill-ground, as well as providing a setting for plays, games, gladiatorial combats and major public ceremonies, like the welcome that would have been given to the Emperor Hadrian when he visited the city in AD 122.

It was a very mixed crowd that would have cheered a visiting emperor. The inhabitants of Londinium gave the city an international character which was maintained by trade contacts and the rotation of officials and military units from abroad. Most were Romanised Britons and some of the top bureaucrats were Romans from Italy itself. Others, like Classicianus, were Roman citizens from neighbouring Gaul and the merchant Aulus Alfidius Olussa, whose tombstone is in the British Museum, was born in Athens. Latin, which was widely spoken and written, provided a binding element in the babel of competing languages.

Within a few years of Hadrian's visit, around AD 125, fire destroyed about a hundred acres of the central city. It was a severe blow and archaeological evidence suggests that for some decades the city passed through hard times, with commerce rerouted to provincial capitals, houses and workshops in outlying areas demolished, baths neglected and even the fort abandoned.

From Renewal to Retreat

By the end of the second century the empire was torn by civil war. Britain, as a frontier province, had a large contingent of regular troops, perhaps a tenth or more of the entire Roman army. It was, therefore, despite being on the inhospitable edge of a world focused on the Mediterranean, a promising base from which to launch a bid for power. In AD 193 the governor of Britain, Clodius Albinus, did just that and took most of his forces to fight on the Continent.

The massive (9-feet thick and 20-feet high) walls which enclosed 330 acres of Londinium made it the largest city in Britain and the fifth largest in the western empire. Coin-finds confirm their date to between AD 190 and AD 220. The walls may have been started by the rebellious governor, anxious to secure his rear; but in any case they were completed by his conqueror, the rightful emperor, Septimius Severus, who came to Britain in person and died at York in 211.

The construction of defensive walls, which incorporated the Cripplegate fort, was accompanied by the rebuilding of the waterfront quay on an even more massive scale. Trade revived but, with the division of Britain into two separate provinces in AD 200, Londinium, capital of Britannia Superior (Upper Britain), became a primarily administrative centre, while Eboracum (York), capital of Britannia Inferior (Lower Britain) became the focal point of military operations.

EGYPTIAN TEMPLE

The fact that London's population was smaller and more dispersed than formerly should not be taken to indicate that the city was in decline but that its occupants could enjoy more gracious surroundings, as befitted life in a capital. Public and private buildings of the period attest to this. A number of houses had fine mosaic floors, red-painted plaster walls and green glass windows. A temple in honour of the Egyptian goddess, Isis, was raised, though its precise whereabouts remains unknown. Around AD 240 a temple to Mithras was built on the east bank of the Walbrook. With a central nave, two side aisles and a rounded apse at the western end, its basilica plan resembles that of an early Christian church. But the cult of Mithras was one of Christianity's strongest rivals and, at the time of the temple's construction it was the mystery religions of the east which were in the ascendant. Mithras was the central figure in a complex cult which came to Rome via Persia. Representing light and renewal he resembled Christ in one important respect – offering the prospect of a life after death. As he also required his followers to display courage and honesty and initiates were subjected to a hierarchy of tests to prove their manhood and devotion, Mithraism appealed strongly to those who risked their lives to do their duty, notably soldiers and merchants. London had plenty of both.

PROSPERITY AND INDUSTRY

The prosperity of Roman London in good times is evidenced by the known existence of brick-fields, flour-mills, potteries, glass-works and workshops turning out furniture, tools, cloth and custom-made foot-wear, from hob-nailed boots to fancy sandals with their owner's initials worked into their decoration. Another indicator of elegant living is the existence of sizeable villas in the surrounding countryside, like Old Ford, near Bow, beyond the cemeteries on the road out to Colchester. Along the valley of the River Darenth in Kent there were villas every two or three miles; an outstanding example, with mosaics, bath-house and its own Christian chapel can still be visited at Lullingstone.

Crisis and Disorder

Disorder returned to Britain in AD 286 when Carausius, admiral of the Channel fleet, declared himself emperor and established London's first mint to turn booty seized from Saxon pirates into coins to buy the loyalty of his troops. In AD 293 Carausius was murdered, ironically by his financial adviser, Allectus, who supplanted him as pseudo-emperor until overthrown by the rightful ruler, Constantius Chlorus, in AD 296. Having beaten Allectus in Hampshire Constantius arrived in London in time to save it from plunder at the hands of his enemy's defeated army. A gold medallion, found in Arras, France, shows the city welcoming its saviour as 'Restorer of Eternal Light' and is the first known representation of London to survive. The fortified gateway it depicts is probably based on the *Porta Nigra* at Trier in Germany where the piece was actually struck. Following Constantine's conversion to Christianity in AD 312, Christians suddenly found themselves in authority. A council at Arles in France in AD 314 is known to have been attended by a bishop representing Londinium. In subsequent years the temple of Mithras was attacked. Some of its fine sculptures were smashed; others seem to have been buried to save them from destruction.

During the mid-fourth century the city once more entered a period of crisis. The usurpers Magnentius and Decentius denuded Britain of troops in AD 350 to make an abortive bid for the throne. In AD 367 Hadrian's Wall was overrun and the coasts ravaged as Picts, Scots and Saxons launched a co-ordinated raid in strength from three directions. The imperial general, Theodosius, came to reorganise defences, including those of Londinium itself. Some 20 solid bastions were added to the eastern wall of the city to carry heavy *ballistae* (catapults). (The fact that they often contained recycled materials from tombs and public buildings does suggest a general dilapidation as well as haste in construction.) Facing downstream these enhanced defences would offer formidable resistance to marauders whose approach would be signalled from new watchtowers built to give early warning of attack. As if to boost morale the city was graced with the honorific title Augusta. The completion of a wall along the river-front and further fortification in AD 396 on the orders of another famous visitor, Stilicho, suggests continuing anxiety.

Stilicho's execution in 408 as a result of palace politics, left the emperor Honorius marooned in his lagoon stronghold at Ravenna. When the British provincial authorities appealed to him for military aid in 410 he replied that they must shift for themselves. This acknowledgement of imperial impotence marked the effective end of Roman hegemony in Britain.

END OF ROMAN RULE

Londinium did not, however, abruptly cease to be a Roman city. The unearthing of military buckles and belts made in the Rhineland suggests the presence of German mercenaries, possibly as a stop-gap defensive measure. But the presence of an eastern Mediterranean pottery amphora of mid-fifth century date in a substantial centrally-heated house in Lower Thames Street implies a continuation of long-distance trade, which in turn implies a means of payment, though this may mean a reversion to the slave business. The house itself evidently decayed until demolished some time before AD 500. The presence of a Saxon brooch among the smashed roof-tiles which littered the floor of the furnace-room conjure a picture of a nervous pagan picking over the debris of a ruin and dropping a valued adornment in sudden fright amid the eerie sounds of a ghost city. Did Roman London end, not with a bang, but a tinkle?

The subsequent abandonment of Londinium was so complete that the basic street pattern of the City today is not Roman but Saxon – which is rather remarkable, given that the Romans liked cities and the Saxons most definitely did not.

Roman Remains

Today's London stands some 20 feet above the level of the Roman city but every time the foundations are dug for a modern high-rise office block an aspect of the City's Roman heritage is almost sure to be brought to light as its recovery and destruction go hand in hand.

The first large-scale unearthing of Roman antiquities came about during the course of rebuilding after the Great Fire of 1666. In 1722 the antiquarian William Stukeley attempted to draw a plan of the city as he thought it might have been in Roman times. The construction of sewers and underground railways during the Victorian era led to many more discoveries, giving a much fuller and more accurate picture of the Roman city. Major finds include the magnificent polychrome

Bucklersbury mosaic, unearthed in 1869 during the construction of Queen Victoria Street and the foundations of the great basilica exposed during the building of Leadenhall Market in 1881. The post-Blitz period of reconstruction uncovered the temple of Mithras, which was resited for public viewing. The line of London's Roman walls is signposted for a 2.8 km walk which runs in either direction from Tower Hill via London Wall to the Museum of London at Aldersgate. The museum's Roman gallery contains not only the Mithraic marbles, a fine bronze portrait bust of Hadrian and extensive collections of coins, tools, pottery and jewellery but also such curiosities as a pair of girl's leather bikini trunks with frilly edging, a stamp for marking sticks of eye-salve with the pharmacist's name and a building-tile inscribed with the tantalising information that 'Austalis has been wandering off on his own every day for a fortnight.'

Other notable exhibits include timbers from a barge found near Blackfriars Bridge in 1962 (complete with its cargo of Kentish ragstone for building the city wall) and fascinating reconstructions of a Roman kitchen and two dining-rooms, fully equipped with authentic utensils and table-ware. Other items from Roman London can be seen in the British Museum. The crypt of St Bride's, Fleet Street, contains traces of a substantial Roman house, and the skeleton of a Roman woman discovered nearby revealed traces of Christian burial. A stone doorway at All Hallows by the Tower incorporates recycled Roman tiles and the crypt there has a small display of Roman finds.

London also possesses two other Roman remains, one of which may actually be so, the other of which probably is not. The London Stone, now set in a niche in the wall of the Bank of China in Cannon Street, was once set in the wall of St Swithin's church and is documented as far back as 1198. From the sixteenth century onwards it has been suggested that it may have been a Roman milestone and possibly even the one from which all distances to London were measured. Standing so near to the site of the governor's palace this is quite plausible, but it may just be the eroded top of a wayside funerary monument. The alleged 'Roman bath' off Strand Lane near Temple station is almost certainly a seventeenth-century attempt to impress the neighbours.

Lundenwic

The *Anglo-Saxon Chronicle* tells us that in AD 457 the remnants of a British army took shelter within the walls of London, following their defeat at the hands of the Saxons in the area of Crecganford (Crayford). By the year 500 London appears to have been largely deserted. Saxon settlers seem to have advanced along the Thames and the valleys of its tributaries, meeting little resistance from the former inhabitants and establishing isolated farmsteads or small villages whose names reveal their tribal origins – Ealing (Gillingas), Barking (Berecingas) and Staines (Staeningas). Excavations imply that the newcomers positively avoided the ruined Roman city, preferring to establish themselves at some distance from it, in areas like Rainham to the east, Hammersmith to the west and Mitcham to the south. Saxon barrows are still visible in Greenwich Park and at Grim's Dyke, Pinner there are traces of an earthwork several miles long, which may have been a boundary marker. Around 600, the London area lay within the territory of the kingdom of the East Saxons, which covered the later counties of Essex and Middlesex, most of Hertfordshire and part of Surrey. Its king, Saebehrt, seems to have acknowledged the suzerainty of his more powerful uncle, Ethelbert, King of Kent.

ETHELBERT, KING OF KENT

Ethelbert was the first English monarch to convert to Christianity, probably because the French princess he married was already a fervent believer. His decision to welcome St Augustine and his fellow missionaries in 597 ensured that Canterbury (and not London as the pope had originally intended) would ever after retain primacy over all other cities in the history of English Christianity. Nevertheless London, at least as a site if not as a settlement, was thought important enough to be selected as the seat of a bishopric soon afterwards. In 604 Saebehrt welcomed a Christian delegation, led by Mellitus, first bishop of reconverted London, and allowed them to build the first cathedral dedicated to St Paul. Legend also credits Saebehrt with founding a church in the Westminster area in 616. On Saebehrt's death, however, the Londoners reverted to paganism and it took another generation for the new faith to reassert itself.

While Christianity struggled commerce revived. A royal charter of ca.670 refers to London as a landing-place for ships. The Venerable Bede, writing the history of the Christian missions in England around 731 calls London 'the mart of many nations resorting to it by land and sea.' This cosmopolitan venue was now known as Lundenwic – the suffix-wic denoting a trading centre, as in Ipswich or Sandwich. Saxon settlement in the London area appears to have clustered outside the city walls, to the west of the Fleet river as far as Charing Cross, where the slope and curve of the river bank may have made it a convenient place for beaching and unloading boats. Finds of imported pottery, wine-jars and German millstones in this locality point up the gradual revival of long-distance as well as purely local trade.

The former city area, within the Roman walls, appears to have been unoccupied, apart from the cathedral and probably a royal palace, as yet unlocated but possibly around Aldersgate where the Roman fort once stood.

SAINTS ERKENWALD AND ETHELBURGA

The most dynamic of the early Saxon inhabitants of London was undoubtedly St Erkenwald, the fourth bishop and founder of the abbeys at Chertsey and at Barking, the latter being headed by his sister, St Ethelburga. Erkenwald established the right to charge a toll on every load of wood which passed into the city along what is now appropriately called Bishopsgate. Mitres on the side of modern office blocks at the junction of Bishopsgate and Wormwood Street recall this shrewd coup. Bishopsgate was also home to a small late medieval church dedicated to St Ethelburga. Her abbey at Barking controlled the church of All Hallows, which predates its neighbour, the Tower of London, by more than four centuries. Its crypt has a Saxon wall and the lower part of its tower has a Saxon arch (made of Roman bricks), the oldest in London.

Little else that is clearly identifiable as Saxon survives in London but the importance of this period for the subsequent development of the city should not be underestimated. It was during these centuries that the boundaries of most of its central wards and parishes were established and a new street-pattern superimposed on the old Roman one as the inhabitants used the metalled roads to provide a firm foundation for their wood-and-thatch dwellings and out-houses. It is Lundenwic rather than Londinium which provides the framework for the London of today.

The Vikings

Having accommodated the Saxons, London from the ninth century onwards attracted the unwelcome attentions of the Vikings. The year 842 was recorded by chronicles as one of 'great slaughter'. In 851 the raiders returned with a huge fleet of 350 ships and reduced London to a charred waste. A series of summer campaigns in the following decade smashed the power of the Saxon kingdoms of eastern England and in 871–2 the Danes felt confident enough to sit out the winter in London.

Alfred of Wessex

In 886, under the inspired leadership of Alfred of Wessex, the English retook London. The king restored its walls and made it, with the 'Sudwerke' (south work – Southwark) at the other end of London Bridge, the anchor-point of his frontier defence system of fortified 'burghs'. The River Lea was negotiated as the eastern boundary of the 'Danelaw' and here one Haakon took possession of an island or 'Ea', thus giving name to 'Haakon's Ea' – Hackney.

RESETTLEMENT

Alfred's son-in-law, the capable Ethelred, ealdorman of Mercia, was appointed governor of London and charged with its resettlement. He was probably responsible for the laying out of streets around two market areas – Eastcheap and Westcheap (now Cheapside) – which served the general public and the royal household respectively. Meanwhile the settled area to the west of the city seems to have reverted to fields, its former condition recalled by its name, 'the old wic' (Aldwych) and by the continuing presence of such churches as St Brides, St Andrews, Holborn and St Martin-in-the-Fields. Within the city walls crafts revived and there is evidence of the presence of skilled cloth-makers and workers in bone and metal. New waterfronts were constructed at Billingsgate and Queenhithe, where finds reveal not only a continuation of trade with Frisia and the Rhineland but amber, ivory and whetstones from Norway as well. By the tenth century London may have had permanent colonies of French and German merchants; by the eleventh century the Danes were certainly present in force.

Danegeld

By the reign of Athelstan (925–39) who styled himself 'King of all Britain', London had more authorised coiners than any other town, a clear indication of its commercial significance; but, although royal councils met in London, they met in other places, too, so it was not yet in any special sense the capital. London's power is, however, attested by the fact that when, in 994, it faced a joint attack by Olaf Tryggvason of Norway and Sweyn Forkbeard of Denmark, the would-be predators 'suffered greater loss and injury than ever they expected.' The vacillating leadership of King Ethelred however enabled the raiders to obtain by threats what they had not been able to take by force. Over the next 20 years London was obliged to contribute mountains of silver to the annual 'danegeld' tribute, paid to buy off the attackers. In 1014 the English, with the assistance of Olaf of Norway, enjoyed a brief moment of glory and literally pulled London Bridge from beneath the feet of their tormentors, but the death of the spirited Edmund, Ethelred's son, in 1016 forced them to accept Cnut, son of Sweyn Forkbeard, as their king and for the next quarter century England was a province of a Danish maritime empire. The Danish impact on London is recalled in the dedication of churches to such otherwise unfamiliar saints as Magnus the Martyr and Olave (Olaf). Tooley Street also takes its name from the corruption of St Olave's name.

The Building of West Minster

The death of Cnut's son in 1042 ended his dynastic line and the throne reverted to the surviving son of Ethelred, Edward; he was so pious that

The burial of Edward the Confessor at Westminster – a scene from the
Bayeux tapestry

his nickname was 'the Confessor'. His piety appears to have taken the
form of a voluntary commitment to celibacy, which left the kingdom
without an heir, and an obsessive ambition to bless his new kingdom
with a church so grand it would out-shine every other. The unpro-
mising site selected for this enterprise was Thorney Island, a swamp at
the mouth of the River Tyburn, approachable only by boat or over
stepping-stones. Edward allocated one-tenth of his entire store of 'gold,
silver, cattle and all other possessions' to the building of his 'West
Minster' and, abandoning Cnut's modest palace within the city walls,
established a splendid new royal residence next to his building site so
that he could pay the closest attention to the supervision of his pet
project.

Westminster henceforth became the centre for royal justice and
administration while the port–city downstream retained its mercantile
character. Modern London grew out of the tension between these two
polarities.

The Confessor's church was consecrated on 28 December 1065. But
the king himself was too weak to attend the ceremony. Ten days later
he was dead and buried in his own creation.

CHAPTER TWO

Conquest and Corporation,
1066–1400

William, King, greets William, Bishop and Godfrey, Portreeve, and all the burghers within London, French and English, friendlike. And I will that both be worthy of all the rights of which ye both were worthy in King Edward's day. And I will that every child be his father's heir after his father's day. And I will not suffer that any man offer you any wrong. God keep you.

As a missive from a conqueror who had smashed his rival's army in a single battle it was a distinctly conciliatory message, but William of Normandy knew when to be conciliatory as well as when to be bold. London's leading citizens had trekked out to Berkhamsted to offer him the throne and their allegiance and he had had himself crowned with full ceremony in the Confessor's new abbey church on Christmas Day 1066.

Norman Strongholds

Immediately afterwards the new king had moved ten miles out of London to the comfort of the abbey at Barking, the second greatest in all England, while 'certain strongholds were made in the town against the fickleness of the vast and fierce population.'

The most imposing of these was eventually to form the core of the Tower of London, while on the western side of London two more castles were hastily constructed, taking their names from their custodians – Baignard (Baynard) and Montfichet (Mountfichet). The exact site of the latter is unknown, though it was probably near Ludgate. Within two centuries it was described as 'old and ruined'. Baynard's Castle served as the headquarters building for London's own army until it was handed over in the late-thirteenth century for the Dominicans to convert it into an extension for their friary. A pub, standing just opposite the Mermaid Theatre, preserves its name today.

The Norman Conquest more or less completely dispossessed the Saxon landowning class throughout England, but within London's city walls its impact was far less disruptive. Most of the land and nearly all of the trade remained in the same hands as before and the city continued to enlarge its privileges under the Conqueror's successors. A chronicler of King Stephen's anarchic reign refers in passing to the 'formidable and large army of the men of London', which implies that there was more than the power of the purse or the threat of riot behind the city fathers when they came to bargain with the crown. And, when the crown needed money, for wars or ambitious building schemes, as it invariably did, a community which owed its very livelihood to hard bargaining could be relied on to negotiate to its own best advantage.

The Corporation

Richard I, desperate for cash to fund his crusading expedition to the Holy Land, is said to have proclaimed, 'I would sell London if I could find a buyer.' During his absence, in 1191, his younger brother John agreed to recognise London as a commune, a perpetual corporation with a legal personality. Tradition variously dates the election of London's first mayor, Henry Fitz Aylwin to 1189 or 1192; whichever it was, it was an office he still held in May 1215 when John, now king, confirmed the right of Londoners to elect their own mayor. A month later, as part of the agreement summarised in Magna Carta, John reaffirmed the rights that the City had squeezed out of the crown over the century-and-a-half since the Conquest. The presence of the mayor of London among the greatest barons of England on that historic occasion affirms the unique standing that London had achieved.

Population Growth

By the beginning of the thirteenth century the population within the city walls is estimated to have been around 40,000 and the earliest

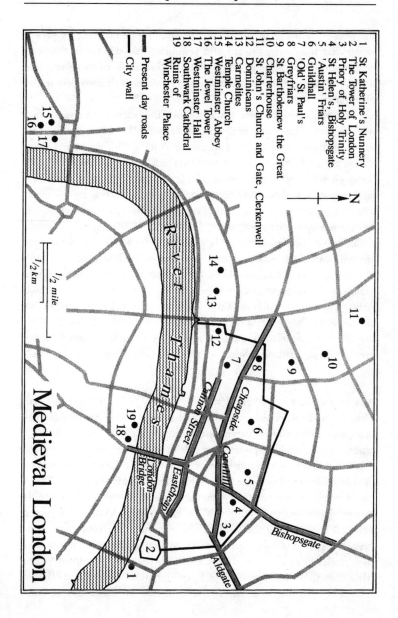

Medieval London

1 St Katherine's Nunnery
2 The Tower of London
3 Priory of Holy Trinity
4 St Helen's, Bishopsgate
5 'Austin' Friars
6 Guildhall
7 'Old' St Paul's
8 Greyfriars
9 St Bartholomew the Great
10 Charterhouse
11 St John's Church and Gate, Clerkenwell
12 Dominicans
13 Carmelites
14 Temple Church
15 Westminster Abbey
16 The Jewel Tower
17 Westminster Hall
18 Southwark Cathedral
19 Ruins of Winchester Palace

▨ Present day roads
— City wall

N →

½ mile
½ km

River Thames

Cannon Street
Cheapside
Cornhill
Eastcheap
London Bridge
Bishopsgate
Aldgate

attempts were being made to enforce building regulations, by prohibiting thatch as a fire hazard and requiring that the lower floors of houses should be built of stone. The reaffirmation of these requirements suggests that they were honoured more in the breach than in the observance.

The population clustered thickest along the edge of the river which was the basis of London's prosperity and around Westcheap, which was its major market area and said to have 800 stalls. Outlying areas, even within the walls, still retained a rural aura and, it was not until 1297 that the city's inhabitants were formally banned from obstructing the streets with pig-styes, and not until 1394 that the ward of Farringdon Without was demarcated to provide formal representation to the suburb which had grown up to the west, along the road to Westminster.

London's population probably peaked in the reign of Edward II at around 80,000, fell back drastically as a result of the Black Death (1348–9), then recovered to about 45,000 as a result of the rejuvenating force which had always sustained it − immigration. Even at this much reduced size it was still three times as big as the next largest cities, York and Bristol. The constant arrival of newcomers ensured that London was always a city of immigrants, English even more than foreign, as the prevalence of surnames which are those of villages and towns attests.

CITIZENSHIP

Any non-citizen was referred to as a 'foreign', even if London-born. Only full citizens could trade and own property and benefit from the protection of the city's courts in case of dispute. After 1319 candidates for citizenship had to be supported by at least six existing men of the trade they intended to live by; otherwise they were condemned to live by casual labour or to flee to the 'Tower Hamlets' east of the city where they could try to practise a craft beyond the searching eye of the increasingly powerful city guilds. The guilds' powers of supervision were given practical assistance by the tendency of craftsmen and retailers to congregate together in particular localities, whose names now memorialise their trades or products − Honey Lane, Fish Street Hill, Bread Street, Milk Street, Wood Street, Shoe Lane and Ironmonger Lane. Billiter Lane was once the home of the 'Bell-yetteres' or bell-founders, Can-

dlewick Street has since become abbreviated to Cannon Street and
Seacoal Lane marks the spot where coals were landed.

Westminster Hall

Apart from the Tower and Westminster Abbey, only about a score of
medieval London's buildings survive, often much altered or restored.
Westminster Hall, now part of the Houses of Parliament, was first built
in 1097–9 on the orders of William Rufus, the Conqueror's son, who
peevishly dismissed the finished building as 'too big for a chamber and
not big enough for a hall.' Originally it was an aisled structure, its roof
resting on a forest of pillars. Richard II's court architect, Henry Yevele,
working in collaboration with master carpenter, Hugh Herland, rebuilt
it between 1394 and 1401, raising the height of the walls and
strengthening them to bear the 660 tons of a stupendous oak hammer-
beam roof, revolutionary in concept and flawless in execution, which
created an immense open space 240-feet long and almost 68-feet wide.
At the centre the roof is 92-feet high above the floor and still the widest
unsupported timber span in the country. Westminster Hall has seen

Henry III and his masons

such historic events as the deposition of Richard II, the trials of Thomas More, Anne Boleyn, Guy Fawkes and Charles I; from the thirteenth century until 1882 it housed the law courts; since then it has been used for the lying-in-state of Prime Minister W.E. Gladstone, King Edward VII and Sir Winston Churchill. A few hundred yards from the hall stands the Jewel Tower, dating from ca. 1380, also from Yevele's hand and the only other part of the old Palace of Westminster to be seen today.

The Great Hall of Eltham Palace, built for Edward IV in 1479, also has a fine roof, as does Crosby Hall, the home of a City merchant, which once stood in Bishopsgate but in 1908 was resited by the river at Chelsea. London's oldest timber structure is, however, a humble but impressively capacious thirteenth-century barn at Ruislip; the nine-bayed tithe barn at Upminster dates from the fifteenth century but shows a mastery of intricate constructional technique.

Norman Churches

Vestiges of Norman masonry can be seen in the Romanesque arches of the crypt of St Mary le Bow and the ribbed vaulting in the crypt of St John's, Clerkenwell, but the most complete survival from the Norman period, though greatly truncated, is the church of St Bartholomew the Great at Smithfield. It was raised at the initiative of Rahere, a former courtier of Henry I who, after a near-fatal bout of malaria induced visions of damnation, established a priory of which he became the head and his great church the core. It was once over 300-feet long but the nave was demolished at the Reformation and other parts of the complex turned over to commercial use, including a print-shop where Ben Franklin worked on first coming to London. The choir still retains its massive Norman arches, an elaborate late-medieval painted tomb and effigy of Rahere and London's only medieval font, in which the painter William Hogarth was baptised. He later became a governor of neighbouring St Bartholomew's Hospital, another of Rahere's foundations, which is the oldest of all London's hospitals and has provided medical care for the city's inhabitants on the same site for almost nine centuries.

In the suburbs Norman churches can be seen at Harmondsworth (St Mary's), Harlington (St Peter and St Paul) and, best of all, at East Ham, where St Mary Magdalene, buffered by its ancient graveyard, nestles beside a thunderous fly-over and in the shadow of an artificial ski-slope. Some of its roof timbers are original, dating from 1130, and its thick walls conceal a cell for an anchorite.

THE TEMPLE CHURCH

The Temple Church, consecrated in 1185 in the presence of Henry II and Heraclius, Patriarch of Jerusalem, is remarkable as one of only five circular churches in the country. Its inspiration was the Holy Sepulchre in Jerusalem. It also shows a very early use of the pointed arch and is noteworthy for its cross-legged effigies of thirteenth-century knights. The spacious and elegant choir was added some time before 1240, which makes it contemporary with the first phase of St Helen's, Bishopsgate. St Helen's was once part of a nunnery and when a second nave was added, doubled up as a parish church. Its rich display of tombs and monuments has won it the title of 'the Westminster Abbey of the City.'

SOUTHWARK CATHEDRAL

London's other Protestant cathedral, at Southwark, attracts visitors who come to see the chapel dedicated to John Harvard, the gaudy tomb of the fourteenth-century poet John Gower, or the memorial window populated by characters from Shakespeare's plays; but the building itself is architecturally significant in its own right. Originally an Augustinian foundation, known as St Mary Overie, it retains a choir and retrochoir, built between 1213 and 1235, which brilliantly exemplify the uncluttered Early English style of Gothic.

A Saint's Story

All his life, the man known to history as Thomas à Becket, called himself Thomas of London. A plaque at the southern end of Iron-monger Lane marks the supposed site of his birth, in the house of his father Gilbert, a wealthy mercer. Appropriately it takes the form of the sort of lead badge a pilgrim would have bought as a souvenir of a visit to

Becket's shrine at Canterbury, the most venerated in all England. A quarter of all the hundreds of pilgrim badges which have been found in London are of this type, striking testimony to the power of his cult, which had devotees throughout Europe.

Trained in both arms and the law Becket's meteoric career led him to become the most trusted counsellor of Henry II, serving his royal master as both Chancellor and Constable of the Tower. Translated almost overnight to become Archbishop of Canterbury, the highest cleric in the land, Becket vigorously defended the rights of the church against the king. Henry's fury resulted in the archbishop's bloody murder in his own cathedral and the king's subsequent repentance and humiliation. Becket's tomb soon became the scene of miracles of healing and he was swiftly canonised. Chapels were dedicated to him on London Bridge and in the Tower of London and his likeness was added to the seals of the Mayor and Corporation.

WILLIAM FITZ STEPHEN

Within a few years of Becket's martyrdom a former member of his secretariat, William Fitz Stephen, wrote his biography, prefacing it with the first recorded personal account of London by a Londoner. Fitz Stephen wrote with an ardour that would have won the approval of a medieval tourist board had there been such a body. According to him the city: 'pours out its fame more widely, sends to farther lands its wealth and trade, lifts its head higher than the rest. It is happy in the healthiness of its air, in the Christian religion, in the strength of its defences, the nature of its site, the honour of its citizens, the modesty of its matrons; pleasant in sports; fruitful of noble men.'

Considering he was a cleric, Fitz Stephen appears to have been extremely appreciative of the pleasures of the senses. While he praised the city for its studious scholars, pious priests and hardworking housewives, he went into positive raptures about the fast-food emporia at the river's edge, where one could buy fish from the sparkling Thames, wine straight off the ship and 'viands, dishes roast, fried and boiled' in spicy sauces around the clock. For amusement one could stroll through the weekly horse fair at Smithfield or wander to marshy Moorfields to watch the youths of the city race three-up on a stallion or wrestle, fence and shoot at the mark; in winter there was an even more spectacular free show: '. . . when the great marsh . . . is frozen . . . (Some) there are . . . who fit to their feet the shin-bones of beasts, lashing them beneath their ankles, and with iron-shod poles in their hands they strike ever and anon against the ice and are borne along swift as a bird in flight or a bolt shot from a catapult.'

Of London's possible shortcomings Fitz Stephen could name only two – 'the immoderate drinking of fools and the frequency of fires.' He was certainly right about the latter. Between 1077 and 1137 London had to be substantially rebuilt on no less than four occasions.

Fitz Stephen was proud to record that London had no less than 13 conventual churches, serving communities of monks or nuns and 126 parish churches, serving the populace at large – roughly one for every three acres of land, with an average congregation of about 300. Between a quarter and a third of all the land in and immediately around the City was owned by the church in one way or another. In the half-century after Fitz Stephen's account was written, a number of substantial new religious foundations appeared as a result of the coming of the friars, a new type of cleric who eschewed the contemplative life of the cloister in favour of active mission and community care, especially among the more deprived classes of the city's population.

The Knights Templars

Approaching London from the west around the year 1250 one would first pass, on the south side of Fleet Street, the extensive precinct held by the crusading Knights Templar from 1128 until their suppression in 1312, when their land was turned over to their rivals, the Knights Hospitaller. As the Hospitallers already had their own estate and priory of St John at Clerkenwell, on the north side of the city, they were to lease the land on to lawyers and law students whose professional descendants still inhabit Inner and Middle Temple to this day.

THE FRIARS

The Templars' neighbours were Carmelite 'White Friars', who established themselves in 1247 on the opposite bank of the Fleet river from where the Dominican 'Black Friars' were already ensconced in the area which is still known as Blackfriars. To their north were the house of the Franciscan 'Grey Friars', the college of St Martin le Grand (where felons, but not traitors or Jews, could seek sanctuary from the law) and the hospital and priory of St Bartholomew. All of these, when built, were just inside or just outside the city walls, away from the crowded lanes of the waterside and city centre, where the press of houses, people and parish churches was most dense. Similarly, on the eastern side of London, were situated, from south to north, the hospital of St Katharine by the Tower (where St Katharine's dock now is), the house of the Friars of the Cross (in 'Crutched Friars'), the priory of Holy Trinity, Aldgate, the convent of St Helen on Bishopsgate, the house of Augustinian ('Austin') Friars, and, set apart from the community, the hospital of St Mary of Bethlehem (a mental asylum) and, further away still, the New Hospital of St Mary without Bishopsgate.

Bishop's Palaces

Along the river, or on the road between London and Westminster, stood the town residences of the great bishops. The bishop of Winchester's palace complex in Southwark had its own prison (the Clink) and outlying properties, used as brothels, which enabled the worthy prelate to draw part of his income from the charms of the notorious 'Winchester Geese', possibly so-called because of their white skin and long necks.

Upriver, at Lambeth, the archbishop of Canterbury maintained a permanent home from 1207 onwards, testimony to the emerging role of Westminster as a fixed centre of royal administration and justice. Between these two extremes were ranged other episcopal edifices commemorated today in the names of Salisbury Court and Ely Place, where the tiny thirteenth-century church of St Etheldreda still survives. In the fourteenth century, the doctrine of purgatory was energetically promoted, giving prayers for the souls of the dead a heightened significance. Wealthy citizens began to endow chantry chapels where stipendiary priests could celebrate mass daily to shorten the time before they could enter heaven. This led to the adornment of many churches and a great augmentation in the clerical population of the city. Chantry priests, whose efforts were clearly devoted to the salvation of patrons rather than the benefit of the community as a whole, became a focus for popular resentment, as did unemployed clerics drawn to London by the lure of such undemanding labour.

Plague and Protest

> The pestilence, which originally started in the country occupied by the Saracens . . . started in England in the region of Dorchester about the time of the Feast of St.Peter (29 June) 1348 . . . and around the Feast of All Saints (November 1) it reached London . . . and it increased so much that from the Feast of Purification (2 February) until after Easter in a newly made cemetery next to Smithfield more than two hundred bodies were buried almost every day . . .

This plague pit on the western fringe of the city covered 13 acres. Twenty years later it was to become the site of the Charterhouse, where Carthusian monks lived a life of poverty and silence. Another emergency cemetery was opened in the Minories, the area occupied by priests in minor orders, on the eastern side of the city. The total death toll appears to have been about 30,000, perhaps half the entire population of the city. The Black Death returned in 1361, a little less virulently than in its first visitation but it still killed off so many of the learned that from thenceforward the law courts at Westminster conducted their proceedings not in French but in English. Further bad outbreaks of plague occurred in 1369 and 1375.

LABOUR MARKET

These epidemics had a dramatic impact on the labour market, despite parliament's panic-stricken efforts to impose a statutory wage-freeze. Now labour, not land, was in short supply and the common man might begin to take a bolder tone with his master and even dream of a better life than his father had ever known. At the same time the continuing wars with France and Scotland gave increasing numbers of men another escape-route from serfdom, as well as the opportunity to learn a skill in arms which they might one day use on their own account. John Ball, whom the French chronicler Jean Froissart dismissed as a 'crazy priest' found many eager listeners to his impromptu wayside harangues: 'We all come from one father and one mother, Adam and Eve; whereby can they say or show that they be greater lords than we be, saving that they cause us to win and labour for what they spend. They are clothed in velvet . . . and we be clad with poor cloth: they have their wines, spices, and good bread, and we have the rye, the bran, and the straw . . .' Ball's populist message was easily reduced to a single rhymed slogan:

> When Adam delved (dug) and Eve span,
> Who was then the gentleman?

The Peasants' Revolt

The death of enfeebled Edward III and the accession of his ten–year-old grandson as Richard II heralded a dangerous moment for the stability of the throne. The imposition of a poll tax in that same year, 1377, caused widespread discontent; as a simple impost on every unprivileged individual, regardless of means, it was bound to press hardest on those least able to pay. The attempt to impose a second poll tax in 1381 turned popular disquiet into a general uprising. This Peasants' Revolt involved disturbances from Hampshire to Cheshire but it was in London that it reached its climax and its resolution.

JACK STRAW AND WAT TYLER

The peasants of Essex, led by a priest, Jack Straw, and their fellows from Kent, led by an ex-soldier, Walter ('Wat') the Tyler, converged on the capital to lay their grievances before a fumbling government. London offered little resistance to the oncoming horde, estimated by one chronicler as 60,000 strong, larger than the entire population of the city itself. Relations between the City fathers and the court were at a low ebb and the City was itself divided by its own rivalries, both within and between classes. It was an alderman who let down the drawbridge and allowed the Kentish mob to surge across London Bridge and it was another who stood by as the Essex contingent poured through Aldgate, their numbers swelling as trouble-seeking apprentices, beggars and thieves joined the throng.

In the confusion there were abundant opportunities to commit outrages with impunity. Seven Flemings were murdered out of hand at Clerkenwell and 35 more at St Martin's, Vintry – the fact that the area was the centre of the wine trade may not have been unconnected with this. The prisons were opened and their inmates recruited into the ranks of the army of protest. At the Temple the lawyers' muniment rooms were ransacked and their records burned. To the west of the city, on the road to Westminster, the luxurious riverside palace of the Savoy, home of John of Gaunt, the boy-king's powerful uncle, was singled out for special attention. The duke himself escaped but his plate and furnishings were hurled onto a bonfire and his jewels crushed and thrown into the Thames as a gesture of hatred towards a man so reviled that his attackers would even steal from him. One who did try to loot on his own account was himself thrown on the bonfire, and when the wine cellar collapsed on 30 more drunken plunderers they were left beneath the wreckage to die of their injuries or starve. A box of gunpowder mistakenly consigned to the flames brought down the Great Hall and rendered the entire palace uninhabitable.

RICHARD II

From the Tower, Richard II courageously sent word that he would meet the rebels at Mile End, a hamlet and patch of open ground to the east of the city. He did so and promised not only an amnesty but a charter of reforms which would have put serfs on a footing with free men. Reassured, the Essex rebels began to disperse; but meanwhile, back in the City itself, a separate band was storming the Tower and dragging the archbishop of Canterbury and the royal treasurer out to Tower Hill, where their heads were hacked off. Returning to London the king took refuge overnight in the royal wardrobe, a high-security facility for his personal finery, (as opposed to state regalia), which stood near the Blackfriars monastery.

The following day Richard faced another mob, this time Wat Tyler's Kentish men, drawn up at Smithfield. What exactly passed between the boy and an evidently disrespectful Tyler is not known for certain – but it was enough to provoke Mayor William Walworth, a leading figure in the royal entourage, into stabbing Tyler dead for it. (His dagger is preserved in Fishmonger's Hall.) As the crowd milled and muttered in

Richard II, the earliest known portrait of an English king

confusion the 14-year-old monarch himself rode boldly forward and, rising in his stirrups, bawled 'I will be your chief and captain!'. Whether startled or bemused by this turn of events, the ranks of armed and sullen men allowed themselves to be led to Clerkenwell where they gradually melted away – after which the government got a grip on itself, reneged on all its promises, and hunted down and hanged all the ring-leaders who could be identified. Jack Straw was beheaded at Smithfield and John Ball was hanged, drawn and quartered as the king looked on. Mayor Walworth was knighted. But there were no more poll taxes.

Money and Merchants

It was Norman policy to encourage the immigration of Jews, many of whom came initially from Rouen. Forbidden to own inheritable land, they held their wealth in cash or precious objects such as jewels, furs, silks and books, pledged as collateral for the loans they made to kings, barons and merchants alike. Christians were forbidden by canon law to lend money at interest but credit was vital to the smooth functioning of government and commerce alike. Jewry Street and Old Jewry in the City recall the presence of a community which both benefited from royal protection and was ultimately the victim of royal ruthlessness. Jews had no political rights and were subject to many discriminatory restrictions. Until 1177 Jews throughout the country (there were substantial communities in York, Oxford, Lincoln and Norwich) were compelled to bring the bodies of their dead to be interred in a special burial-ground at Cripplegate, a burden in itself in violation of Jewish sacred law requiring interment within 24 hours of death. After 1181 Jews were forbidden to bear arms even in their own defence. And in 1222 Archbishop Langton decreed that: 'To prevent ... the mixture of Jewish men and women with Christians of each sex, we charge ... that the Jews of both sexes wear a linen cloth, two inches broad and four fingers long of a different colour from their own clothes, on their upper garment, before their breast.'

Jews were constantly liable to exceptional taxation at the whim of the monarch and were frequently caught up in disturbances which had nothing whatever to do with them. In 1189 they were attacked because some of their leaders had, to show loyalty to the throne, attended the coronation of Richard I.

Some Jews practised medicine but even this profession had its perils. When one lost a prominent patient in 1130 the entire community was fined £2,000 'for a sick man whom they killed.' Despite all these discouragements many Jews prospered, living in fine houses. A century after the Conquest it is estimated that they may have held as much as a third of all the movable wealth in England; through mortgages they may have had an indirect hold on much land as well. By 1188 they were raising about a twelfth of the crown's entire annual income.

MASSACRE

In 1262, when the kingdom was torn by the struggle between Henry III and the baronial opposition led by Simon de Montfort, 'the King's Jews' became the victims of a terror which could not be visited upon the king himself. The chronicler Thomas Wykes recorded sorrowfully:

... the slaughter of the Jews which was perpetrated at that time in London should not be passed over in silence.... Rushing ... in unexpected tumult on the Jews, of whom a very great multitude dwelt with all confidence in London, little thinking that harm would happen to them, they, enticed not by the zeal of the law, but by their lust for worldly goods, most cruelly slew as many as they could find in the city ... nearly four hundred Jews of both sexes and all ranks being killed. And although they were not signed with the mark of our faith, it seemed an inhuman and impious deed to slay them without cause.

The 'cause' was, of course, apart from prejudice and plunder, the chance to destroy documentary records of all outstanding debts. Henry III established a 'Domus Conversorum' (House of Converts) in what is now Chancery Lane (then New Street), where Jews who renounced their faith and their property in favour of Christianity could find succour and a stipend of one-and-a-half pennies a day. Few seem to have wished to take advantage of this dubious bargain, except to prey upon their former fellows. Under Edward I collection of a special poll tax on all Jews over 12 was sub-contracted to one 'William le Convert', who had thought up the idea in the first place. Between 1263 and 1273 the Crown extorted some £420,000 from the Jews who 'enjoyed' its 'protection'. The insecurity of the Jews' position is well illustrated by an incident in the reign of Edward I when the corpse of a Christian boy was found to bear puncture marks alleged to resemble Hebrew letters. Unknown Jews were charged with ritual murder and, after the body was buried in St Paul's with some pomp, the entire community was fined 60,000 marks, payable over five years. In 1286 some 600 Jews were accused of coin-clipping and incarcerated in the Tower; almost half were subsequently hanged.

EXPULSION

In October 1290 the entire Jewish population of the kingdom, some 16,000, was finally expelled to Flanders. Royal protection was extended to their persons and movables but their houses, shops, synagogues and cemeteries were forfeited to the crown. Not until 1656, under Cromwell's Commonwealth, was a Jewish community to be re-established in London.

Cosmopolitan London

The enforced exodus of the Jews left a financial vacuum which was filled by Italian bankers whose favoured area of operations became known as Lombard Street. Other significant foreign communities included Flemings, concerned with the traffic in fine wool, England's main export, to the cloth-making towns of Flanders, and Gascons, engaged in the wine trade with Bordeaux, which was still under the rule of the English crown. The presence of permanent foreign communities did not, however, make the capital a sunny scene of cosmopolitan harmony. In 1308 Edward II was obliged to warn Londoners to be on their best behaviour at his forthcoming coronation: 'The King doth command that all persons shall receive and pay honour to the French and the other folks from abroad who have come, and shall come, to the said coronation; and that no one shall do them wrong in word or deed, on pain of imprisonment for a year and a day, and of forfeiture to the king in the loss of all that they have.'

THE HANSEATIC LEAGUE

Near Dowgate Hill stood the Steelyard, London headquarters of the powerful Hanseatic League, a federation of merchants from north German and Baltic cities who prudently kept their daily contacts with Londoners to the minimum, avoiding even the playing of games, lest they should lead to quarrels and blows. Drinking their preferred Rhenish wine, using their own currency, excluding all women and electing their own aldermen in their own guildhall, they remained in occupation for some four centuries until their privileges were revoked in 1551 and they were finally banished in 1598.

There were, of course, wealthy English merchants, too. One such was Gybon Maufeld of Billingsgate, who rose to be both an alderman and a sheriff. He dealt in everything from pearls to millstones and, as a moneylender, made loans not only to merchants and courtiers but also the royal architect, Yevele, and the poets Gower and Chaucer. But he evidently over-extended himself and died bankrupt in 1397, his estate being seized by the king, which is why his account book has survived.

Dick Whittington

Far different was the story of medieval London's best-known businessman, the legendary – and also historical – Dick Whittington. Alas, the pantomime hero did not arrive in London a poor boy but the third son of a wealthy Gloucestershire family. And his famed 'cat' was not a faithful feline but the name commonly given to a type of boat much used in coastal trade. The story that he was urged on to destiny by hearing Bow Bells ring out 'Turn again, Whittington, thrice Lord Mayor of London', dates from a play produced in 1605 (by when the term 'Lord' Mayor had become current), long after Whittington's death in 1423. The spot where this is supposed to have happened, on Highgate Hill, is marked by a nineteenth-century stone inscribed with two errors – he was four times mayor, not three, and was never knighted as the stone says.

PHILANTHROPY

Dick Whittington's fame probably derives from his great philanthropy. His will left money for the founding of a College of Priests (part of whose duties was to pray for his soul) and an almshouse on what is now College Hill, next to the church of St Michael Paternoster Royal, where he was buried and is commemorated by a charming memorial window (with cat!). He also left money for the paving of the new Guildhall and the refurbishment of Newgate prison. This generosity was the product of no death-bed repentance for he made many donations during his lifetime, including one for a ward for unmarried mothers: '... a new chamber with eight beds for young women who had done amiss, in trust of a good amendment ... all things that had been done in that chamber should be kept secret ... for he would not shame no young woman in no wise, for it might be the cause of their letting (hindering) their marriage.'

Geoffrey Chaucer (c. 1342–1400)

If the facts of Dick Whittington's life are tantalisingly fragmentary, the life of his most famous contemporary, Geoffrey Chaucer, is far better documented. 'The Father of English poetry' was born around 1342 in the Vintry, where the hall of the Vintners' Company still stands (Chaucer and his father were both members). The nearby church of St Michael Paternoster Royal reveals in its name not a connection with the throne but with La Reole, a centre of the wine trade near Bordeaux. Chaucer's bourgeois background was no barrier to royal employment and in the course of a varied career he travelled in Flanders, France and Italy, served as a soldier, spy, customs official, member of parliament, diplomat and building project manager. It was the latter connection, which involved supervising work at Westminster, which probably secured him burial in the abbey. The funeral monument which celebrates his literary status was not added until Tudor times.

For more than a decade Chaucer lived in a suite of rooms in the gatehouse of Aldgate, from which he could observe the traffic and travellers on the main eastern route out of the City. This experience, and the opportunities which his official position gave him to meet all sorts, from courtiers and clerics to merchants and masons, helped him to develop that broad knowledge of human types he used to such effect in the prologue to his *Canterbury Tales*, introducing us to very individual pilgrims, each of whom tells a tale which is true to their character.

The Chaucer family's wine trade connections may help to explain the poet's early fluency in French. Where he acquired Italian is not known, perhaps in Italy, perhaps from Italian merchants in London. His unique standing in the history of English literature rests, however, on the fact that despite his mastery of courtly French, learned Latin and fashionable Italian, he deliberately chose to compose his masterpiece in the language of his native city.

CHAPTER THREE

From Medieval to Modern, 1400–1600

Livery Companies

The munificence of a Dick Whittington symbolises the ascendancy of the great City companies and the oligarchy which controlled them in late medieval times. But there is an even more potent symbol. In 1411 the chronicler Robert Fabyan recorded that: 'In this year was the Gild Hall of London to be new edified, and an old and little cottage made into a fair and goodly house ...'. Ever since then this has remained the heart of the City's government and it is of the utmost significance that it has always been called Guildhall and not City Hall.

The City companies have their origin in the frith guilds of the Saxon period. These mutual aid societies provided their members with a range of economic and spiritual benefits, serving as a cross between a religious brotherhood and a social security system. Over the centuries these functions were taken over by associations of craftsmen or traders who were additionally concerned to regulate the conditions of their livelihood, and in particular such matters as training, pricing and quality control. The earliest surviving document incorporating a craft gild is that of the weavers, around 1155. Their agreement, witnessed by Thomas Becket, gave them control of their craft in return for an annual payment to the king. By the fourteenth century, some of the major gilds were being given powers which were national rather than merely local in scope. As their powers grew so did the ambition of the companies to affirm their status by building fine halls for their meetings and holding elaborate processions and lavish banquets on major royal or civic occasions or on the 'holyday' of their gild's patron saint. Such pageants are the ancestors of today's annual Lord Mayor's Show.

POLITICAL POWER

On such special days all those granted the privilege of doing so wore splendid 'livery' or uniforms, made up from expensive cloth and gorgeously embroidered or trimmed with fur. As only 'liverymen' were entitled to take part in the election of the lord mayor and sheriffs, the livery companies, as they became known, wielded political as much as economic and social power. Clashes occurred both within and between companies. Ordinary craftsmen sought to challenge the virtual monopoly of office exercised by the wealthiest members of their trade. 'Non-victualling' companies worked together to make life difficult for

𝕷𝖔𝖓𝖉𝖔𝖓

The earliest printed view of London

the Grocers or Fishmongers by stirring up the poor to protest against food prices. Conflict could go as far as pitched battles, with lives lost and ring leaders hanged. But even the deadliest rivals would close ranks when it came to keeping out foreigners.

CHARITY

More constructively, livery companies continued to echo their frith guild origins by endowing charitable causes, particularly almshouses and schools. St Paul's, established in 1510 by John Colet, the cathedral's Dean, pioneered the teaching of Greek and Latin and thus established the model for subsequent 'grammar schools'. Colet was the son of a mercer and placed the governance of the school in the charge of the Mercers' Company. Other livery companies which came to establish schools included the Merchant Taylors and Haberdashers and, in Victorian times, the Coopers and Stationers.

In 1514 the Court of Aldermen established an order of precedence which confirmed the status of the 12 'Great Companies' – Mercers, Grocers, Drapers, Fishmongers, Goldsmiths, Skinners, Merchant Taylors, Haberdashers, Salters, Ironmongers, Vintners and Cloth-workers. After the establishment of the Fanmakers in 1709 no new companies were created until 1929 when the Air Pilots and Air Navigators Guild came into existence. In 1992 the Information Technologists became the one-hundredth city company. Although they have largely shed their religious character, apart from the rituals of annual services to mark special occasions, the city companies have retained many of their charitable activities, especially in the field of education, and through the sponsorship of prizes and research relating to their professional field of interest.

Crown and Corporation

When Henry V returned to his capital after his great victory over the French at Agincourt in 1415 he made a triumphal progress over London Bridge, attended a service of thanksgiving in St Paul's and was given a gargantuan feast at Guildhall. Legend has it that, as a gesture of admiration and generosity, Dick Whittington concluded the joyous proceedings by taking the promissory notes issued by the king against City loans to finance his campaign and hurled them into the fire. True or not the story attests to the closeness of crown and corporation. When the crown itself became the object of contending aristocratic factions during the Wars of the Roses London was largely untroubled. Although there was sympathy for the Lancastrian cause among the poor the ruling élite was solidly Yorkist. In 1471 London's loyalties were twice put to the test. At Easter, contingents of troops were despatched to Barnet, some ten miles north of the City, where they helped Edward IV to a decisive victory. In May 'The Bastard Fauconberg', self-proclaimed 'Captain of King Henry's People in Kent', demanded to pass through the City on his way to join the Lancastrian army. When the mayor refused him passage Fauconberg sent an assault party which burst through Aldgate only to find itself trapped. Fauconberg there-upon withdrew into Kent where he was hunted down and in September 'Thos Fauconbrydge his head was yesterday set upon London Bridge, looking into Kentwards.'

Edward IV

Edward IV remained ever mindful of the support that London had given his cause. Handsome and affable, he went out of his way to cultivate cordial relations with the merchant princes of the capital, inviting them to hunt with him in Waltham Forest, dining in their houses and even raising five aldermen to become Knights of the Bath.

A Publishing Revolution

The stability established by Edward IV provided a suitable setting for the introduction and rapid development of a new technology which would revolutionise the art of book production within a generation and confine the scribe to writing charters and other legal documents.

WILLIAM CAXTON

In 1476 William Caxton set up the first printing press in England in the shadow of Westminster Abbey. Long domiciled in Bruges and

Cologne Caxton, upon returning to England, brought back the magical machine with his baggage. Over the next 15 years he was to produce more than 90 books, involving 18,000 pages, hand-set in eight different type-faces, and ranging from *The Game and Play of Chess* to an edition of Chaucer's *Canterbury Tales*. He also became a large-scale importer of books from abroad, challenging the Hansa merchants already established in this field.

When Caxton died he bequeathed his press to his assistant Wynkyn de Worde, and the enthusiastic amateur gave way to the hard-headed professional. One of de Worde's first business decisions was to relocate in the Fleet Street area, which has been associated with printing ever since; another crucial commitment was to print texts to suit the curriculum of the new grammar schools.

Henry VIII's concern to damp down the spread of heretical ideas led in 1534 to the passage of an Act which, referring to the 'marvellous number of printed books' imported over the previous 50 years, effectively banned the trade henceforth thus securing for English printers a virtual monopoly of the domestic market. Another restrictive practice to their advantage was the decision to limit editions to 1,250 copies, after which the type had to be broken up and reset, thus creating more employment.

THE STATIONERS

In 1557 the Stationers, established as a Brotherhood in 1403, were recognised by royal charter and became in effect the instrument of official censorship, registering the publication of all books until 1911. Stationers' Hall still stands a stone's throw from St Paul's churchyard which by the sixteenth century had become established as the centre of London's publishing and bookselling business. Caxton would no doubt have been gratified to know that a century after his death no less than 50 printing presses were at work in London.

Law and a Lawyer

If one required any proof that the Tudors had made even their mightier subjects feel the smack of firm government, it can be seen in the greater willingness of the powerful to resolve their disputes not on the battlefield but in the courts, with serjeants-at-law rather than sergeants-at-arms.

THE INNS OF COURT AND CHANCERY

By the early sixteenth century it was reckoned that almost 2,000 students were enrolled in the Inns of Court or the less prestigious Inns of Chancery. For many sons of landowning or merchant families they offered an education far more attractive than the ancient universities of Oxford and Cambridge. Few had any intention of completing the seven years of study required of a professional lawyer. Most came for a year or two, making useful social and business connections and taking part in the lively, sometimes rowdy, cultural life of the capital. And, as many of them would, in later life, find themselves disputing land boundaries, contesting wills or serving as justices of the peace a smattering of jurisprudence was no bad thing to have picked up either.

Thomas More

One student who did stay the whole course was Thomas More (?1477–1535), destined to become Henry VIII's Becket. Like Becket More was London-born, like Becket well-educated and of outstanding ability. He rose like a rocket to become Lord Chancellor of England, the first layman to hold that office. Like Becket, More became not only the king's most trusted counsellor but his friend as well. And even a king might think himself fortunate to have the company of such a man. An ascetic who had voluntarily endured the privations of the Charterhouse before deciding that he was not suited to the cloister, More was cultured as well as learned. His riverside house at Chelsea, where Hans Holbein lived for three years before moving on to become court painter, was so attractive to the king that Henry built himself a similar country retreat virtually next door.

Like Becket, More perished because he would not, could not, budge on an issue of principle. Refusing to accept the validity of the king's marriage to Anne Boleyn, he resigned his great office and declined to attend her coronation. His refusal to take the Oath of Supremacy, acknowledging the king as head of the church in England, sealed his fate and he was imprisoned in great privation in the Bell Tower at the Tower of London. More's stout-hearted wife wrote to him uncomprehendingly: '. . . And seeing you have at Chelsea a right fair house, your books, your gallery, your garden, your orchard and all other necessaries so handsome about you, where you might in the company of me your wife, your children and household be merry, I muse what a God's name you mean here still thus fondly to tarry.'

TOWER HILL EXECUTION

But tarry More did until, emaciated and bedraggled, he was led forth to Tower Hill for an execution he faced with uncharacteristic levity, saying to the Lieutenant of the Tower as he stood at the foot of the scaffold, 'I pray you, Sir, see me safe up and for my coming down, let me shift for myself.'

More's Chelsea home has long since vanished but a modern statue of him stands in front of Chelsea Old Church where he worshipped. As if to symbolise his renunciation of worldly allegiance he bears his chain of office not around his neck but spread across his knees.

Monks and Martyrs

'Who is she that will set her hand to work to get 3d a day and may have at least 20d a day to sleep an hour with a friar, a monk or a priest?'

By the beginning of the sixteenth century this sort of gibe would find ready endorsement in London, where so many clerics were concentrated. Citizens increasingly resented the fact that clergy, and laymen attached to the church, were outside the common law and that such taxes as they did pay went to Rome rather than the king or the city. In the north of England where the monasteries still provided valuable welfare services to the community, Henry VIII's Dissolution provoked protest and rebellion; but in London those who might have mourned their passing were swept aside by those who were eager to grab their assets. Although ten of the monastic chapels took on a new lease of life as parish churches, most monastic buildings were either converted to secular uses or demolished. The Austin Friars church became a wine warehouse, Greyfriars was used to store herrings and Charterhouse to stow the king's tents. Crutched Friars' priory was plundered for stone to repair the Tower and the land built over. The Leathersellers acquired the dormitory of the former nunnery of St Helens, Bishopsgate.

MONASTIC RUINS

In 1551 the Venetian ambassador noted disapprovingly that the City was 'disfigured by the ruins of a multitude of churches and monasteries'; but by releasing monastic properties which could become building sites the Dissolution did temporarily relieve the City's overcrowding. The discontinuance of monastic services however obliged both crown and corporation to take on more responsibility for the care of the insane and the aged as well as the education of the young. Henry VIII himself was persuaded to refound St Bartholomew's Hospital; his statue stands over its gateway to this day. Edward VI turned Bridewell Palace over to the City to serve as a home for orphans and a house of correction for petty offenders. The buildings of the former Greyfriars monastery he converted into a new school – Christ's Hospital. Elizabeth I refounded Westminster School.

Because there was very little active resistance to the Dissolution in London it was accomplished with little bloodshed, except in the case of the Charterhouse, where six brothers were executed for their defiance and nine more chained up until they starved to death.

RELIGIOUS PERSECUTIONS

London was not, however, to be spared the horrors attendant upon religious persecution. In the last year of Henry VIII's reign 25-year-old protestant Anne Askew was burned as a heretic at Smithfield in the presence of the Lord Mayor. Under Mary Tudor more than 40 were to perish in the flames there. The first was John Rogers, within sight of the church of St Sepulchre, Newgate where, as vicar, he had preached against the papacy – '... the fire was put unto him; and ... he, as one feeling no smart, washed his hands in the flame as though it had been in cold water.'

The sufferings at Smithfield were vividly chronicled by John Foxe, a protestant cleric, whose *Book of Martyrs*, illustrated with woodcuts, was published in 1563. Its sales were surpassed only by those of the Bible itself and it helped to whip up a tide of anti-Catholic feeling which enabled Londoners to yell their approval when, under Elizabeth, it was no longer protestants being burned at Smithfield but catholic recusants and Jesuits being carted off to Tyburn to be hanged, drawn and quartered.

'Evil May Day'

In 1437 there were only about 500 registered aliens in London; by 1583 there were over 5,000. The increase in their number was welcomed by thoughtful citizens, who appreciated the technical skills they invariably brought with them; but ordinary Londoners were likely to be less enthusiastic. In 1497 an Italian visitor recorded that: 'Londoners have such fierce tempers and wicked dispositions that they not only despise the way in which Italians live, but actually pursue them with uncontrolled hatred. They look askance at us by day, and at night they sometimes drive us off with kicks and blows of the truncheon.'

A century later the duke of Württemberg came to the remarkably similar conclusion that even though London was: '. . . a large, excellent and mighty city of business . . . its inhabitants are extremely proud and overbearing; and because the greater part, especially the tradespeople, seldom go into other countries . . . they care little for foreigners, but scoff and laugh at them, and moreover one dare not oppose them, else the street boys and apprentices collect together in immense crowds, striking to the right and left unmercifully. . .'.

CURFEW

Anti-foreign feeling did, on one occasion, rebound on the Londoners themselves. In Easter Week 1517, the City authorities, concerned at the growing number of incidents involving insult and injury to innocent foreigners, proclaimed a special curfew on the eve of May Day lest the customary revels got out of hand. Ironically it was the very attempt to enforce this unaccustomed ban which, in fact, provoked the very riot it was intended to avert. Apprentices defied the aldermen charged with shooing them indoors and began breaking windows and jeering at foreigners, most of whom had the good sense to stay safely locked up indoors. Those unfortunate enough to be caught on the streets were likely to be forced up against a wall and told to identify the left-overs of an apprentice's lunch. If they made the mistake of saying *Brot und Kase*, instead of bread and cheese, they were in for a beating.

Enemies of the City, particularly at court, saw a grand chance to make mischief, alleging that the authorities had completely lost control of the situation, which would greatly damage the king's amicable relations with foreign powers and was, therefore, little short of treason. While volunteers from the Inns of Court mustered and the Lieutenant of the Tower fired off artillery to no very clear purpose, Sir Thomas More toured the streets, successfully persuading many of the rowdies to go to their homes. But he was too late to save all of them from royal wrath and 13 'younglings' were summarily hanged for their part in the disturbances. Further pleading by More and the mayor persuaded the king to commute the punishment of the rest to a humiliating parade through the streets with each boy wearing a hangman's noose about his neck. The Venetian ambassador recorded smugly but accurately, 'this has been a great commotion, but the terror was greater than the harm.'

An Elizabethan Tycoon

The career of Sir Thomas Gresham (1519–79) is a prime example of the close connection between royal service and commercial eminence in Tudor times. Such was Gresham's fame in his own day that the story of his life quickly became overlaid with fanciful legend; the grasshopper that became his emblem was said to have been adopted because he had been abandoned in a field as an infant and was found because the chirping of grasshoppers had attracted the attention of passers-by. In fact Gresham was no foundling but the son of a leading mercer and lord mayor, who had the grasshopper as part of his coat of arms before Gresham was even born.

In 1543 young Gresham entered the Mercers' Company and government service simultaneously, being sent to Antwerp to buy gunpowder for the royal arsenal. His role gradually expanded into that of a general agent on behalf of the crown, both making purchases and gathering information. Under Mary, Gresham's career did little more than mark time, but on the accession of Elizabeth he rode post haste to put himself at her disposal and was 'made a young man again' by the warmth of her welcome. Resuming his position as royal agent on the Continent, he also served as English ambassador at Brussels, for which he was knighted. Even after his return to England he continued to be involved in diplomacy in an informal way, offering semi-official hospitality to visiting dignitaries such as Cardinal de Chastillon and Count Casimir of the Palatinate.

GRESHAM'S LAW

Gresham's other major role was to act as a confidential economic adviser to the crown. Even today he is remembered as the formulator of 'Gresham's Law' – that bad money drives good money out of circulation. As an expert on credit and coinage he helped stabilise English currency during the crucial early years of Elizabeth's reign. He then went on to whittle away the privileged position of the Hansa merchants and to make the government so far independent of foreign financing that by 1570 he could boast that, 'Her Majesty cannot lack in money matters, if it were for £40 or £50,000 within her City of London.'

The Royal Exchange

Vital though Gresham's expertise may have been to the development of public finance and the encouragement of commercial enterprise his most visible contribution to his native city was the realisation of a scheme projected a generation previously by his own father who, having been mightily impressed by the bourse at Antwerp, was fired with the vision of building one in London. Gresham agreed that it was absurd that businessmen should have to conduct their negotiations standing about in Lombard Street and even 'walk in the rain when it raineth, more like pedlars than merchants.' So, at his own expense, he built London its own trading centre, employing a Flemish architect and Flemish bricklayers and even importing the slate, glass and other building materials from the Low Countries as well. Queen Elizabeth, after visiting it, decreed that it should thenceforth be known as the Royal Exchange. A huge grasshopper sign on the roof left no one in any doubt about the identity of its creator. Gresham's Royal Exchange was destroyed in the Great Fire of 1666 and its replacement by fire again in 1838. The present Royal Exchange, opened in 1844 still incorporates a statue of Gresham and a Turkish pavement from his original building.

Under the terms of Gresham's will his house in Broad Street was to go to his wife for her lifetime and then to become Gresham College, where free lectures would be given by resident professors whose annual stipend of £50 would be provided from the rents of the shops in the Royal Exchange. Seven subjects were covered, one on each day of the week – divinity, astronomy, music, geometry, law, medicine and rhetoric. The Royal Society, Britain's premier scientific institution, was to develop out of the weekly meetings of the seven professors. Gresham College is now part of City University and Gresham Street honours in its name the memory of its founder.

JOINT-STOCK COMPANIES

During Gresham's lifetime a decisive shift took place in the centre of gravity of north European commerce and finance, away from Antwerp and in favour of London. In no small part this was due to Gresham's own efforts but in part also to the destruction wrought in the Low Countries by Spanish occupation forces. Much credit, however, must also be given to the effort and enterprise of London merchants in perfecting a new form of trading organisation to spread the risks inherent in long-distance commerce – the joint-stock company. These specialised ventures concentrated on particular markets. The first, founded in 1555, was the Muscovy Company which established links with Russia and later with Persia. This was followed by the Turkey Company and Levant Company, trading with the Middle East, the Guinea Company trading with Africa, and the Virginia Company to settle and exploit America. The Hudson Bay Company, formed to control the fur trade of Canada, went far beyond its original remit to play a major role in administering the western regions of that vast country, while the East India Company, originally intended to spearhead English efforts to get into the vastly profitable Indian spice trade, became over the centuries the effective government of the entire sub-continent.

Alarums and Excursions!

If the Tudor monarchy was strong, its strength did not go unchallenged and on several occasions, these threats reached the capital itself.

In 1553 Mary's plan to marry King Philip of Spain provoked a rebellion by Sir Thomas Wyatt of Allington in Kent, son of the poet of the same name. Mary acted decisively and, riding to Guildhall, made a stirring speech, which reminded her subjects of their allegiance and seemed to imply a reconsideration of the marriage project. Twenty thousand men enrolled to defend her throne and the city. Wyatt, after a skirmish at Hyde Park, pressed on with a depleted and disheartened force as far as Ludgate, which was barred and defended against him. He surrendered – aged 33, a father of 11, he was beheaded on Tower Hill.

In his death-speech Wyatt had taken care to emphasise that Elizabeth, then princess, had had no knowledge of his plot. As queen she was to be the intended victim of no less than six major attempts at *coup d'état*. But no domestic subversion was as dangerous as the huge Spanish armada which bore down on England in the summer of 1588.

SPANISH ARMADA

London was prepared. At Tilbury a boom made of 120 masts and 40 anchors, lashed together with nine-inch cables, blocked the Thames, providing at the same time a floating platform for artillery and a bridge which would allow the earl of Leicester to move his men to the Kentish shore should a Spanish landing take place there. As further precautions nine more batteries were sited at bends in the river to rake an oncoming fleet broadside and at Blackwall a second boom was laid. In London itself a force of 10,000 irregulars was raised, headed by the Honourable Artillery Company, and under the command of Lord Hunsdon, the queen's cousin and Lord Chamberlain (and later patron of Shake-speare). In villages and towns along the Essex shore, from Brentwood to Stratford, volunteers mustered behind barricades.

On 8 August the queen reviewed her troops at Tilbury, making a speech which has become legendary for its majestic defiance. Adjourning for a meal she then received despatches informing her of the defeat of the Spanish fleet. In the heady days that followed a military review was held at St James's and captured Spanish flags were displayed in St Paul's cathedral, where, in November, a commemorative service was held at which Queen Elizabeth 'gave God's public thanks for that triumphant and ever memorable victory over the Spanish Fleet proudly called the Invincible.'

The Play's the Thing

London's earliest known theatrical performances took place on trestle stages erected in the courtyards of inns. And almost from the start they were the subject of fierce opposition, condemned as lewd, time-wasting and a health hazard, liable to spread the plague by creating unnecessary crowds. In 1574 the lord mayor and aldermen were empowered to censor plays and regulate their presentation – which was enough to provoke carpenter-turned-actor James Burbage to erect London's first purpose-built playhouse, 'The Theatre'. Located at Shoreditch it stood outside the City walls and therefore beyond the jurisdiction of its censors; but it was no more than a stroll away for the potential playgoer. (The site, in Curtain Road, is now marked by a plaque.)

WILLIAM SHAKESPEARE

Equipped with a permanent stage and proper dressing-rooms The Theatre could accommodate an audience of about a thousand. It opened in 1577 and was such an immediate success that it inspired the establishment of a rival, The Curtain, barely 200 yards away. Eventually the two companies merged and, more important, acquired the powerful protection of Lord Hunsdon to become 'the Lord Chamberlain's men'. The star of the company was Burbage's son, Richard and its major creative support, William Shakespeare, who joined it in 1594, having already been in London some eight years. Other members of the troupe included John Heminge and William

The Globe Theatre

Condell, who took it upon themselves, after Shakespeare's death, to collect and publish the First Folio edition of his plays, which would almost certainly otherwise have been lost to posterity. Their memorial, surmounted by a bust of the bard approved by his widow as a good likeness, stands in the churchyard of St Mary Aldermanbury, where they themselves lie buried. (The church itself was taken down after World War Two and re-erected at Fulton, Missouri as a memorial to Winston Churchill.)

When Burbage's lease ran out he coolly disassembled The Theatre (thus cruelly disappointing the ground landlord who intended to claim it for himself) and used the timbers to erect The Globe over on the south side of the river at Bankside and right next to the company's only serious rivals, 'the Lord Admiral's Men.' Their patron was Lord Howard of Effingham, hero of the Armada and their theatre was The Rose. Here between 1594 and 1600 manager, Philip Henslowe, and actor, Edward Alleyne, produced no less than 55 plays, including Marlowe's *Tamburlaine* and *Faustus*. Alleyne was so successful that he retired from the stage in 1597, returning to the boards three years later at the express request of the queen. In that year the company migrated to The Fortune, a new playhouse, modelled closely on The Globe but situated in Golden Lane, on the north side of the city. When Alleyne finally did retire, before the age of 40, he was so wealthy that he could buy the manor of Dulwich outright and endow a foundation which was to establish 'Alleyn's College of God's Gift at Dulwich' and eventually to benefit half-a-dozen other schools.

Although it is customary to hail the period which produced Shakespeare, Marlowe, Jonson, Fletcher, Chapman, Massinger, Ford and Dekker as a 'golden age' of theatre, it is as well to remember that the audiences who thronged to see their plays were equally eager spectators of 'sports' which involved the merciless tormenting of chained bulls and blinded bears. And even the great Alleyne owed at least part of his fortune to the income he derived as 'Master of the Royal Game of Bears, Bulls and Mastiff Dogs.'

Surveying Change

In 1604 James I gave a royal licence to beg to 'a very aged and worthy member of our city of London, who hath for 45 years to his great charge and with neglect of his ordinary means of maintenance, for the general good as well as posterity, compiled and published divers necessary books and chronicles.' The man was John Stow, London's first true historian. A tailor by trade, Stow was really a frustrated academic. In 1561 he published an edition of Chaucer's works and in 1565 *A Summarie of Englyshe Chronicles* which went through 11 editions. Throughout his long life Stow remained endlessly curious about his native city. Born in 1525 he had quizzed old men who could recall the Wars of the Roses; but he was no mere fact-grubbing antiquarian and fully deserves the title historian for his relentlessly methodical gathering of source materials.

JOHN STOW

Retiring from his trade Stow spent years on 'the discovery of London, my native soil and country.' He walked every street, visited every church, noted every monument. He examined the archives of the Tower, the parishes and the livery companies. Had he never written a line his efforts in rescuing priceless documents from the decaying collections of former monasteries would have earned him the gratitude of all subsequent historians. Without formal scholarly training or the support of a wealthy patron, he undertook a herculean task which he confessed himself 'hath cost me many a weary mile, many a hard-earned penny and many a cold winter night's study.'

The result of Stow's labours appeared in 1598 as *A Survay of London*, dedicated to the lord mayor and citizens of the city. For his pains Stow received £3 and 40 free copies of the book. That the book found an eager readership is clear from the fact that it was reprinted within a year and a second edition, with additional material, appeared in 1603. Meanwhile Stow literally put begging bowls in the street outside his house by Aldgate Well. When he died in 1605 he was buried in nearby St Andrew Undershaft, where his widow raised an effigy of him, holding a quill pen. Each year on the anniversary of his death a memorial service is held and the lord mayor replaces the quill pen with a new one.

Stow's motive appears to have been incurable curiosity compromised by pride in his native city. Claiming to write without fear or favour he nevertheless got back at the Vintners' Company, who refused him access to their archives, by simply leaving them out of his story. And he tells with evident satisfaction the story of: 'Sir John Champeneis, Alderman and Major . . . built a high tower of brick, the first I ever heard of any man's house to overlook his neighbours in the city. But this delight of his eye was punished by blindness some years before his death.'

MUSHROOM GROWTH

A man who referred to Wat Tyler as a 'presumptuous rebel' was assuredly a man who deplored change, particularly when it was motivated by greed and unchecked by taste. The mushroom growth of London throughout Elizabeth's reign was a change so great it was impossible to ignore and, to Stow's mind, so horrendous that it could only be deplored:

> (Hog Lane) ... within these forty years, had on both sides fair hedgerows of Elm trees, with bridges and easy stiles to pass over into the pleasant fields, very commodious for citizens therein to walk, shoot and otherwise to recreate and refresh their dulled spirits in the sweet and wholesome air, which is now within a few years made a continual building throughout, of garden houses, and small cottages; and the fields on either side be turned into garden plots, tenter yards (areas for finishing cloth), bowling alleys and such like ...

Wapping, Stow observed, was, 'a continual street or filthy straight passage with alleys of small tenements', while east of Aldgate, 'both sides of the street be pestered with cottages.'

When Stow was born, London had a population of about 50,000, when he died it was about 200,000. All this despite repeated epidemics; the outbreak of 1563 alone carried off 25,000 and there were further major visitations in 1582 and 1592–3. And if the plague couldn't check the growth of the city the government was even less likely to be able to do so. In 1580 the queen issued a proclamation forbidding anyone: '... of what quality so ever they be, to desist and forbear from any new buildings ... within three miles from any of the gates of ... London ... and also to forbear from ... suffering any more families than one ... to inhabit from henceforth in any house ...'

Despite the fact that the proclamation was backed by statute in 1593 it remained a dead letter. Houses spread north to Shoreditch, east towards Whitechapel, west along the Strand and, on the other side of the river, southwards from Bankside. Courtiers and officials fled the city to escape its noise and enjoy pleasant gardens. Tradesmen went to evade gild controls and find cheaper premises. Immigrants, English and alien, settled for what they could where they could get it.

CHAPTER FOUR

Revolutions and Rebuilding, 1600–1700

'As he was going through Lusen by Greenwich, he asked what town it was? They said, Lusen. He asked a good while after, what town is this we are now in? They said, still, 'twas Lusen. On my soul, said the King, I will be King of Lusen.'

And if that was what James VI of Scotland thought of Lewisham, what must he have thought of London itself, whose citizens waited to hail him as James I of England? In fact, he thought of it with some trepidation as it was in the grip of yet another ferocious bout of plague. He may still have been impressed by its sheer size, ten times larger than any other city of his new kingdom, but he had even greater ambitions for it, for he proclaimed that he wanted to be able to say that he 'had found our Citie and suburbs of London of stickes, and left them of bricke, being a material far more durable, safe from fire and beautiful and magnificent.'

Ironically the king's wish was to be granted, for between the establishment of the Stuart dynasty and its demise London was indeed transformed from a city of timber and plaster to a city of brick and stone. But the transformation was to be wrought not by royal initiative but by catastrophe.

Water and Wheels

The unrestrained expansion of London during Elizabeth's reign inevitably imposed new strains on the city's infrastructure and, in particular, on its water-supply. The Thames had served from the city's very foundation both as its main highway and as its source of water for drinking, cooking and washing. The growth in London's population increasingly polluted it, not merely with human and animal refuse, but with the noxious effluents from such processes as tanning, brewing and the manufacture of soap and glue. Non-riverine sources, such as the wells at Goswell and Clerkenwell, had also become polluted. From the thirteenth century onwards arrangements were made to bring water in from outlying springs and streams by means of conduits which were connected to wealthier homes by pipes of elm or leather. Lambs Conduit Street in Holborn commemorates the sponsor of one such network. But by 1600 there were less than 20 in operation and most citizens had to rely on the 4,000 'Water Tankard Bearers' who filled their three-gallon vessels at the conduit heads.

Parliament fumbled the issue and it was left to a methodical Welsh businessman, Sir Hugh Myddelton, to analyse and solve the problem using his own initiative. The result was the aptly named New River which brought water almost 40 miles from rural Hertfordshire to the edge of the city at Islington. The engineering involved the construction of over a 100 wooden aqueducts and 40 sluices, plus pumps for 13 subsidiary feeder wells.

FROST FAIR

The River Thames, obstructed by refuse, its flow impeded by the massive piers of London Bridge, could, in a long, hard winter freeze solid from bank to bank. When it did so in 1564–5 dancing and archery contests were held on the ice. The winter of 1608 saw a Frost Fair complete with football matches and temporary taverns. Another, in 1648–9, saw the erection of a printing press, which became a regular feature of later fairs, enabling visitors to buy a souvenir certificate of attendance with their name printed on it. Charles II did so in 1683–4 when there was an entire street of booths and a whole ox was roasted on the ice. Frost Fairs continued to be held until 1813–14. The demolition of Old London Bridge in 1831 so accelerated the river's flow that it never froze enough again to hold another.

CARRIAGE TRANSPORT

Another pressing need in an expanding city was transport. In 1622 the 'Water Poet' John Taylor observed, 'This is a rattling, rolling and rumbling age. The world runs on wheels'; as a Waterman who got his living from rowing people up and down the river he could only deplore the growing popularity of carriage transport. There were soon new fashions for him to deplore. Around 1625 the hackney carriage – a coach cruising the streets for hire – first made its appearance in the capital. The more leisurely sedan chair followed in 1634, but took a century to become popular. Not so the hackney. King and Cromwell alike tried to set a limit to their number. In 1661 Charles II set the total at 400, increased to 700 in 1694 and 800 in 1710.

Inigo Jones

If any one person can be said to have brought about an architectural revolution in England single-handed it was Inigo Jones (1573–1652). Welsh by background but a true cockney by birth, he was trained as a joiner before venturing to Italy, where he acquired a knowledge of both classical architecture and the art of staging elaborate masques. After a brief period in the service of the king of Denmark, Jones reappeared in England as the producer-designer of a court masque written by Ben Jonson and organised primarily for the amusement of James I's consort – who just happened to be a Danish princess.

In 1613–14 Jones returned to Europe as guide and tutor to the young earl of Arundel on a leisurely journey through northern Italy. This second visit gave him abundant opportunity to make detailed sketches of Roman buildings. It also enabled him both to nurture and to benefit from his charge's extravagant enthusiasm for the antique. Arundel was to become the greatest collector of his day, importing no less than 37 full-size statues, 128 busts and 250 inscribed marbles. Apart from affording Jones an invaluable study tour, Arundel was later to be instrumental in bringing to London the brilliant Czech engraver Wenceslaus Hollar. He was to produce the most detailed views of Stuart London and is commemorated in Southwark Cathedral, which he often used as a vantage-point.

KING'S SURVEYOR

On returning to England in 1615 Inigo Jones was appointed King's

Inigo Jones

Surveyor. Over the next 20 years this fussy workaholic was to be engaged on as many projects but, of these, only three major ones survive. The earliest of these is the Queen's House at Greenwich (*see p 259*). The next was the Banqueting House in Whitehall (*see p 261*), which has been called 'the most revolutionary piece of architecture ever to rise in London ... the first fully Italianate edifice to grace the metropolis.' The last is the Queen's Chapel, which is part of St James's Palace; like the other two buildings it is a double cube, whose beauty rests in part on an understanding of the formal mathematical theory on which it is based. Above the altar light blazes through an imposing Venetian window, the first of its kind in England.

Much of Inigo Jones' time was taken up with minor works, alterations and refurbishments; but he also acted as adviser to Charles I on his art collection and gave much time to a grandiose scheme for rebuilding Whitehall Palace which was never realised.

Despite his closeness to the royal family Jones also found time to work for aristocratic patrons, the most important being the earl of Bedford, for whom he designed Covent Garden as London's first Italian-style piazza, although the actual model seems to have been the Place des Vosges laid out in Paris in 1605. Covent Garden is dominated, albeit discreetly, by the church of St Paul's. The earl had instructed his architect to keep it plain, not much more than a barn; Jones in reply promised him 'the handsomest barn in England.' To the modern eye it still meets his three basic tenets of correct style – 'masculine, solid, simple.'

Civil War

Throughout the civil wars London stood solidly for parliament. As the largest city, chief port, centre of finance and traditional seat of government, it was surely a trump card against the royalists. London had seen the most dramatic events leading up to the crisis – the trial and execution of the earl of Strafford, the king's chief minister, and the abortive attempt by Charles I to arrest five MPs in the House of Commons itself only to find that 'the birds have flown.'

When hostilities did break out in 1642 the king was obliged to raise his standard at Nottingham and was later to make Oxford his capital. The recapture of London was naturally the prime aim of royalist strategy. In the autumn of 1642 London anticipated an attack from the west.

BARRICADES

Barricades were thrown across the main routes into the city and, on a Sunday morning in November, 24,000 men mustered at Turnham Green to face the impending assault. Most were raw recruits with a stiffening of blooded veterans of the previous month's indecisive encounter at Edgehill in the Midlands. As they outnumbered the royalists two to one the king, after a token artillery barrage, retired appropriately to Kingston.

Royalist strategy was more co-ordinated the following year and aimed at a three-pronged attack on the capital from the north and west.

London prepared frantically, conscripting even children to dig trenches. Expert engineers were brought over from Holland and work was continued even on a Sunday – a hard decision for the Puritan conscience. The result of these labours was a circuit of more than 20 forts and batteries, linked by a nine-foot high earth rampart and a nine-foot deep ditch, which gave London the largest defensive fortifications in all Europe. The scale of the works can be judged from the fact that the ironically named Fort Royal, which stood where the Imperial War Museum now stands, held no less than 3,000 men. But the attack never came. The king was defeated in the field and after 1647 the defences were so thoroughly dismantled that almost no trace of them remains.

THE PUTNEY DEBATES

With the defeat of the king dissensions within the ranks of the opposition came into the open. At Putney church an extraordinary debate was staged between senior officers of the parliamentary army and 'Levellers' who proposed the revolutionary step of granting the vote to all 'free Englishmen' – which did not, of course, include servants or women, i.e. the majority of adults. A handsome plaque records this historic flirtation with democracy, which was upstaged by the king's escape from captivity at Hampton Court and the outbreak of a series of royalist uprisings. These were easily crushed by Cromwell's New Model Army but served to convince the parliamentarians that there could be no living with the king. In January 1649 Charles I was tried in Westminster Hall for treason, having levied war 'against the parliament and kingdom of England.' He refused to acknowledge the legitimacy of the court or even to remove his hat. The outcome of the four-day trial was a foregone conclusion, even though half the commissioners ordered to serve as a jury had failed to answer their summons, including even General Fairfax, the parliamentary army's commander-in-chief. To defeat a king was one thing, to kill him quite another. When the verdict of death became known Londoners wept in the streets.

EXECUTION

On 30 January the diminutive monarch, who stood less than five-feet tall, prepared for his execution by putting on an extra shirt lest his subjects should think he shivered from fear. He then walked from St James's Palace across St James's Park to Whitehall Palace, where he took the last sacrament. He was then led through the magnificent Banqueting House, decorated with scenes of his dynasty's splendour, and guided through a first-floor window onto the scaffold erected outside. At 2 o'clock Charles I turned to the bishop of London and uttered his last word – 'Remember!' As the axe fell an eye-witness recalled that 'there was such a dismal universal groan amongst the thousands of people who were in sight of it, as it were with one consent, as I never heard before, and desire I may not hear again.'

Nowadays the fine equestrian statue of Charles I, cast by Huguenot Hubert Le Sueur in 1633, stands at the north end of Whitehall, gazing towards the execution site. Its location marks the notional centre of London, from which all distances are measured. The statue, originally intended by Lord High Treasurer Weston for the garden of his house at Roehampton, was not to be set up until 1676. In 1655 Cromwell's men found it in the crypt of St Paul's, Covent Garden, where it had been hidden by royalists. A Holborn brass-worker, John Rivett, was given the job of melting it down; but he cannily sold off souvenirs allegedly made from the bronze of the statue while preserving it safely until he could hand it back to a grateful Charles II after the Restoration. Charles I's last command has indeed been fulfilled for, every year on the anniversary of his death, a wreath is laid at his statue by a contingent of royalists, dressed in the uniforms of his defeated army. Meanwhile, at the opposite end of Whitehall, Cromwell's statue stares broodingly across the street at the church of St Margaret's, Westminster, where, from a niche above a doorway, his gaze is returned by a bust of Charles I – head only.

A Merry Monarch

This day, his Majesty, Charles the Second came to London after a sad and long exile ... This was also his birthday and with a triumph of above 20,000 horse and foot, brandishing their swords and shouting with inexpressible joy; the ways strewed with flowers, the bells ringing, the streets hung with tapestry, fountains running with wine; the Mayor, Aldermen and all the

Companies, in their liveries, chains of gold, and banners. Lords and Nobles, clad in cloth of silver, gold and velvet; the windows and balconies, all set with ladies, trumpets, music, and myriads of people flocking...

Considering its role as the former citadel of rebellion, the capital took a brazenly self-indulgent path back to royal favour, eschewing remorse in favour of excess; but that was to be thoroughly in keeping with the coming age. Charles II himself observed cynically that had he known he would receive such a welcome he would have come back sooner. The diarist John Evelyn, who knew the king well, described him as being:

... of a vigorous and robust constitution ... a prince of many virtues, and many great imperfections; debonaire, easy of access, not bloody or cruel; his countenance fierce, his voice great, proper of person ... a lover of the sea, and skilful in shipping; not affecting other studies, yet he had a laboratory and knew of many medicines, and the easier mechanical mathematics; he loved planting and building, and brought in a politer way of living. He had a peculiar talent for telling a story ... of which he had innumerable.

ST JAMES'S PARK

Shrewd, cultured, genial, and idle the king enjoyed the company of clever men and beautiful women. He had more than a dozen mistresses but left no legitimate heir, though he did leave a typically personal imprint on London itself. He had St James's Park landscaped in the severe French style and added an aviary which was to become Birdcage Walk. Graciously accepting an exotic gift of pelicans from the Russian ambassador the king established the now traditional association between the park and its abundant and varied bird life. A brisk walker, he often took his daily 'constitutional' along what is now Constitution Hill. Alternatively he might stroll in the opposite direction, past the back garden wall of his most celebrated mistress, the witty and warm-hearted Nell Gwyn, the first great comedy actress of the English stage.

The broad avenue in which Nell's house once stood is now Pall Mall, which takes its name from a French game, favoured by the king, which seems to have been a cross between golf and croquet. Another of the king's pleasures is recalled in the name of the Theatre Royal, though in fact theatre combined two of the king's pleasures for, accustomed by his French exile to seeing females on stage, Charles insisted, when granting charters to theatrical companies the puritans had closed down, that they should all employ actresses rather than continue the ancient convention of having boys play women's parts.

THE KING'S ROAD

At the weekends Charles, like generations of well-to-do Londoners ever since, aimed at a speedy getaway to his rural retreats at Hampton Court or Windsor; his private escape-route through Chelsea is still known as the King's Road.

Samuel Pepys

To many English readers the name 'Pepys' is synonymous with diarist – which may be fair to Samuel Pepys but does scant justice to his friend, John Evelyn. They are equal, however, in one respect – both are regarded as key witnesses of their times, though ironically neither intended his writings for publication.

Samuel Pepys (1633–1703) was a Londoner, born and bred. The son of a tailor (and with a life-long weakness for well-cut clothes) he was educated at St Paul's and Cambridge. After marrying a 15-year-old Huguenot girl he took advantage of family connections to become an official in the Navy Office. Able and industrious, he rose steadily in authority and royal favour, was on close terms with the leading figures of his day and also served as an MP and president of the newly-established Royal Society. In 1678 he became an innocent victim of the so-called 'Popish Plot' which aimed at the overthrow of the king and was for a while imprisoned in the Tower. A further four years in office enabled him to press forward with his invaluable naval reforms but his close association with the deposed Catholic James II, forced him into an early retirement and cost him a huge sum in unpaid salary. Evelyn described Pepys as, 'universally beloved, Hospitable, Generous, Learned in many things . . . for near forty years . . . my particular friend.'

Pepys kept his diary from 1 January 1660 to May 1669, when he gave it up for fear that his eyesight was failing. These momentous years

Samuel Pepys

cover the Restoration, the Great Plague, the Great Fire and the second war against the Dutch, all events in which Pepys was personally involved. As a boy of 12 he saw Charles I executed and, as a young man, he was on the ship that brought Charles II back to England and was in the abbey for the coronation. The million-and-a-quarter words of the diary, written in a mixture of Pepys' own invented shorthand and a number of European languages, also give an unashamed account of the writer's ambitions, advancement and escapades. It is quite clear that for Pepys 'wine, women and song' was not a proverbial saying but a recipe for a good night out.

John Evelyn

John Evelyn (1620–1706) was, by contrast, a man who never had to work to make his way in the world and gave little away about his personal life in a diary which is more a history of his times than a portrait of the man. The visit of Tsar Peter the Great to the Deptford dockyards in 1698 provides a rare instance of the urbane mask slipping. The tsar, being huge, ham-handed and boorish, thoroughly deserved his epithet. He hired Evelyn's conveniently-sited house near Deptford and filled it, in the words of Evelyn's bailiff 'full of people and right nasty.' In the course of his stay the tsar and his people managed to smash 300 window panes and to wreck Evelyn's prize holly hedges by insisting on being hurtled through them headlong in a wheelbarrow. Evelyn's account of the interlude is clearly written through gritted teeth.

Thoughtful and public-spirited, Evelyn published treatises on such diverse subjects as engraving, medals, vineyards, navigation, salads, the undesirability of foreign fashions, the necessity of tree-planting programmes (to provide timber for the navy) and how to cure London of fog (answer – move out every industry using coal.) Like Pepys, Evelyn stayed in London throughout plague and fire, helping to organise relief efforts after both disasters. Like Wren, he submitted an imaginative plan for the rebuilding of London after the Great Fire. Evelyn's diary, like that of Pepys, remained forgotten until it was rediscovered and published in the early nineteenth century.

The Great Plague

It is no exaggeration to call the epidemic of 1665 the Great Plague, for it exceeded all previous visitations in scale and severity. Despite the fact that there had been only four years since 1603 without some occurrence of the disease and major outbreaks in 1625, 1630, 1636 and 1647 Londoners were overwhelmed by the magnitude of the disaster. Official statistics put the death-toll at 68,576 over a period of 18 months. The figure was probably around 100,000 because, in the alleged interests of public morale, the parish clerks making out the weekly Bills of Mortality frequently falsified the cause of death and attributed plague fatalities to anything from 'worms' to 'lethargy'.

The epidemic began in earnest in April, after a severe winter which had held it in check. Within the month those who could afford to do so

Burying the dead with a bell before them.

The victims of the Great Plague being buried. In the background is St Paul's Church, Covent Garden

had begun to flee the capital and the authorities were hastily putting up new 'pesthouses'. The warm summer helped spread the infection rapidly, as did the official policy of exterminating all dogs and cats – the only effective check on the rats which were the actual carriers of the disease.

By July 1,000 were dying each week and by August 2,000; September saw the peak, over 12,000 in a single period of seven days. Many priests, doctors and apothecaries courageously stayed at their posts and many quacks filled the ranks of those who did not. There was little enough that any of them could do. The standard 'treatment' was to light fires in the sweltering streets to purge 'infectious air' and to impose quarantine, which involved locking up an entire household for 40 days if any of its members fell sick. The door was marked with a red cross and armed guards posted to prevent break-outs. Isolation could lessen the risks of infection. Some 10,000 Londoners marooned themselves on boats moored in mid-river; their survival rate was higher than any other group which remained in the capital.

ECONOMIC COLLAPSE

Wholesale disruption of normal daily life led to a collapse of the metropolitan economy. Shops went bankrupt for lack of customers.

Because the Newcastle colliers refused to put in coal, workshops closed for lack of fuel. Unemployed servants and apprentices were thrown onto the streets to live by begging or looting deserted houses. Grass grew in the streets.

Not until November and the onset of cold weather did the weekly death-toll dip below a thousand. Not until February 1666 did the king and court judge it safe to return from Oxford to St James's.

The Great Fire

The summer of 1666 was long, hot and dry. In retrospect it is easy to see how it must have reduced a city of wooden buildings to the condition of a tinderbox. The spark was provided in the small hours of the morning of 2 September by a neglected fire in the bakehouse of royal baker Robert Farriner in Pudding Lane. Although the baker and his family escaped safely, the fire spread quickly to neighbouring properties, fanned by an unseasonally strong wind. When he was awakened with the news, the lord mayor, Sir Thomas Bludworth, dismissed the danger with the fateful sneer that 'a woman might piss it out,' and went back to bed. By mid-morning Samuel Pepys reckoned that 300 houses, several churches and half of London Bridge had been consumed. The riverside warehouses added greatly to the conflagration, being packed with combustibles such as rope, timber, tar, hides, tallow and spirits. Meanwhile householders frantically tried to salvage their goods by cart or, better still, get them away to the safety of a boat on the river. Pepys hurried on to Whitehall to report to the king who sent him straight back to the lord mayor with orders to pull down houses to create fire-breaks. Pepys found the luckless first citizen at his wit's end – 'Lord, what can I do? I am spent, people will not obey me. I have been pulling down houses, but the fire overtakes us faster than we can do it.'

John Evelyn's terse account reveals how the sheer scale of the catastrophe overwhelmed its victims: 'The conflagration was so universal and the people so astonished that from the beginning ... they hardly stirred to quench it, so as there was nothing heard or seen but crying out and lamentation, running about like distracted creatures. ...

God grant mine eyes may never behold the like, who now saw above ten thousand houses, all in one flame.'

The following day the duke of York (the future James II), a brave and experienced seaman, was put in charge of fire-fighting operations. Teams of soldiers and volunteers manned an arc of fire-posts from which they could sally forth to beat back flames or create fire-breaks. Foreigners and catholics were locked up for their own protection as rumours spread that the fire had been deliberately started as part of a plot.

On 4 September unsuccessful attempts were made to halt the fire's spread westwards by pulling down houses either side of the Fleet River. The failure is scarcely surprising as the flames, at times 300-feet high, had crossed the open ground around St Paul's by throwing huge sparks onto its roof. But sailors did manage to save the Tower by blowing up surrounding houses with gunpowder. From the steeple of All Hallows, Barking Pepys saw 'Everywhere great fires. . . . The wind had dropped but there was still a blaze at the Temple, Holborn and Cripplegate, where the King himself was seen helping the soldiers.'

END OF MEDIEVAL LONDON

By the time the fire had run its course almost 400 acres had been wiped out within the City walls and another 60 outside. Four-fifths of medieval London had gone for ever at a stroke. Eighty-seven churches had been burned down, plus the halls of 44 livery companies and over 13,000 houses, with over 100,000 made homeless. St Paul's was gutted and so were Guildhall and the Royal Exchange and the Custom House. Remarkably, though, the number of lives lost could be counted on the fingers of two hands; and the city, purged by the flames, was never to suffer from plague again.

Bewildered Londoners camped out as best they could in the days after the fire and the king rode amongst them, promising relief and countering rumours of foreign plots against the throne. In fact a Frenchman, Hubert, confessed to setting the fire and was hanged for it although he was almost certainly deranged and innocent. A parliamentary enquiry concluded soberly that the causes were 'the hand of God upon us, a great wind and the season so very dry.'

Rebuilding and Wren

On 5 September 1665 Charles II issued a series of proclamations announcing immediate measures to aid those made homeless by the fire. Emergency arrangements were made to bring bread to special markets on the northern and eastern edges of the City, from Clerkenwell round to Ratcliffe, and it was also ordered that churches, schools and other public buildings should be opened for the temporary storage of household goods rescued from the fire. A week later a 'General Fast' of atonement throughout the entire country was fixed for 10 October, when a collection would be made for the victims of the disaster. York alone sent almost £400 in response to the appeal.

The king, zealous in fighting the fire and compassionate in relieving its effects, saw in its aftermath an unprecedented opportunity to realise the dreams of his father and grandfather and rebuild London as a planned city, with a nobility worthy of its eminence. He called for plans. Within six days he had one from Christopher Wren, the brilliant young astronomer–turned–architect, who already had in hand building projects at both the ancient universities. Among others who submitted plans were John Evelyn, the diarist, and Robert Hooke, the scientist and City Surveyor. Wren's scheme envisaged a rebuilt St Paul's and Royal Exchange as the focal points from which major thoroughfares would radiate. An underlying grid pattern would be overlaid with broad diagonal avenues and circuses to create grand vistas and provide an overall framework which would be rational, efficient and comprehensible but not monotonous. The halls of the 12 'Great' livery companies would be grouped around Guildhall to make a handsome square. A continuous quay would be built from Blackfriars to the Tower and so on.

Wren's vision was eventually to provide inspiration for the planning of Washington DC over a century later. But London was in too much of a hurry to rebuild. A complete replanning would have required complex negotiations over property rights and values and hence long delays. As it was a specially-convened Fire Court of 22 judges was tip-toeing through a legal minefield trying to adjudicate just who did own what underneath all the ash and rubble. The state had neither the funds nor the bureaucracy to undertake the huge task of reconstructing a capital from scratch. Even the first prerequisite – to compel or compensate existing property-owners into giving up their land – would have been quite beyond its resources, as well as being a very imprudent move for a dynasty so newly reestablished in the affections of its subjects. The rebuilding of the city more or less as it had been was to prove an immense labour. In October 1666 the lord mayor ordered all householders to clear their sites of rubbish and salvage and stack any bricks or stone that could be used for rebuilding. (Total enforcement of even that decree proved impossible.) Wren and Hooke were, at the same time, commissioned to undertake a preliminary survey of the burned-out area. A detailed map was later prepared by John Ogilby and William Morgan and finally published in 1677. In 1682 Morgan alone put out an even more detailed version, on a scale of 300 feet to the inch. These two maps are of the greatest historical value, being the first really scientific surveys of the city and also revealing how quickly much of the rebuilding was achieved. Already by 1671 no less than 9,000 homes had been rebuilt. But the following year it was reckoned that some 20,000 former inhabitants had still not returned.

IMPROVEMENT AND RENEWAL

Although the chance to reconstruct London on grand continental lines was lost many significant elements were incorporated in the city's renewal. Over 100 streets were widened to a minimum of 14 feet. King Street and Queen Street were laid out as entirely new thoroughfares to connect Guildhall with the river. The Fleet was dredged and canalised. Several quays were improved. The first raised pavements for pedestrians were provided. New building regulations required houses fronting onto main streets to be four storeys high, in 'streets and lanes of note' three storeys and in by-streets two. Walls were to be of brick or stone and of a minimum thickness. Later Acts of 1707 and 1709 required doorway cornices to be of stone, not wood, and as a further fire precaution decreed that windows should be recessed rather than built flush with the outer brickwork.

The Monument

As one of the six appointed 'Commissioners for Rebuilding the City of London' Wren took special responsibility for the rebuilding of St Paul's (*see p 253*) and no less than 51 City churches. Fifteen were under way by 1670 and most were completed by 1686, though in many cases their steeples were added later, as funds allowed. In addition to this prodigious output Wren also designed 'The Monument', which commemorates the Great Fire and celebrates the city's rebirth from the ashes, portrayed allegorically on the low relief sculpture at its base in which the Danish sculptor Cibber shows Charles II and the duke of York, attended by various figures representing Art, Commerce, Liberty etc., raising the fallen figure of London to her feet. A column 202-feet high from plinth to capital, The Monument, surmounted by a golden blaze of flames, is located 202 feet from where the fire started. Wren's alternative designs for it included one twice as big with a statue of Charles II on top and another four times as big with a telescope on top.

Even as he worked on the reconstruction of the City's churches and cathedral Wren was also supervising the building of the Great Armoury at the Tower of London, veterans' homes for soldiers and sailors at Chelsea and Greenwich respectively, the east and west wings of Hampton Court Palace, major extensions at Kensington Palace, Marlborough House in Pall Mall, and the Royal Observatory at Greenwich – not to mention alterations and repairs to the House of Commons, Westminster Abbey, St James's Palace and Whitehall Palace. All this – plus architectural work outside London (such as stabilising the leaning spire of Salisbury Cathedral) as well as membership of the Royal Society and three terms as a member of parliament. Wren was, in brief, a genius; but, although he knew the measure of his own talents, he never thought they excused him from hard work.

The West End

While Wren was rebuilding the City what we now call 'The West End' was being born. Driven from their accustomed homes by the fire, many

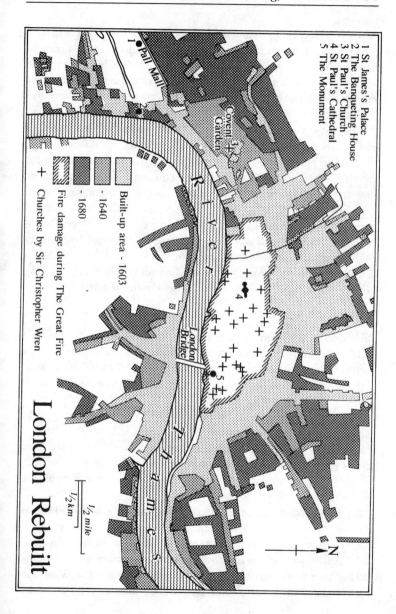

London Rebuilt

1 St James's Palace
2 The Banqueting House
3 St Paul's Church
4 St Paul's Cathedral
5 The Monument

Built-up area - 1603
- 1640
- 1680

Fire damage during The Great Fire

+ Churches by Sir Christopher Wren

1 Pall Mall

Covent Garden

River Thames

London Bridge

N

½ mile
½ km

of the wealthier refugees found that living outside the walls could have positive attractions. At the same time the re-establishment of a court at St James's made its immediate neighbourhood a highly desirable address. The last third of the seventeenth century saw, therefore, the emergence of a new type of planned development which was to give the London scene one of its most characteristic elements – the square.

The first square actually to be called such was laid out by the fourth earl of Southampton on his land at Bloomsbury. In doing this the shrewd earl pioneered a procedure which was to set a precedent for the development of half of London. Building himself a fine residence along one side of the square he leased off the other sides in uniform plots at rents low enough to attract speculators into putting their own cash into the construction of houses on the sites. At the end of the 42-year leases, however, both the land and the houses reverted to being the property of the Southampton family who were free to re-let them on new terms entirely to their own profit. For those who could afford to take the long view it was a highly profitable and low-risk form of investment.

'LITTLE TOWNS'

John Evelyn described Southampton (now Bloomsbury) Square as 'a little town', for apart from the square itself there were also side-streets, a carriage-mews and a market to serve the needs of the local inhabitants. Foreign visitors were soon being taken to view the new community as one of the wonders of London.

The other major enterprise of the period was the building of St James's Square by the diplomat Henry Jermyn, Lord St Albans, a favourite of Charles II who arranged for him to lease the necessary land from the crown. Jermyn went one better than Southampton and built his people a new church – St James's, Piccadilly. Almost inevitably it was designed by Wren.

These were grand schemes, seeking to express their sponsor's taste, as well as make a profitable return. But there were other property developers at work, even more energetic, often less securely-financed and frequently quite unscrupulous. The most notorious was a smooth-talking ex-doctor, Nicholas Barbon, who built up much of Soho and part of the Strand and created an ancillary income for himself by inventing fire insurance and running his own private fire brigade. Other entrepreneurs included the gambler Col. Panton (Panton Street), the ex-bricklayer Richard Frith, who built Frith Street but went bankrupt before he could profit from it, and the herald and engraver Gregory King, whose King's Square is now known as Soho Square. Sir Thomas Bond's Bond Street, now the very byword for exclusive elegance, went so slowly that at his death in 1689 it was still said to look 'like the ruins of Troy.'

SPITALFIELDS

In the East End expansion was equally dramatic and even less lovely. The Spitalfields area was colonised by Huguenots, protestants whose flight from France had been going on for a century but became a mass exodus of 30,000 after the revocation of the Edict of Nantes in 1685 ended the official policy of religious toleration. Thrifty, skilled and hard-working, they brought with them valuable skills in the manufacture of silks, silver and clocks and taught the ignorant English not to throw away ox-tails but to turn them into the nourishing soup that has ever since been considered a quintessentially English dish. To the north, London's Italian community was consolidating itself around Clerkenwell. Their impact on English cuisine was to come much later. Restoration London valued them as painters, makers of ornate plaster ceilings and teachers of the civilised arts of fencing, dancing and coffee-making. Further east the growth of river traffic created jobs for labourers whose tumbledown tenements spread northwards from the riverside to embrace Stepney, which soon lost the air of a wholesome country retreat.

Allies of a Kind

Anglo-Dutch relations were at their closest during the seventeenth century, when apart from trading and fishing rivalries which led to three short and indecisive wars, both nations were to accept refugees from the other and the Dutch were to provide England with a king, William III. The estuary of the Thames faces those of the Scheldt, Maas and Rhine and thus the stretch of sea between them developed into one of the great axes of European trade. Until the coming of the railways the Low Countries were, for many practical purposes, much closer to London than many parts of northern or western England were, certainly in terms of time and ease of travel. The Dutch language was closer to English than French was and seamen of both nationalities found ready employment on each other's ships, which naturally led to occasional residence in each other's countries. In 1567 the bishop of London reckoned that of 3,760 foreigners in the city 2,993 were Dutch, though this figure almost certainly included Flemings and Germans as the English found it too difficult – or simply failed to bother – to distinguish between them.

In Spain, and then France, the great catholic powers of Europe, the two protestant nations found common enemies, but mutual support scarcely led to mutual admiration. The Dutch historian, Van Meteren, who settled in England, found the English 'clever, handsome and well-made' as well as brave and hospitable. But he also thought them frivolous, gluttonous and 'very suspicious, especially of foreigners, whom they despise.' More to the point, they were basically lazy:

> The people are not as laborious and industrious as the Netherlanders or French, as they lead for the most part an indolent life like the Spaniards; the most toilsome, difficult and skilful works are chiefly performed by for-eigners, as among the idle Spaniards ... They keep many lazy servants, and also many wild animals for their pleasure.... The English dress in elegant, light and costly garments, but they are very inconstant and desirous of novelties, changing their fashions every year, both men and women.

As early as 1593 the House of Commons was debating a bill to ban Dutch shopkeepers from selling cheap imports because, according to counsel retained by the City Corporation:

> ... strangers' wares are better than ours, which causeth that our retailers have no sale of their wares.... And by this reason they have factors (agents) beyond the seas that are their friends and kinsfolk.... Their retailing, beggaring our retailers, makes a diminution of the Queen's subjects. Their riches and multitude makes our estate poorer and weaker.

One member put the contrary, liberal view that 'the riches and renown of the city cometh by entertaining of strangers and giving liberty to them.' But Sir Walter Raleigh caught the mood of the house better when he declared: 'The nature of the Dutchman is to fly to no man but for his profit. . . . The Dutchman by his policy hath gotten trading with all the world into his hands. . . .'

CO-OPERATION AND CONFLICT

Throughout the seventeenth century Anglo-Dutch relations veered between co-operation and conflict, but economically the ties remained strong and the benefits which England derived from the Dutch are evident in fields as diverse as taxation and domestic architecture. The fact that the words buoy, ahoy, yacht, keel, skipper and smuggler all entered English from Dutch attests to their influence in maritime matters, just as easel, landscape and still life do in art. Englishmen imitated Dutch technology in the manufacture of cloth, pottery, maps and paper, the building of ships and the draining of land; they admired Dutch frugality, charitableness and cleanliness; and, impressed by the contribution of Jews to Amsterdam's commercial life, they were per-suaded thereby to admit them to London.

Glorious Revolution

It was a Sephardic Jew, Francisco Lopez Suasso, whose loan financed William III's 'Glorious Revolution' in 1688. Without a Dutch Jew to put up the money it is possible that England might never have got its Dutch king. And it was the Bank of Amsterdam which provided the model for the Bank of England, founded to finance Dutch William's wars against the French and backed by the security of the state itself, not by private creditors. London merchants had wanted such a bank for almost a century; but they didn't get one till a Dutch king was on the throne. In the sixteenth century the English and the Dutch shared a common liking for hops, herrings and heresy. During the seventeenth century, the English gratefully accepted from their North Sea neigh-bours such further additions to their national lifestyle as tulips and topiary, grandfather clocks, gilt-framed mirrors and gin, tiled fire-places and tea-drinking and the consumption of cabbage on a scale to make a Frenchman despair.

CHAPTER FIVE

Elegance and Violence,
1700–1780

The Face of the City

St Paul's Cathedral was officially completed in 1710. Anyone who had strolled round the gallery which encircled its dome would have been able to get not just a good view of London but to see all of it. In the course of the century the city was to expand, but discontinuously and more in some directions than others. Expansion to the east and south was largely fuelled by continuing inward migration from other parts of the British Isles; given London's horrendous mortality rates its continual growth of population would have been impossible without the constant renewal that these job-seeking young people represented. The expansion of the city to the west and north, by contrast, was largely the outcome of the efforts of the well-to-do to escape the growing hazards of inner-city life – air pollution, disease and street violence.

Lord Burlington

One of the earliest trendsetters of change was Lord Burlington, who spent the summer of 1719 in Italy and returned to London, like Inigo Jones a century before, afire with enthusiasm for the works of Andrea Palladio, the sixteenth-century reviver of classical architecture. The fruits of Burlington's passion were the 'Palladianising' of his family's Piccadilly mansion and the construction of an idealised classical villa at Chiswick, not to live in, but to serve as a gallery for his art collection. (The waspish Lord Hervey dismissed it as 'too small to inhabit and too large to hang to one's watch.') Burlington's circle of collaborators and protégés embraced Colin Campbell, the architectural writer; Giacomo Leoni, who published an English edition of Palladio's writings; William Kent, architect of the Horse Guards building which still stands in Whitehall; Henry Flitcroft, who designed what is now Chatham House in St James's Square and the church of St Giles-in-the-Fields; and John Vardy who built Spencer House, the grand Palladian mansion over-looking Green Park which has recently been restored to its old splendour and opened to visitors.

BUILDING BOOM

In the eighteenth century, building booms alternated with periods of warfare as resources of men and money were diverted from one major national enterprise to the other. The first boom began after the Treaty of Utrecht in 1713 at the end of the War of the Spanish Succession and lasted about a quarter-of-a-century. Large-scale residential develop-ments of this period included Hanover Square, named for the new ruling dynasty and inhabited by Tory generals; Grosvenor Square, focal point for the building of Mayfair as a whole and, at six acres, the largest purely residential square in London; Berkeley Square, where the house

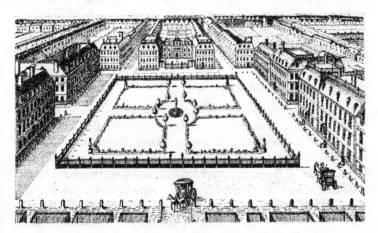

King's Square in Soe Hoe, now Soho Square, after early eighteenth-century engraving

of Robert Clive, hero of the Battle of Plassey, fabulously wealthy 'nabob' and suicide, still stands; and the Cavendish-Harley estate north of Oxford Street.

Major public buildings ranged from new offices for the Admiralty, Treasury and Paymaster-General to a face-lift for St Bartholomew's Hospital. When private initiatives slackened non-commercial enterprise soldiered on with an imposing new Mansion House for the lord mayor and the building of new hospitals, almshouses and schools.

Urban expansion provided an incentive for loosening the bonds that constricted the movement of traffic through the city. In 1756 the 'New Road' (now Marylebone Road and Euston Road) was laid out as London's first bypass to allow cattle to pass from the west of the capital round to the meat market at Smithfield without causing chaos in Oxford Street and Holborn. In 1760–61 the old City gates were finally demolished and the houses cleared off London Bridge. At Westminster and Blackfriars two new bridges were built across the Thames (*see p 269*). Many more changes would have been desirable in the eyes of the visionary, John Gwynn, who, in 1766, published a pamphlet entitled 'London and Westminster Improved', in which he argued the case for a strategic development plan for the capital as a whole and proposed schemes of improvement which were not to be realised until well into the next century, such as Trafalgar Square and the Embankment.

William Chambers

A second major boom began around the end of the Seven Years' War (1756–63). The Portman estate led the way with Portman Square, begun even before the war had ended. The years that followed were dominated by two Scottish architects – William Chambers and Robert Adam. Born in Sweden, Chambers (1723–96) spent his youth as a merchant in Asia, then trained as an architect in Paris and Rome, where he lived for five years with the great Piranesi and met both the painter Joshua Reynolds and his future rival, Robert Adam. Chambers' career took off in 1757 when he published a book of *Designs for Chinese Buildings* and was appointed tutor of architecture to the future George

III. This led to a commission to lay out the grounds of the royal retreat at Kew as a botanical garden and to decorate them with temples and the ten-storey Chinese pagoda which stands there to this day. Royal favour and Chambers' own talent and industry enabled him to build up a large practice, but the only one of his works that survives in central London is the handsome Somerset House (1776–86) in the Strand, Britain's first purpose-designed set of office buildings.

Robert Adam

Robert Adam (1728–92) worked in close consort with his brothers to offer his clients an 'all-through' design service which co-ordinated the architecture of his buildings with their interior decor and fittings. His most ambitious enterprise was the Adelphi (Greek for 'brothers'), a riverside residential block which combined exquisite private accommodation with a wharf and basement chambers for handling and storing merchandise. It was brilliantly designed, well built yet a financial disaster which all but bankrupted its creators and had to be disposed of by lottery. The Adam brothers' surviving London masterpieces include 20, Portman Square, 20 St James's Square and Chandos House, just off Cavendish Square. More impressive, however, are the effects they achieved in remodelling a number of great houses which were, in their day, well out in the country, Osterley and Syon to the west of the city, and Kenwood, up the hill at Hampstead.

CADOGAN AND SLOANE

One further scheme merits mention. In 1771 the second Earl Cadogan married Elizabeth Sloane, daughter of former royal physician Sir Hans Sloane, whose collections formed the basis of the British Museum. Her marriage portion included a sizeable chunk of Chelsea which was rapidly transformed from meadows and market gardens into a fashionable residential district in which the Cadogan family is memorialised in the names of one pier, two squares and four streets and the Sloanes in nine streets, two squares and a crescent.

While aristocratic enterprise was extending the boundaries of the city, its overall look was transformed within a few years by the substitution of street numbers for signs. Traditional shop signs were brightly painted and even gilded to advertise the standing of each establishment and the quality of its goods; but they creaked alarmingly on windy days, were rather a fire risk and sometimes were so over-sized that they broke their supports and fell down. In 1718 a sign in Bride Lane brought down the entire front of the house it was attached to and killed four pedestrians. Legislation in 1762 and 1766 finally required the removal of all such signs and forced the inhabitants of the metropolis to adopt the more prosaic system of numbering each house, a custom which was in general use by 1770.

Crime and Charity

'The rope being put about his neck, he is fastened to the fatal tree when, a proper time being allowed for prayer and singing a hymn, the cart is withdrawn and the penitent criminal is turned with a cap over his eyes and left hanging about half an hour . . .'.

Thus, with cool detachment, *The Foreigner's Guide to London* of 1740 described one of the city's chief attractions, the public executions at Tyburn, which themselves became a scene for petty crime on such a scale that the *Guide* prudently advises its readers that 'these executions are always attended with so great mobbing and impertinences that you ought to be on your guard when curiosity leads you there.'

Crime was probably at its most blatant in London in the middle years of the eighteenth century, when the demobilisation of soldiers and sailors from foreign wars loosed a class of potentially violent criminals on a city in the grip of 'gin mania' as 6,000 'dram shops' dispensed 'mother's ruin' to the populace at large for the price of a few coppers.

'Drunk for a penny, dead drunk for twopence. Clean straw to lie on' was the brutally direct promise of those who offered the over-worked and malnourished under-class a short cut to oblivion. Average *per capita* consumption by the 1730s was estimated at two pints a week – a figure that included children. The novelist, Henry Fielding, predicted in 1751 that 'should drinking this poison be continued in its present height during the next twenty years, there will, by that time, be very few of the common people left to drink it.' But in that very year parliament at last resisted the lobbying of the distilleries that profited from the misery of the masses and passed legislation imposing duties which raised the price of spirits to the point where they could no longer be drunk without heeding the cost.

Foreign visitors frequently remarked on the bravado with which condemned felons, dressed in their best, clutching bouquets and often roaring drunk, met their end at Tyburn. Others observed how Londoners perversely lionised those who preyed on them. Highwaymen were the most romantic of the criminal fraternity. Claude Duval, a former French page at the court of Charles II, had set the style and created a legend by dancing in the moonlight on Hounslow Heath with a lady whose coach he had stopped. James Maclean 'The Ladies Hero' lodged in St James's, passed himself off as an Irish squire and conducted his robberies with the 'greatest good breeding' until captured. He went to the gallows decked in a lace-trimmed silk waistcoat and danced at the rope's end in yellow slippers of the softest Moroccan leather.

Highway Legends

Even law-abiding citizens could scarcely grudge the legendary Jack Sheppard his fame. Graduating from pickpocket to burglar to highwayman, he escaped twice from Newgate prison, first from the condemned cell, using a smuggled file and then, even more sensationally, from a cell on the third storey of a 60-foot tower, where he had been handcuffed, manacled and chained to the floor. Recaptured, he entertained hundreds of visitors while awaiting execution and had his portrait done by Sir James Thornhill, the king's own painter. When his body was cut down after his death he was found to be carrying a small, concealed knife with which he had evidently once more intended to cheat the hangman.

Sheppard was cheered the whole three miles from Newgate to Tyburn in 1724; not so Johnathan Wild the following year. Wild had made himself a hero with the propertied classes by offering to recover their stolen valuables in return for a fee. In fact these goods had often been stolen in the first place by one of Wild's own gangs, whose members he kept in order by periodically betraying them to the authorities, thus sending over 60 of his accomplices and dupes to the gallows. Eventually the 'Thief-Taker General' was himself caught out and, on his journey to meet his maker, pelted mercilessly all the way.

HANGING OFFENCES

Cool-headed modern research tends to play down the significance of the colourful characters whose exploits were dramatised in the *Newgate Calendar* and emphasises that the general level of crime in the capital was closely tied to trade depressions and harvest failures which made work scarce or bread dear. Theft was the most common crime and, as it most often involved food or petty items of daily use, poverty appears to have been the usual motivation. It is also apparent that the authorities only gradually learned to get a grip on a situation which they clearly found both alarming and confusing. Simply adding to the number of hanging offences until they passed the 150 mark might give vent to the indignation of victims but did little to aid the actual enforcement of the law. Judges and magistrates refused to put a lad who stole washing from a clothesline on a par with a daylight robber such as the one who waylaid a woman in Hyde Park and cut her open with his sword to get at her wedding-ring when she thought to defy him by swallowing it.

Juries, aware of the savage penalties attendant on conviction, often acquitted the guilty in the face of clear evidence. During the last two decades of the century over half of those condemned to death were pardoned or transported rather than hanged. Imprisonment could, of course, itself amount to a death sentence as 'gaol fever' often proved fatal to condemned criminal, remand prisoner and distrained debtor alike. Alternative punishments included the treadmill, flogging, branding and being pilloried to be stoned by the mob.

STREET CRIME

Street crime was gradually diminished by the extension of lighting which deprived thugs of dark corners and alleys from which to pounce on their victims. Even more effective was the formation by the half-brothers, John and Henry Fielding, magistrates at Bow Street, of a private police force of six plain clothed 'thief-takers'. 'Mr Fielding's People' eventually found fame as the 'Bow Street Runners', ancestors of the modern 'Flying

Squad'. But there was no overnight revolution in the security of the streets and in the 1770s the prime minister, lord chancellor and prince of Wales were all to be calmly robbed in broad daylight in the West End and the lord mayor held up at pistol point at Turnham Green. Travellers still found it a wise precaution to assemble in convoys at taverns on the edge of the city before proceeding to hazard themselves across such dangerous places as Finchley Common or Epping Forest.

Thomas Coram

Paradoxically in a century and a city so remarkable for its callousness outstanding charitable projects were also to be undertaken. Life, and particularly young lives, may seem to have been held cheap when three out of four children died before reaching the age of five. But some consciences were sorely troubled by the sight of babies literally abandoned on doorsteps or even left to die in the streets, and none more so than that of kindly Captain Thomas Coram (1668–1751). Returning after long years in the American colonies, Coram was scandalised by London's indifference to the fate of orphans and the illegitimate offspring of prostitutes and of luckless servant girls who had been seduced and then thrown out by their employers. After 17 years tireless lobbying and agitation, he finally obtained a charter in 1739 to establish a Foundling Hospital which moved into purpose-built premises in Lamb's Conduit Fields in 1747. It soon became a most fashionable cause and won the patronage and active interest of the capital's intelligentsia. Hogarth and Handel were both diligent fund-raisers and Reynolds hit on the novel idea of getting painters to lend their works for a public exhibition whose proceeds would be donated to the upkeep of the charity. From this germ the Royal Academy shows were to grow.

FOUNDLING'S HOSPITAL

Coram's Hospital so far proved itself that parliament eventually gave it financial support; but even so it could not admit all who sought entrance. Those children who were fortunate enough to be taken in by the charity were taken to be reared out in the healthy countryside until they were past five and had avoided the worst risks of epidemic disease, then they were brought back to London where they were taught a trade by which they could support themselves as adults. Many were given the surnames of the institution's illustrious governors. Amateur genealogists with aristocratic names should therefore be warned that their origins may not be as distinguished as they might imagine.

New Hospitals

Considering the relatively unspectacular progress of medical science in the course of the eighteenth century, the establishment in London of five major new hospitals by private philanthropists is perhaps all the more noteworthy. The Westminster was the first to open its doors, in 1720. In 1724 Thomas Guy established a hospital which was funded by the fortune he had made out of the 'South Sea Bubble', a stupendous speculative scam which had crashed in 1720. Some, like Guy, who bailed out early, made a killing, others lost heavily, their numbers including Kneller, the court painter, Pope, the poet and essayist, and John Gay, the composer. St George's was the next hospital to open, in 1733, followed in 1740 by the London, the capital's oldest 'teaching hospital'. Finally came the Middlesex in 1745. In addition to these general hospitals specialist institutions were developed for the treatment of particular ailments such as smallpox and venereal disease or the provision of 'lying-in' services to expectant mothers.

As far as the poor were concerned the growth of a network of charitably-endowed public dispensaries was probably even more valuable. By the end of the century these proto-health centres were providing basic treatment, often heavily larded with moral exhortation, to 50,000 Londoners.

Education

Education was the other main activity to benefit from the charitable impulse, though sectarian rivalry provided a hidden motivation for much of the effort. During the late-seventeenth century a number of excellent schools had been set up by the Nonconformists. The Church of England therefore counter-attacked with a 'Charity School' movement which aimed to provide the offspring of the poor with basic literacy, decent uniforms and sound instruction in Anglican dogma. Thus moulded into biddable citizens it was intended that, on graduating, pupils from these schools should be apprenticed to a suitable trade or entered into domestic service. By 1718 over 5,000 boys and girls were attending one or other of the 127 charity schools scattered throughout the London area.

Mixing Business with Pleasure

'These houses are extremely convenient. You have all manner of News there: You have a good Fire which you may sit by as long as you please; you have a Dish of Coffee, you meet your friends for the Transaction of Business, and all for a Penny, if you don't care to spend more.'

When the Swiss visitor Henri Misson de Valberg wrote thus warmly in praise of coffee-houses they were already so firmly entrenched as a part of the London scene that a royal attempt to suppress them as places 'where the disaffected meet and spread scandalous reports' had to be hastily withdrawn. Half-a-century later, indeed, the French Abbé Prevost would see in them no less than 'the seats of English liberty' because there 'you have the right to read all the papers for and against the government.' But when Misson de Valberg saw them the coffee-houses were barely 20-years-old and, in their origin, like so many English institutions, more the product of circumstance than contrivance.

COFFEE-HOUSES

Daniel Edwards, an English merchant who traded out of Smyrna on the Turkish coast, returned home accompanied by a servant from that city's old-established Greek community, Pasqua Rosee. Every morning the servant would prepare coffee for his master as he had done in Smyrna and the novelty attracted so much attention that Edwards set him up in business in St Michael's Alley, Cornhill in 1652. Initially the exotic beverage was presented to a curious, but slightly wary, public as being of medicinal benefit on the grounds that 'it is a very good help to digestion, quickens the spirit and is good against sore eyes.'

Pasqua Rosee's venture soon found many imitators who competed by offering their clientele facilities other than simple refreshment. In 1680 a private postal system (in violation of the official government monopoly) was devised to enable customers to use their regular coffee-house as a place where they could both post and receive letters. By the reign of Queen Anne regular newspapers, rather than occasional news-sheets, began to appear, carrying gossip from court, advertisements for goods and services and news of the arrival and departure of shipping on the river. A Swiss traveller noted that 'what attracts enormously to these coffee houses are the gazettes and other public papers. All Englishmen are great newsmongers.'

With the proliferation of coffee-houses came a diversification which led many to attract a distinctive clientele with specific interests. The clergy frequented Truby's or Child's near St Paul's, while booksellers went to the appropriately named Chapter in nearby Paternoster Row. Nando's in Fleet Street was the centre for lawyers. Financiers used Jonathan's in Exchange Alley, which over the century was to grow into the Stock Exchange. Merchants trading with the Atlantic colonies used the American in Threadneedle Street; those who dealt with the East could be found at the Jerusalem in Cowper's Court, off Cornhill; West Indies merchants naturally went to the Jamaica (which, not surprisingly, was also noted for its excellent rum) in St Michael's Alley (still trading, but since 1869 as the Jamaica wine bar).

Merchants with a special interest in shipping went to the premises of Edward Lloyd in Abchurch Lane. Within 20 years of its establishment it became not only the place where reliable information could be had but also the place where ships could be insured. In 1769 a New Lloyd's Coffee-House was established in Pope's Head Alley with membership strictly limited to those in the marine insurance business. From that modest beginning the world-famous Lloyd's of London insurance market has developed.

STEELE AND ADDISON

If men of business naturally congregated in the City, the West End coffee-houses were the favourite haunt of courtiers, politicians and gentlemen of leisure. Scholars foregathered at the Grecian in Covent Garden. Will's in Russell Street rose and fell in popularity with the life and death of its most celebrated patron, the poet John Dryden. Nearby Button's boasted the essayists Steele and Addison among its customers. In Devereux Court stood Tom's, much used by the actor-manager David Garrick and other 'theatricals'. The poet Cowper used to breakfast daily at Dick's near Temple Bar. The British in Cockspur Street was a stronghold of Scotsmen. The St James's in St James's Square served as the informal headquarters of the Whig party, while Tories plotted and muttered at the Cocoa-Tree in Pall Mall. In the very first issue of the *Tatler* Sir Richard Steele wittily confessed to changing his accommodation address to suit whatever he happened to be writing: 'I date all gallantry from White's; all poetry from Will's; all foreign and domestic news from St James's; and all learned articles from the Grecian.'

Pleasure Gardens

If coffee-houses were for the morning, pleasure gardens were for the evening. The most famous were at Vauxhall on the south side of the river. Known as New Spring Gardens in the reign of Charles II they were a great favourite with Samuel Pepys: '. . . for a man may go to spend what he will, or nothing, all is one – but to hear the nightingales and other birds, and here fiddles and there a harp . . . and here laughing and there fine people walking, is mighty divertising.' A century later a German visitor, Sophie Von la Roche, showed a shrewd appreciation of the commercial side of this capital attraction: 'Half this excellent area is occupied by boxes where people can . . . eat and drink during the evening. The rest of the garden is divided into attractive walks. . . . In the evening there are 3,000 lamps alight . . . 60,000 guineas profit are reckoned during the summer.'

Vauxhall, which appears as a setting in the novels of Richardson, Fielding, Smollett and Fanny Burney, as well as the plays of Wycherley, Congreve and Vanbrugh, could not but inspire imitators.

RANELAGH

The most successful of the imitations was Ranelagh, on the Chelsea side of the river, which opened in 1742 with a rotunda 150-foot in diameter as its centrepiece. Mozart played there as a child and no doubt viewed with delight the nearby ornamental lake and Chinese pavilion, which Canaletto was to paint. The critic and aesthete Horace Walpole pronounced emphatically, 'It has totally beat Vauxhall ... You can't set your foot without treading on a Prince ...' The entrance fee of 2s 6d included tea and coffee. On fireworks' nights the charge was 5 shillings. The historian Edward Gibbon cynically thought Ranelagh 'the most convenient place for courtship of every kind – the best market we have in England.'

For those who could not afford to pay the entrance fee of any of the 200 other pleasure gardens, traditional fairs still provided a free chance to let off steam. Bartholomew Fair in Smithfield was dignified by the presence of the lord mayor, and typically afforded such distractions as conjurors, rope-dancers, boxers and fortune-tellers. In 1728 there was a performance of John Gay's *Beggar's Opera* which had only just been premiered in the theatre. The equivalent fair on the south side of the river took place in Southwark. Hogarth painted a picture of it in 1733, documenting the presence of a waxwork show of 'the whole court of France', a German giant and an illusionist with 'curious Indian birds'. Abounding in pickpockets and prostitutes, Southwark fair was finally banned in 1763. The 'Mayfair' held in the Shepherd Market area over the first fortnight in May was likewise suppressed in 1764 as the city's 'chiefest nursery of evil' – but basically because it outraged Mayfair's increasingly up-market inhabitants.

Silks, Silver and Shops

In his *Tour Through the Whole Island of Great Britain* the author, Daniel Defoe, observed how every part of the kingdom found a market for its goods in London. Coal came hundreds of miles by coastal barge from Tyneside; hops were brought by cart from Kent for the breweries; Welsh and Scottish drovers herded cattle from the remotest ends of the realm to Smithfield; and every autumn thousands of turkeys were literally marched in procession from Norfolk in time for the Christmas trade. The pull of the London market was irresistible to an enterprising businessman. Defoe, a Londoner himself, claimed to have made and lost a dozen fortunes there. And, because London represented the largest concentration of purchasing power in the country, it naturally also became the centre of the luxury trades and those which demanded the highest degree of craft skill.

The Huguenot silk weavers of Spitalfields found ready customers for their product among the wealthy. It was used not only for clothes for both sexes but also for pillows, bags, slippers and the upholstering of expensive furniture. Silk was never cheap but it was versatile and durable; many surviving garments show evidence of having been cut and altered to follow new fashions or fit a new owner. It was normal practice for wealthy people to pass on discarded garments to their servants who in turn would, when they considered them too shabby, sell them on to a second-hand clothes dealer.

Silversmithing was another craft in which Huguenots were well represented. Silver was used not only for tableware and tankards but also for candlesticks, snuff-boxes and other personal items of daily use. The less wealthy made do with pewter, a mixture of tin and lead, which was made into a wide range of household goods, from plates to chamber-pots.

PORCELAIN

One of the growth industries of the eighteenth century was the manufacture of porcelain. For centuries the Chinese had preserved the secret of its composition but around 1700, Italian craftsmen evolved a formula which enabled them to produce an acceptable substitute for the oriental original. From there the knowledge spread to northern Europe, to Meissen in Germany and Sèvres in France.

London manufacture was located at Bow and Limehouse on the eastern side of the city, and Chelsea and Vauxhall on the west. Both sites had easy access to the river, which offered a cheap means of bringing in raw materials and a relatively safe way of transporting out the precious and fragile products which would scarcely have survived a few miles had they been entrusted to the jolting of carts or pack-horses. Another common factor in the location of porcelain works was the presence of marshy ground where large quantities of spoiled goods could be dumped. Standards were so exacting that in some instances as much as 90 per cent of a particular line may have been eliminated as unfit for sale.

Chelsea really took off under the direction of Nicholas Sprimont, yet another Huguenot, who was clearly in touch with Sèvres and eager to emulate and surpass both its technology and its designs. Much of the prosperity of this new industry can, of course, be explained by the fashion for drinking tea, which came almost entirely from China, and was naturally prepared and consumed in vessels modelled on those the Chinese themselves would have used. Other favourite porcelain products were decorative figurines and candlesticks. The London demand for high-quality ceramics of all kinds was such that the Staffordshire potter Josiah Wedgwood kept a permanent showroom in Soho.

FURNITURE

Furniture-making was an established industry which reached a new apogee of excellence under the inspiration of designer-craftsmen such as Hepplewhite, Sheraton and Chippendale. The importation of exotic woods, such as mahogany and teak, from Britain's widening overseas empire was an important stimulus to innovation in both styling and decoration. Coach-building and the manufacture of ornate mirrors and musical instruments were associated London crafts drawing on a similar range of wood-working skills.

METAL-WORKING

As the nation's largest port London was inevitably the leading centre for the manufacture of navigational instruments, telescopes, barometers and chronometers which enjoyed a world-wide reputation as second to none. Other precision metal-working crafts included clockmaking, the manufacture of guns and swords and the production of scientific, medical and surveying equipment, with many shops and workshops concentrated in the Charing Cross area or along Fleet Street. Cutlers and locksmiths clustered in Clerkenwell while jewellers were to be found around Hatton Garden, still the largest centre of the trade in gold, silver and gem-stones.

Noxious and noisy industrial processes were pushed outwards to the city's edges. At Islington white lead (for paint) was manufactured. Along the river's banks to the east was a muddle of small foundries, mixed up with boilers of soap, sugar, glue and tallow, while to the west, at Chiswick and Hammersmith large new breweries were erected and at Paddington and Kensington brick and tile works blackened the air.

OXFORD STREET

As the fashionable classes increasingly deserted the City in favour of the West End so the commercial centre of gravity of the metropolis shifted westwards, with Oxford Street replacing Cheapside as the major shopping street. Sophie Von la Roche was entranced by it in 1786: 'First one passes a watchmaker's, then a silk or fan store, now a silversmith, a china or a glass shop … Behind the great glass windows absolutely everything one can think of is neatly, attractively displayed, in such abundance of choice as almost to make one greedy.' Another foreign visitor noted approvingly that even 'the richest merchant never shows ill-humour, even if asked to unfold more than a hundred pieces of stuff.' Typically the shopkeeper followed Defoe's counsel and was willing 'to bear all impertinence. A tradesman behind the counter must have no flesh and blood about him; no passions; no resentments.' Shops often stayed open until ten at night, gave indefinite credit and delivered gladly.

Prices were invariably negotiable. But a retail revolution slowly began to get under way. A Mr Palmer, proprietor of a general store near London Bridge, made a radical departure from existing practice by ticketing all his goods with a fixed price and requiring cash on the nail. His blunt methods shocked many of his competitors but he made a fortune. Another major retailing breakthrough was made by Mr Gedge, a linen-draper of Leicester Square, whose large iron-framed display windows allowed potential customers an unobstructed view of his stock; the shop-front had arrived.

MARKET GARDENS

Most Londoners, of course, still did their daily shopping at the city's thirty-odd markets, which were supplied with meat, fruit, milk, vegetables and fodder from the surrounding countryside, as well as shipborne supplies from as far away as Cheshire, the usual source of cheese and salt. What is now suburban London then consisted largely of orchards, meadows and market gardens whose produce went to feed the capital. The fact that these same areas were being colonised by processing industries banned from the city proper may help to explain the disparaging comments of a French visitor of 1765 – 'All that grown in the country about London, cabbage, radishes and spinach, being impregnated with the smoke of sea-coal ... has a very disagreeable taste.'

Hogarth, Handel and Johnson

Georgian London may have struck contemporaries as huge, being both the largest city in Europe and, in effect, the focus of the entire world trading system then emerging; but to the modern eye it was still remarkably compact. A brisk walker could cross it from side-to-side, Westminster to Whitechapel, in a couple of hours. More to the point it was still, at least for the propertied and educated minority, a community. Looking back it is easy to classify Hogarth, Handel and Johnson as commanding figures in the history of art, music and literature respectively. It is all too easy to forget that they all actually knew each other as well. One of Hogarth's best portraits was of the philanthropist Captain Coram, and the novelist Henry Fielding was one of his most fervent admirers. Johnson's statue in St Paul's Cathedral was designed by his old friend, the painter Sir Joshua Reynolds. And Johnson in turn complained that John Wesley, the religious reformer, although always civil was also always in a hurry.

To understand the way in which these networks of contacts overlapped and interconnected is to understand the full import of one of Johnson's most frequently-quoted sayings, of which the crucial prefatory sentence is invariably omitted. When James Boswell, Johnson's confidant and biographer, dared to suggest that permanent residence in London might prove less exhilarating than periodic visits, Johnson retorted with majestic self-confidence: 'Why, Sir, you find no man, at all intellectual, who is willing to leave London. No, Sir, when a man is tired of London, he is tired of life; for there is in London all that life can afford.'

THE CLUB

For Johnson life meant people and London had not only the greatest quantity but also the greatest quality; almost everyone who counted in the kingdom either lived there or was obliged to visit it regularly.

Johnson's own circle of friends which met weekly as 'The Club' at the (now vanished) Turk's Head in Gerrard Street included his ex-pupil, David Garrick, fellow author Oliver Goldsmith, Reynolds the painter and two of the most dissimilar talents of the age, the radical Charles James Fox and the arch-conservative Edmund Burke. It was a dazzling company and Johnson was the star.

Samuel Johnson was, like Dickens, a Londoner by adoption; the composer Handel, like the American novelist, Henry James, was to become a naturalised Englishman; but William Hogarth (1697–1764) was a Londoner born and a roast-beef-and-beer Englishman to his core. Hogarth is described in a Tate Gallery catalogue as 'the first of the great native British painters.' It is a title he would have gloried in. Born in the reign of William III, he was named for the Protestant king. He only went abroad once, to France, and hated it, returning with all his prejudices confirmed. Trained as an engraver, he aspired to become a painter, a high ambition for a Briton in a field still dominated by foreign masters – German-born Kneller, the Swedes Dahl and Hysing, the Dutchmen Hovemans and Nollekens, the French Laguerre and Van Loo and the Italians Verrio, Ricci, Amiconi and Pellegrini.

The main native challenger to these interlopers was Sir James Thornhill, who spent 19 years adorning the ceilings of Wren's Royal Naval Hospital at Greenwich and also decorated the interior of the dome of St Paul's. Hogarth took Thornhill as his mentor, and also eloped with his daughter, much to Thornhill's initial displeasure. Hogarth was, at least, fortunate enough to swim on a rising tide. In 1723 George Vertue, the would-be founding father of English art history, listed 23 'painters of note in London', mostly foreign; by 1748 the *Universal Magazine* could list 56, mostly English.

Hogarth's father, a classics teacher, took the unlikely career-shift of trying to run a coffee-house in which everyone had to speak Latin. Its not entirely unpredictable failure led to his imprisonment for debt, an experience which left the young Hogarth with an enduring hatred of poverty and injustice. Prisons, gaolers and debtors were to occur repeatedly as motifs in his art.

Hogarth first achieved notoriety with a satirical engraving at the expense of aristocratic connoisseurs of art *The Taste of the Town*. It was a highly appropriate triumph, for he was to have an antagonistic relationship with patrons throughout his career. But the fact that poverty had obliged him to undertake initially the humble trade of an engraver ironically enabled him to publish his own works, reaching a far wider audience than he could ever have done through painting alone and generating an income which largely freed him from dependence on wealthy collectors.

While Hogarth was a more than competent producer of the kind of group portrait known as a 'conversation piece' he developed his own variant which was essentially a comment on the follies and foibles of the London of his day, what he called 'modern moral subjects.' The first was based on John Gay's *Beggar's Opera* which combined two subjects of perennial fascination to the artist – the theatre and the criminal underworld.

The Harlot's Progress followed, chronicling the downfall of a country rector's daughter, corrupted by London from innocent maiden to imprisoned whore. On the strength of the paintings, before the plates were even engraved, Hogarth collected 2,000 advance subscriptions at a guinea each. So successful was the series that cheap pirate copies began to appear. Hogarth responded by getting parliament to pass the Engravers' Act, which became law on 15 June 1735, the day on which, secure in the protection of the new legislation, he published *The Rake's Progress*.

'Hogarth's Act' was to become the basis of all subsequent copyright law. Hogarth's later commentaries include *Marriage à la Mode*, an attack on marriages based on property, not love; *Industry and Idleness*, the contrasting fates of a good and bad apprentice, and *Gin Lane*, whose misery is opposed with the geniality of *Beer Street*. His last great moral series, *An Election*, villifies the political corruption of his times. Hogarth's friend Fielding understood the stature of his achievement when he wrote in the preface to *Joseph Andrews*: 'It hath been thought a vast commendation of a painter, to say his figures seem to breathe; but surely it is a much greater and nobler applause, that they appear to think.'

The essayist Charles Lamb was to put it neatly half-a-century later – 'other pictures we look at – his prints we read.'

Hogarth's work now enjoys appropriate prominence in both the Tate and the National Gallery.

COURT COMPOSER

Hogarth was English because he couldn't be anything else, Handel was English because he wanted to be. Yet another protégé of Lord Burlington, he had arrived from Saxony in 1710. In 1714 Britain acquired a German king, George I. Handel, a fellow German, became his court composer. In 1723 he moved into No.57 (now 25) Brook Street, Mayfair, then a newly-built and highly fashionable thoroughfare leading up to patriotically-named Hanover Square. It was there that he was to compose a work which has, from its first performance, been a mainstay of English choral performance, *The Messiah*. It was there that he was to die 36 years later. A loyal servant of the Anglo-German dynasty he was also to compose the *Water Music*, a lively but soothing instrumental suite, to be played as the royal barge rowed up the Thames, and the *Music for the Royal Fireworks*, which was commissioned to accompany the pyrotechnic display in Green Park to celebrate the peace treaty of Aix la Chapelle in 1749. The 'Dead March' from his oratorio *Saul* is still played on solemn occasions and his anthem *Zadog the Priest* is still incorporated into the ritual of royal coronation. His statue in Westminster Abbey, sculpted by the French master Roubiliac, gazes down on the grave of his great contemporary, Samuel Johnson.

TWO STATUES

Johnson has the rare honour of two statues, one in St Paul's, the other at the western end of Fleet Street, where he lived, standing outside the church of St Clement Dane's, where he regularly worshipped. Opting for dignity, rather than accuracy, the sculptor barely suggests his subject's legendary scruffiness and fails to convey his bear-like proportions and shambling gait. But then, as Johnson himself once said, 'in lapidary inscriptions a man is not on oath.' The inscription, however, tells no untruths in describing him as: 'Critic Essayist. Philologist. Biographer. Wit. Poet. Moralist. Dramatist. Political Writer. Talker.'

Indeed he was. Johnson is said to be, after Shakespeare, the second most quoted author in the English language. His portrait adorns the front cover of the *Cambridge Guide to English Literature*, and the *Oxford*

Dictionary of Quotations lists more than 300 of his pronouncements, pithy, elegant and thunderous by turns:

'Shakespeare never has six lines together without a fault.'

'Marriage has many pains, but celibacy has few pleasures.'

'Wickedness is always easier than virtue; for it takes the short cut to everything.'

Language and London were the twin poles around which Johnson's life revolved. His great *Dictionary* was not technically the first; but its predecessors were mere word-lists by comparison. He gave not only definitions but also derivations and illustrations of correct usage taken from his voracious reading. His other writings are little known nowadays, but contemporaries would perhaps have thought of him as a scrupulous editor of Shakespeare's plays and author of dozens of *Lives of the Poets* – scholarly works which constitute a paradoxical achievement for a man who said that 'no man but a blockhead ever wrote, except for money' and who composed his only novel, *Rasselas*, in a single week to raise the cash to give his mother a decent burial.

James Boswell

That we know so much of Johnson's personality is entirely due to the world's first great literary biography, composed by his devoted friend, James Boswell. The Scotsman's portrait appears as a plaque on the plinth of Johnson's statue and looks fittingly downcast, for, after Johnson's death, Boswell declined from conviviality into sottishness, surviving his much older mentor by scarcely a decade.

The two men literally bumped into one another in a bookshop, Davies's in Russell Street, Covent Garden. There is still a coffee-house there now, as there was then. Boswell apologised for being a Scot, to which Johnson replied teasingly that it was a fault he shared with many of his countrymen. Years later, touring Scotland together, Johnson was to remind Boswell of their first encounter and confirm that 'the noblest prospect that a Scotchman ever sees, is the high road that leads him to London.'

Johnson himself had followed just such a road, tramping almost 200 miles from his native Lichfield. In London he endured much poverty before achieving literary success, an honorary degree from Oxford (he had been too poor to stay long enough to graduate) and a royal pension. Cursed by depression and a morbid fear of madness, slovenly in his manners, he was yet rich in friendships and coined the word 'unclubbable' to condemn a man who was not. Johnson himself proclaimed that 'there is nothing which has yet been contrived by man, by which so much happiness is produced as by a good tavern or inn.' One of the good doctor's favourite 'locals', Ye Old Cheshire Cheese, still does brisk business in a turning just off the eastern end of Fleet Street, within a short walk from the house in Gough Square where the visitor can still stand in the attic room which Johnson paced for eight years dictating 40,000 dictionary definitions to six frantic assistants – five of them Scotsmen!

Religion and Riots

Toleration in matters of religion is a relative term. Compared to much of contemporary Europe, Britain in the eighteenth century was a tolerant country; compared to Britain in the seventeenth century it was a tolerant country. But, if those whose beliefs or behaviour were different from the mass of nominal Anglicans were unlikely to be butchered, they still ran the risk of being beaten up. It is a paradoxical truth that, while the Anglican church passed through a period of somnolent corruption, it still constituted a spiritual community powerful in its prejudices against catholics, nonconformists and quakers alike.

In such an environment the position of the Jews remained marginalised. Resettled under Cromwell, they moved into a handsome new synagogue in Bevis Marks, on the eastern edge of the City, in 1701. It was designed by Joseph Avis, a quaker, who returned his fees to the congregation. Queen Anne herself donated a main beam for the building. It stands to this day, the oldest synagogue in Britain. Fifty years after its opening, however, Jews were still regarded as sufficiently alien for a well-meaning Naturalization Act to have to be hastily withdrawn in the face of popular hostility. Daniel Mendoza, the Jewish bare-knuckle boxer might become a popular hero; with Jews as individuals Londoners could live easily enough, but as a community they weren't so sure. Perhaps this reflected confusion within the ranks of the anglicans themselves. After the Restoration of 1660 not only catholics but protestants who would not accept the authority of the bishops and dogma of the Church of England (e.g. baptists, congregationalists or quakers) were banned from parliament or from holding official positions in the army or the law.

'FIFTY NEW CHURCHES'

The success of these 'nonconformists' in commerce and in gaining converts alarmed the anglican-dominated parliament into voting money for 'Fifty New Churches'. Most never got built but those that did include the unmistakable creations of Wren's protégé, Nicholas Hawksmoor – St Alfege's, Greenwich; Christchurch, Spitalfields; St Anne's, Limehouse; St George's, Bloomsbury; St George in the East, Shadwell; and St Mary Woolnoth, by Bank Junction. Other major eighteenth-century churches include Thomas Archer's St John's, Smith Square (now famed for its concerts) and James Gibbs' St Mary-le-Strand and St Martin-in-the-Fields, which daringly combined a Greek temple with a soaring steeple in a way which outraged some contemporaries but became a model for many wooden imitations in New England.

The Wesleys

New churches did not necessarily mean new churchgoers. The anglican establishment occasionally expressed itself alarmed at the decline of religious observance among the lower orders. But it became even more alarmed at the revival of religious enthusiasm kindled by the brothers John and Charles Wesley. The Wesleys' devout commitment to their faith in a sceptical age, their regular private prayer and study sessions, their willingness literally to 'comfort the afflicted' by visiting prisoners in gaol won them the derisory nickname of 'Methodists' even before they left Oxford. Their attempt to promote the gospel among transported London felons and whores in the new penal colony of Georgia was not an altogether positive experience, but it did bring them into contact with the German Protestant sect of Moravians who had sought refuge in the New World. On returning to London John attended a Moravian meeting in the area of London Wall, where the Museum of London now stands, and found his heart 'strangely warmed' by a sudden conviction of the certainty of salvation. Determined to re-energise the Church of England from within rather than to form a separate body he worked tirelessly for the rest of his long life, preaching an estimated 40,000 sermons, while brother Charles wrote 6,500 hymns. The disused foundry in Moorfields which was Wesley's first London base has long since gone but his house and chapel in City Road still stand while, in Bunhill Fields opposite, lies the grave of his mother. Wesley's fellow student, George Whitefield, became a similarly charismatic preacher. His church in Tottenham Court Road has a long association with London's American community and nowadays makes a special effort to help people of all nationalities to feel at home in London.

Helping people of all nationalities to feel at home did not, however, always come naturally to the eighteenth-century Londoner. Black people from Africa and the Caribbean were relatively few in numbers and not perceived as threatening. Some even achieved a modest prosperity. Ignatius Sancho, butler to the duchess of Montagu, ran a successful delicatessen and had his portrait painted by Gainsborough. The Irish, by contrast, were numerous, poor and willing to work for whatever they could get. In 1736 Spitalfields weavers (themselves mostly French in origin) rioted when Irish linen weavers started to undercut them.

John Wilkes

It was usually a sharp rise in the price of bread that brought the mob onto the streets but they could also be manipulated by a shrewd politician like the radical MP, John Wilkes. His defiance of the government of the day – from somewhat mixed motives – made it possible for him to pose as a champion of individual rights. So the mob turned out more than once for 'Wilkes and Liberty'. A new statue of cross-eyed, womanising Wilkes can be seen in Fetter Lane, just off Fleet Street, an appropriate site for a man who made the political headlines so often.

It was, however, old-fashioned religious bigotry that sparked the century's most terrifying outburst of mob violence. In 1780 parliament,

Arson and looting during the Gordon Riots

largely preoccupied with the disastrous progress of the war in the American colonies, gave less than its full attention to petitions presented with some ardour by the Protestant Association. Headed by the half-demented Lord George Gordon, this body demanded the repeal of proposed legislation which would restore to Roman catholics the right to buy and inherit land.

At the head of a mob, at least 30,000 strong, Lord George Gordon stormed the City with the cry of 'No Popery' and opened both the prisons and the distilleries. The combination of the contents of the two proved lethal and the mob turned from burning the chapels at the embassies of catholic countries to looting and arson of a fairly unfocused kind, setting fires at some 36 different points throughout the capital. Ironically John Wilkes, now an alderman, was to find himself fighting spiritedly in defence of the Bank of England. It was to take the deployment of regular troops and the infliction of over 450 fatalities and serious woundings to restore a semblance of order to the streets again. Toleration is, indeed, a relative term.

CHAPTER SIX

The Great Wen,
1780–1837

The half-century between the death of Dr Johnson in 1784 and the accession of Queen Victoria in 1837 witnessed the apparently unstoppable expansion of what choleric controversialist, William Cobbett, was to rail at as 'this hellish and all-devouring Wen.' A passionate lover of the English countryside, Cobbett saw London as essentially parasitic, consuming rather than creating the nation's wealth, as much a symptom of the distemper of his times as the new-fangled paper money and government office-holders which the capital likewise seemed to spawn.

1801 Census

Britain's first census in 1801 showed the population of the capital and its environs accounting for some 10 per cent of the entire population and the second (1811) showed it passing the million mark, making it by far the largest city of the most advanced industrial and commercial economy in the world's most dynamic continent. The most populous district was still the City itself, closely followed by fashionable Marylebone and then by Whitechapel, which absorbed the City's overflow of poor.

NOUVEAUX-RICHES

To modern eyes London was still a bewildering mixture of elegance and squalor. The wealth of the *nouveaux-riches* was reflected in the opening of purpose-designed shopping areas, such as the Burlington Arcade in Piccadilly, the Royal Opera Arcade, off Haymarket, Woburn Walk, St Pancras and, on a far grander scale, Regent Street itself. The removal of the public gallows from Tyburn in 1825, the creation of a police force in 1829 and of a fire brigade in 1833, and the spread of gas-lighting in the West End, all represented undoubted advances in the provision of what are now regarded as the basic facilities essential for civilised urban existence.

NEW HOSPITALS

Apart from the almost single-handed efforts of quaker Elizabeth Fry to humanise the treatment of prisoners and the insane the tide of social concern was at a low ebb in the capital. Rather more progress was made in the field of medicine.

An Act of Parliament of 1815 gave the London-based Society of Apothecaries the power to set examinations for the emerging profession of pharmacy. In 1823 crusading Thomas Wakley founded *The Lancet* as a campaigning journal to expose medical malpractice. In 1818 Charing Cross Hospital was founded as an act of private charity by Benjamin Golding; among its early students was to be the missionary-explorer David Livingstone. The Royal Free Hospital was established in 1828 by surgeon William Marsden, with the support of the Cord-wainers' Company. Known at first as 'The London General Institution for the Gratuitous Care of Malignant Diseases' it changed its name at the request of Queen Victoria when she became its patron in 1837.

Welcome though these advances may have been they were marginal when set beside the needs of the times, as the growth of slums far out-paced the extension of the sewer system. In 1834 the Rev Sydney Smith wrote with habitual flippancy: 'I am better in health ... drinking nothing but London water, with a million insects in every drop. He who drinks a tumbler of London water has literally in his stomach more animated beings than there are men, women and children on the face of the globe ...'.

Outbreaks of cholera in 1832 and typhus in 1837 showed that Smith's levity was, perhaps, misplaced.

Duke of Wellington

Britain's titanic struggle with revolutionary France made this an age for heroes, whose memorials rapidly began to fill St Paul's. Of these none was more heroic in stature than the duke of Wellington, vanquisher of 'Boney', whose threats to invade Britain had thrown the capital into feverish panic in 1798 and again in 1804.

Wellington's relationship with the Londoners was an up-and-down one. Sometimes he was cheered on the streets; sometimes he had to be rescued from jeers and stones by an impromptu posse of Waterloo veterans. The diarist Benjamin Haydon recorded how, during the agitation for parliamentary reform in 1831, when the mob broke the windows of houses without lights, the symbol of support for the cause: 'They began breaking the Duke's; but when the butler came out and told them the Duchess was lying dead in the house, they stopped. There is something affecting in the conqueror of Napoleon appealing for pity to a people he had saved.'

Wellington was not, however, a man to rely on the sentiment of a mob and, pragmatic as ever, installed iron shutters to cover the windows of handsome Apsley House, winning himself the nickname 'the Iron Duke'. Equestrian statues of the hero, mounted on his favourite horse Copenhagen, stand outside Apsley House at Hyde Park Corner and in front of the Royal Exchange at Bank. The latter statue was cast from captured French guns, as was the statue of Achilles (London's first nude) which stands in Hyde Park, just behind Apsley House, and was erected by 'the women of England to Arthur, Duke of Wellington and his brave companions-in-arms.' Wellington is the only historical figure, royal or common, to be honoured with three outdoor statues in London. Apart from serving as prime minister and constable of the Tower of London (where he reorganised the administration and drained the stinking moat as a health-hazard) Wellington was also instrumental in the founding of King's College, London and in securing funding for the reconstruction of London Bridge. His state funeral in 1852 was an occasion of unparalleled national mourning as half-a-million people lined London's streets to see his cortège pass by and 13,000 people crammed into St Paul's for the burial service.

Trade, Traffic and Transport

Despite the political turmoils of the period trade continued to be the engine of London's growth, notwithstanding the challenge of the west coast ports of Bristol and Liverpool. If they benefited from the upsurge in Atlantic trade which followed the ending of the American war, London retained its lead vis-à-vis Europe and Asia, specialising in the importation of such precious commodities as tea, coffee, spices, silk, ivory and ceramics, as well as relatively high-value raw materials like wool and fine woods for the furniture industry. At a more mundane level there was domestic coastal traffic which supplied the capital with food, fodder, fuel and building materials. The number of coal barges equalled, and with timber barges far surpassed, the number of ocean-going vessels using London as a port. As a port it was clearly the greatest in the world but the price of its success was inefficiency as vessels invariably waited at least a week, and sometimes over a month, for a berth at one of the 20 'Legal Quays' which lined the north side of the Thames below London Bridge.

NEW DOCKS

To meet the needs of an ever-expanding commerce a corresponding expansion of dock facilities was undertaken, despite the opposition of those who benefited from the current situation. The West India Docks, cut through the neck of the Isle of Dogs, opened in 1802. In 1803 the aptly named Commercial Road linked this new facility with the City itself. East India Docks and London Dock followed in 1805, Surrey Commercial Docks on the south side of the river in 1807 and St Katharine's Dock, in the shadow of the Tower, in 1828. They were accompanied by the construction of massive and well-guarded ware-houses, enclosed by 30-foot walls and ditches 12-feet broad and six-feet deep to improve storage and cut losses from pilferage. These improvements were, of course, achieved at a price. Clearing the site for St Katharine's, for example, involved the demolition of 1,200 houses and made 11,300 homeless.

THE REGENT'S CANAL

Meanwhile the construction of the Regent's Canal (1812–20) joined the Grand Junction Canal at Paddington with the Thames at Lime-house to provide the capital with a water link to the booming manufacturing districts of the Midlands and the north. Less successful was the projected canal from Portsmouth to London, which actually opened between Croydon and Rotherhithe in 1809 but proved such a commercial disaster that it was eventually filled in and built over as a railway line.

THREE NEW BRIDGES

The upgrading of facilities for handling cargo was matched by the development of better communications within the metropolis itself.

Three new bridges were opened over the Thames – Vauxhall, the first iron span, in 1816, Waterloo the following year and Southwark in 1819. London Bridge itself was rebuilt in 1831. Future possibilities were glimpsed in the opening of the horse-drawn Surrey Iron Railway, from Wandsworth to Croydon in 1803, Richard Trevithick's demonstration of a steam locomotive at Gower Street in 1804 and the inauguration of the first steamboat service on the Thames in 1815.

THE OMNIBUS

Far more important in practical terms was the introduction in 1829 by Bloomsbury coach-builder, George Shillibeer, of a Parisian novelty, the omnibus. For the not inconsiderable sum of 1/6d each it would transport 18 passengers from Paddington to Bank. By 1832, 90 buses were plying this route and another route had been established from Hammersmith to Somerset House on the Strand. By 1835, 600 buses were in operation throughout the capital, carrying an estimated half-a-million passengers daily. Competition was so fierce that pioneer Shillibeer was forced out of business and had to convert his buses to hearses. Another Parisian innovation of the era was the *cabriolet de place* – soon shortened to 'cab' in English – which offered, in effect, a taxi service.

BETTER ROADS

The knock-on effects of London's continuing expansion created a need for better roads as the number of coach passengers travelling to and from London rose 16 times between 1790 and 1835. On the eve of the coming of the railways some 1,500 coaches were arriving in or departing from the capital each day. New North Road, through Islington, opened in 1812, Camden Road in 1825 and Caledonian

Road the following year. A well-to-do businessman could, therefore, live in a fine house in the outlying village of Hampstead or Hackney and still have an easy enough drive down to his office in the City. South of the river, Dulwich and Camberwell were also becoming fashionable commuter suburbs. The father of the artist William Morris, lived in some style on the edge of Epping Forest and commuted in daily from Walthamstow, using the last leg of the regular stage-coach service, rather than his own carriage.

Architects and Builders

SIR JOHN SOANE

Of London's many architects few have made a more distinctive individual contribution than Sir John Soane (1753–1837). Entering the office of George Dance the Younger, his 'revered master', he trained at the Royal Academy and visited Italy before attaining major professional recognition by being appointed to design the new Bank of England (1788). Soane eventually succeeded Dance as professor of Architecture at the Royal Academy in 1806. The imposing windowless curtain wall of his bank still survives, as does his severe Dulwich College Picture Gallery (1811–14) and his Holy Trinity Church (1824–8) on the Marylebone Road. The house which Soane designed for himself at Lincoln's Inn Fields (1812–14) is now a museum containing his models, drawings and vast collection of antiquities, sculptures and paintings including Hogarth's original oils for his engravings of *The Rake's Progress* and *The Election*.

SIR ROBERT SMIRKE

Soane's pupil, Sir Robert Smirke (1781–1867) is chiefly remembered for the British Museum but he was also responsible for the General Post Office (demolished 1913), Covent Garden Theatre (burnt down 1856), the Royal College of Physicians (now Canada House) on Trafalgar Square, the Royal Mint and the Millbank Penitentiary, which covered 18 acres where the Tate Gallery now stands and from which convicts were transported to Australia.

JOHN NASH

In 1815 Soane and Smirke were both appointed architects to the Board of Works. So was John Nash (1752–1835). Unlike the others this son of an impoverished Lambeth millwright had not had the benefit of a formal academic training and foreign travel, and he had also had the misfortune to bankrupt himself through unwise investments in speculative building projects. But he still became the most commercially successful architect of his day, largely through the patronage of his royal master, George IV, whose discarded mistress he obligingly married.

As prince of Wales George had lavished money on his personal residence, Carlton House, which stood in Pall Mall, overlooking St James's Park. A distinguished visitor like Count Munster could declare that it surpassed in elegance and richness even the tsar's palace at St Petersburg, though Smirke sniffily condemned it as 'overdone with finery'. Posterity would probably vote with Smirke. Classical without, Carlton House was just about everything within, from Gothic to Corinthian, and even boasted a Chinese drawing-room.

REGENT'S PARK PROJECT

Soon after becoming regent for the demented George III, the prince began to favour an ambitious plan to lay out a fine boulevard which would link Carlton House with Marylebone Park, a large open space north of Portland Place, which reverted to crown control when the leases ended in 1811. The first plan for this grand venture was drawn up by Nash in 1812. In many ways as vulgar, flashy and affected as his royal employer, Nash was similarly a man of vision and bravura style. His initial scheme envisaged dotting what became Regent's Park with over 40 large individual villas. These were never built; but much was and remains – the flamboyant stuccoed terraces overlooking the park, the charming villas of adjacent Park Village, the elegant curve of Park Crescent, the sinuous sweep of Regent Street itself, which required the demolition of some 700 small shops and houses to realise a purpose which was as much social as aesthetic and divided the *bon ton* of Mayfair from the 'narrow streets and mean homes occupied by mechanics and the trading part of the community' in teeming Soho.

A Nash Terrace: Park Crescent, Regent's Park

Other features of the project included the creation of Piccadilly Circus (known as Regent's Circus until 1880), the building of the Theatre Royal, Haymarket, the laying out of Waterloo Place (now dotted with statuary and quartered by thundering traffic) and the construction of the controversial church of All Souls, Langham Place, whose novel needle spire, encircled with classical columns, outraged architectural purists and whose entrance today shelters a bust of its creator, gazing south along his much-altered thoroughfare.

George IV

On becoming king in 1820 George IV went further still, ordering the destruction of Carlton House after 30 years of non-stop embellishment and bamboozling parliament into paying for the refurbishment of what was to become Buckingham Palace. Nash, now in his seventies, not only supervised these efforts but also put up huge new blocks – Carlton

Gardens and Carlton House Terrace – on the site of Carlton House, and remodelled St James's Park, transforming its rather uninspiring canal into the present graceful curving lake. Nash was however dismissed on the death of the king in 1830 and himself died before he could see the realisation of his notion to raze the stables of the old Royal Mews and replace them with what was to become Trafalgar Square.

The impact of Nash's efforts was summarised in 1826 by Prince Pückler-Muskau as follows:

> London is ... extremely improved ... Now, for the first time, it has the air of a seat of Government, and not of an immeasurable metropolis of 'shopkeepers', to use Napoleon's expression. Although poor Mr Nash ... has fared so ill at the hands of connoisseurs – and it cannot be denied that his buildings are a jumble of every sort of style ... yet the country is, in my opinion, much indebted to him for conceiving and executing such gigantic designs.... It's true one must not look too nicely into details. The church, for instance, which serves as *point de vue* to Regent St, ends in a ridiculous spire.... It is a strange architectural monster. There is an admirable caricature in which Mr Nash ... is represented booted and spurred, riding spitted on the point of the spire. Below is the inscription 'National (sounded nashional) taste.

DECIMUS BURTON

The momentum of Nash's work was partly kept up by his protégé, Decimus Burton (1800–81), the tenth son of Nash's collaborator, James Burton, a speculative builder. Decimus Burton's London designs include Cornwall and Clarence Terrace in Regent's Park, the lay-out of Hyde Park Corner, including both the Constitution Arch and the screen entrance to the park itself, which, like his design for the Athenaeum Club on Waterloo Place, incorporates a frieze based on the Parthenon marbles which, thanks to Lord Elgin, had recently arrived in London. Burton's most original contribution was, however, the Palm House at Kew Gardens, a truly revolutionary structure of iron and glass.

The long wars against France diverted resources away from both speculative and aristocratic building which, taking their cue from royal initiatives, resumed with the coming of peace. The Bloomsbury area was particularly active. Fitzroy Square, begun by the Adam brothers in 1790 was completed in 1829. Euston Square was built in 1827. Nearby St Pancras New Church (1819–22) modelled on the Erectheion at Athens and complete with terracotta caryatids rose as a pure example of 'Greek Revival' taste and the most expensive church of its day.

THOMAS CUBITT

The most energetic developer was Thomas Cubitt (1788–1855), who built Gordon Square, Endsleigh Place and Tavistock Square in Bloomsbury for the Bedford Estate, and Belgrave Square in Belgravia for the Grosvenor estate. Both of these represented a spin-off from opposite ends of the grand Nash scheme, Bloomsbury at the Regent's Park end and Belgravia in the shadow of Buckingham Palace. Cubitt, unlike so many in the boom-and-bust business of building, showed himself adept at juggling the competing requirements of finance, design and management and proved capable of organising a steady stream of projects which enabled him both to keep a large permanent body of craftsmen in constant employment and to establish his own building materials yards on the Grays Inn Road and at Pimlico, within short distances of his major ventures. Having such tight control over both labour and materials Cubitt was able to achieve a quality of finish which impressed customers and contrasted strongly with the work of Nash whose constructional sins were frequently veiled by a screen of stucco. Cubitt's ingenuity is neatly illustrated by his use of spoil from the excavations of St Katharine's dock to provide firm footings in the marshy ground of Belgravia which he was simultaneously developing. The marshy clay itself was turned into bricks to make the actual houses. Cubitt's standing as a professional was confirmed by his ability to see that those houses were designed by George Basevi (1795–1845), Soane's star pupil, and financed by three Swiss bankers. It was Cubitt also who suggested to parliament that it should purchase the land which subsequently became Battersea Park.

Cubitt's Belgravia was hailed by one Mrs Gascoine with unrestrained poetic licence:

> A fairer wreath than Wren's should crown thy brow–
> He raised a dome – a town unrivalled thou!

(Actually it was Cubitt's brother, William who raised a town – Cubitt Town, an early model estate for workers on the Isle of Dogs.)

SOMERS TOWN

Cubitt's orderly and expensive triumph at Belgravia should be contrasted with botches that were perhaps more typical of the period. In 1784 Lord Somers leased some scrubby pasture-land north of Bloomsbury to a Frenchman, Jacob Leroux, who proposed to build a pleasant suburb. He did manage to put up a single, eccentric, 15-sided block before his entire scheme foundered. Nevertheless 'Somers Town' continued to grow as a nucleus of French emigrés was swelled by refugees from the revolution until it had its own French church and four charity schools. After 1823 more refugees came, this time from the failed liberal revolt in Spain. One, Alcala Galiano, eventually became professor of Spanish at newly-founded University College nearby but most shivered, and survived as best they could. The building of Euston station gave a new boost to the area in 1838 but, although public baths and wash-houses were opened there in 1840, the area remained one renowned for its filth and disorder. The only consolation its inhabitants might have had was that neighbouring Agar Town, where St Pancras station now stands, was even worse.

Art and Artists

One of the less obvious side-effects of Europe's revolutionary upheavals was to stimulate the development of London as a centre for dealers and collectors, as fine works of art made their way across the Channel in the baggage of exiles, smugglers and conquerors alike. The fine art auctioneers Christie's benefited greatly from increased business and Phillips was established in 1796 by one of Christie's former head clerks. Apsley House, the Adam mansion presented to the duke of Wellington by a grateful nation, now displays paintings by Goya, Velazquez and Murillo, once part of the Spanish royal collection, which were captured from the French in 1813 and subsequently confirmed in the Duke's possession by the restored Spanish throne.

DULWICH PICTURE GALLERY

The Dulwich Picture Gallery, opened in 1814 as Britain's first-ever public art gallery, owes its existence to the enforced abdication of the king of Poland, who had commissioned the dealer Noel Desenfans to gather exhibits for a projected National Gallery in Warsaw. When the project was aborted by the king's abdication Desenfans offered the 400-picture collection to the British government, which declined the offer, enabling him to pass it on to Sir Francis Bourgeois, who in turn bequeathed it in 1811 to Dulwich College, which already had a modest existing collection. Both benefactors are buried in a mausoleum incorporated in Soane's sober top-lit classical suite of a dozen rooms, which now houses works by Rembrandt and Rubens, Claude and Canaletto, Watteau and Hogarth.

NATIONAL GALLERY

Despite the dithering of the British government London did at long last acquire a National Gallery. Unlike most of its European counterparts, however, it is based on a private, rather than a royal, collection. In 1824 George IV and the connoisseur Sir George Beaumont persuaded the government to buy 38 Old Masters collected by John Julius Angerstein, a Russian-born merchant, advised by Sir Thomas Lawrence, the portrait-painter. Beaumont added some of his own collection and the resulting core exhibition was exhibited in Angerstein's former Pall Mall home until the completion of William Wilkin's National Gallery (1832–8) on the north side of Trafalgar Square.

John Constable

Two of the National Gallery's most famous paintings are Constable's *The Hay Wain* (1821), possibly the most celebrated of all English landscapes, and Turner's *The Fighting Temeraire* (1838) which shows this veteran of Trafalgar being towed to the breaker's yard in a blaze of gold and glory. Both painters were active in London during this period.

John Constable (1776–1837), best known for his depiction of the Essex-Suffolk border country, trained at the Royal Academy under the American Benjamin West but won little recognition until the 1820s, when he also gained the admiration of the French Romantic artist Delacroix. In 1824 *The Hay Wain* was awarded a gold medal in Paris. Constable's revolutionary technique of painting direct from nature in the open air was to exert a powerful, if indirect, influence on generations of French painters. Constable eventually settled at 40 Well Walk, Hampstead but kept a studio at what is now 76 Charlotte Street, just off Tottenham Court Road, in the former home of his mentor Joseph Farrington (1747–1821) whose diaries give a lively picture of the art world of his day. Constable is buried in the churchyard of Hampstead parish church.

J.M.W. Turner

Success came far more swiftly to London-born Joseph Mallord William Turner (1775–1851) who was elected to the Royal Academy at 27, the year in which he took advantage of the Truce of Amiens to view an exhibition of pictures looted by Napoleon in the course of his conquests. Turner's wide range of subject-matter reflected his extensive travels but also includes many sketches of Thames scenery near London. The tower of Putney's riverside parish church was a favourite spot from which to view sunsets on the river. Turner's highly original colouration won him both violent critics and ardent champions, like the young John Ruskin. Despite his wealth and fame, Turner became increasingly reclusive in his later years, living at 119 Cheyne Walk, Chelsea under the assumed name of 'Mr Booth' and dying alone in a Chiswick lodging-house. He bequeathed to the nation the vast body of his work, consisting of some 300 paintings, plus as many sketch-books and 20,000 drawings; these were given on condition that they should be exhibited free and never split up. The Tate Gallery now exhibits the Turner bequest in a special gallery, designed by James Stirling.

THE ART OF CARICATURE

If Constable's views of Hampstead Heath, or Turner's 'Richmond Hill', showed how the foremost landscape masters of the day could be inspired by the still rural fringes of the capital, then the vicious caricatures of Rowlandson, Gillray and Cruikshank went to the anti-

Romantic extreme in exposing the foibles of those who inhabited its very heart. In 1802 a French emigré noted sardonically that, 'If men be fighting over there for their possessions and their bodies against the Corsican robber, they are fighting here to be the first in Ackerman's shop and see Gillray's latest caricatures. The enthusiasm is indescribable; when the next drawing appears it is a veritable madness.'

This observation was ironic, indeed, as Gillray's career was abruptly cut short by insanity in 1811. Cruikshank's subject-matter ranged from the private life of the prince regent to jerry-building, as in his fantastical *March of the Bricks* cartoon of 1829. He also illustrated Pierce Egan's *Life in London* (1820–1) whose heroes, the original Tom and Jerry, personify the manners and slang of the 'man about town', taking boxing-lessons in Bond Street, hanging about the horse-sales at Tattersalls and idly watching the hangings at Newgate. Tom and Jerry's imaginary adventures were so popular that they inspired a musical and plays so numerous that at one time they were said to be being performed at ten theatres simultaneously.

Benjamin West

Regency London was also home to a coterie of young American painters who benefited greatly from the tuition and encouragement of their fellow countryman, Benjamin West (1738–1820) who kept a fine house and studio (now gone) at 14 Newman Street (north of Oxford Street) from 1775 until his death, when he was honoured with a state funeral and burial in St Paul's. A Pennsylvania quaker, born on what is now the campus of Swarthmore College, West studied in Italy before settling in London and idiosyncratically launching his career with a virtuoso display of ice-skating on the frozen Serpentine. West graduated from bread-and-butter portrait work to pioneer the large-scale depiction of contemporary historical subjects, such as the death of General Wolfe (1771), and thereby win appointment to the newly-created position of history painter to King George III. In 1792 West succeeded Reynolds as president of the Royal Academy.

West's protégé John Singleton Copley (1738–1815), also settled and died in London; his *Death of Major Peirson* (Tate Gallery) is in West's grand manner. Another pupil, Robert Fulton, turned from painting to inventing steamboats and submarines and a third, Samuel Morse, stuck to painting intermittently but also invented the telegraphic code which bears his name.

London was no less attractive to European artists. Gericault visited in 1820–1 to exhibit his masterpiece *The Raft of the Medusa*. Fascinated by the capital's street-life, he published a series of prints, using the new technique of lithography to reveal an oppressive scene of smoke and suffering. In remarkable contrast are the cheerful tinted touristic views produced by Eugene Lami which show the Abbey, the Tower, a cock-fight, boxing-match, horse-race, boat-race and smart riders on Rotten Row. Lami's friend, the artist-actor Henry Mannier, drew humorous caricatures, in the style of Cruikshank, whom he knew and admired. German artists included George Scharf, a Waterloo veteran who made detailed records of the rebuilding of London Bridge, and Carl Hartmann whose composed panoramic views of the capital as seen from the top of the duke of York's monument, which was completed in 1834.

Police! Fire!

Despite the orgy of looting which accompanied the Gordon riots of 1780 and the complete failure of the constables of the city and Westminster to check the destruction, the propertied classes remained deeply suspicious of the concept of a police force. Speaking in a parliamentary debate in 1781 the playwright Sheridan observed that the word 'police' itself was 'not an expression of our law, or of our language', for it carried with it overtones of continental despotism, of spies and informers. Perhaps the prejudice in favour of liberty at the expense of a little anarchy was justified. The Gordon rioters had not, after all, attempted to massacre aristocrats, merely to smash their windows. And the royal family felt no need to treat Windsor as a high-security fortress rather than a convenient rural retreat. Despite his considerable personal unpopularity even the prince regent felt perfectly safe living at showy Carlton House, while William IV continued to stroll the streets unescorted, good-humouredly ignoring the jostling of fellow Londoners who attempted either to buffet him or kiss him on his incognito excursions. However divided by rank and wealth, the inhabitants of the capital were united by a fervent patriotism and victories over the king's enemies were sincerely celebrated by all sections of society. Friedrich Wendeborn, a German visitor, concluded that: 'A foreigner will at first hardly be pleased with the manner of living in London but if he has sense enough to perceive and value that freedom in thinking and acting which is to be enjoyed in England, he will soon wish to conclude his days there.'

A bill to authorise a single police authority for the whole of central London was thrown out of parliament in 1785, but piecemeal reform came as the government began to realise, against a background of foreign revolutions and uncontrolled urban expansion, the impossibility of controlling a million people with a few hundred untrained and poorly-equipped constables and night-watchmen. In 1798 a Thames force was set up to suppress piracy on the river, the initial cost being borne by the West Indies merchants who were its prime victims. Patrick Colquhoun, the Scottish founder of this unit, argued in his *Treatise on the Police of the Metropolis* that 100,000 of its people lived off 'pursuits either criminal, illegal or immoral.'

MOUNTED PATROLS

From 1805 onwards a mounted patrol, operating under the supervision of Bow Street magistrates, provided protection from highwaymen for travellers within a 20-mile radius of the city centre. As the ending of the Napoleonic wars discharged hundreds of thousands of veterans onto a distorted and depressed labour market parliamentary committees called with increasing urgency for a wholesale reform of the capital's police arrangements; but it was not until 1828 that Home Secretary Sir Robert Peel set out to convince Londoners that 'liberty does not consist of having your house robbed by organised gangs of thieves.' The City, still jealous of its privileges, was purposely excluded from the Metropolitan Police Bill, which came into force on 29 September 1829.

THE MEN IN BLUE

Commanded by Colonel Rowan, a Waterloo veteran and Richard Mayne, an Irish lawyer, the new police had their headquarters at 4 Whitehall Place, backing onto a courtyard which was once the site of the London residence of the kings and ambassadors of Britain's northern kingdom – hence Scotland Yard. The uniform of the new force was deliberately designed to imitate the cut of civilian dress and was blue because red was the traditional colour of the military. This may, however, have seemed a fairly transparent gesture to a suspicious public because most of the men initially recruited were indeed ex-soldiers. To avoid accusations of working as spies the new police were required to wear uniforms even when off-duty; not for 20 years would a 'plain clothes' detective branch be formally established.

Peel knew that 'angels would be far above my work' but the police manual warned that 'there is no qualification so indispensable to a police officer as a perfect command of temper.' It must have been disheartening for the men at the top to have to discharge so many of their initial intake for drunkenness or dishonesty and even more a matter of dismay at continuing public hostility to the 'Blue Devils'. When an unarmed policeman was stabbed to death during a riot at Clerkenwell the coroner's jury decreed it 'justifiable homicide'. Within four years less than one-sixth of the original intake remained on the strength of the force.

Within a decade, however, the 'Met' had so far proved itself as to be authorised to absorb the river police and Bow Street Runners, while the City paid it the compliment of establishing its own separate police force on similar lines. (The two forces remain separate to this day.) Metropolitan Police officers went on to play a leading role in training provincial and county forces hastily established to combat the activities of criminals driven out of London by the ever-growing efficiency of the 'Peelers'.

Fire-fighting

Like the police London's fire service emerged through a process of crisis and compromise. Serious conflagrations destroyed the Custom House in 1814 and much of the Royal Mint the following year. Fire-fighting was the task of brigades run by different insurance companies, whose responsibility extended only to properties carrying the distinctive metal 'fire-mark' of the particular company for which they worked. *De facto* co-operation between the brigades led to a pooling of resources in

1833 to form the London Fire Engine Establishment, which was placed under the command of James Braidwood, former chief of Britain's first municipal fire service, set up in Edinburgh in 1824.

The 'Jimmy Braiders' consisted of only 80 full-time professionals and, hampered by their chief's conservative preference for manually-operated pumps, proved utterly helpless to save the old Palace of Westminster when its heating boilers exploded and it went up in flames on 16 October 1834. Other spectacularly uncontrolled disasters included the burning of Lloyd's Coffee-House and the Royal Exchange in 1838, of the Grand Armoury of the Tower of London in 1841 and of the warehouses along Tooley Street in 1843. A second Tooley Street fire in 1861 set the whole south waterfront of the Upper Pool ablaze, carried off the luckless Braidwood himself and smouldered on for six months afterwards. This catastrophe led to the establishment of a reconstituted Metropolitan Fire Brigade in 1865. Its commander, Captain Eyre Massey Shaw, up-graded its equipment, built 26 new fire-stations and was immortalised for his efforts in Gilbert and Sullivan's *Iolanthe*.

Intellectual diversions

Despite the impact of the Lakeland poets and the passing of Johnson and Goldsmith, London remained the firm focus of the nation's literary life. The eccentric genius of Soho-born William Blake (1757–1827) both explored the fantastical visions of his inner spiritual journeys and raged against the alienation and exploitation he saw around him:

> In every cry of every man,
> In every infant's cry of fear,
> In every voice, in every ban,
> The mind-forged manacles I hear.
> (*Songs of Experience* 1794 'London' Stanza 2)

Blake's circle included the Swiss painter Henry Fuseli and the sculptor Flaxman, who introduced him to the mysticism of the Swedish philosopher Swedenborg and to the formidable blue-stocking group who gathered at the home of the Revd A.S. Mathew in Rathbone Place.

WILLIAM HAZLITT

Another inhabitant of Rathbone Place was William Hazlitt (1778–1830), a prolific and controversial journalist and critic whose chequered career included debt, divorce, desertion and the laborious composition of an ill-regarded, and spectacularly ill-timed, four-volume biography of his hero – Napoleon. Hazlitt's other writings were, however, so extensive as to form virtually a critical history of English literature at a time when no such work existed. Hazlitt also formed lasting friendships with two other ubiquitous figures of the London literary scene – Lamb and Leigh Hunt.

CHARLES LAMB

Lamb, an old boy of Christ's Hospital, is now best remembered for his *Tales from Shakespeare*, written to introduce children to the Bard, but in his day was better known for the essays, written under the pen-name 'Elia', which appeared in the *London Magazine* and reflected gently and whimsically on the small change of the city's life. In an age when the majesty of Nature was all the rage Lamb confessed in a letter to Wordsworth himself – 'Separate from the pleasure of your company, I don't much care if I never see a mountain in my life.'

LEIGH HUNT

Leigh Hunt was another Christ's Hospital boy who learned to scrape a living as an essayist and publisher while attempting to establish his reputation as a poet and dramatist. An early and enthusiastic supporter of John Keats, the good-natured Hunt became the chief target of the Edinburgh-based *Blackwood's Magazine's* splenetic campaign against what it sneeringly pilloried as the 'Cockney School of Poetry', whose members – Hunt, Hazlitt and Keats – were castigated as 'the vilest vermin' and 'of extreme moral depravity', with Hunt specially singled out on account of his alleged 'low birth and low habits'. This accords ill with the experience of a man who, imprisoned for two years for referring to the prince regent as 'corpulent', was visited in his confinement by a range of acquaintance which ran from Byron to Bentham. From 1833 to 1840 Hunt lived at 22 Upper Cheyne Row, Chelsea, a few minutes walk from Carlyle's house. Hunt's later writings include a *London Journal*

(1834–5), *The Town* (1848) an evocation of London, and *The Old Court Suburb* (1855) a series of essays on Kensington.

WASHINGTON IRVING

Of literary visitors to London few can have been more successful than Washington Irving (1783–1859), the New York-born son of a British merchant who had chosen to side with the American rebels during the Revolutionary War. Struggling unsuccessfully to stave off the impending bankruptcy of his family business, Irving visited England and while there was introduced to the poets Moore and Campbell, the influential publisher John Murray and the venerable Sir Walter Scott. His suave and witty reflections on his first encounter with London, published as *The Sketch Book* (1820) won him acclaim on both sides of the Atlantic. Many even of his metropolitan readers would have agreed with his shrewd but flattering observation that 'An immense metropolis like London, is calculated to make men selfish and uninteresting. In their casual and transient meetings, they can but deal briefly in commonplaces. They present but the cold superfices of character – its rich and genial qualities have no time to be warmed into a flow. It is in the country that the Englishman gives scope to his natural feelings. . . .'

The author took his applause modestly enough but could not forbear to observe that 'It has been a matter of marvel to my European readers that a man from the wilds of America should express himself in tolerable English.'

Washington Irving returned to London in 1829 to serve for three years as secretary to the United States Legation and to glow in the pleasure of being the first professional American writer to have achieved a reputation outside his own country.

The Stage

The early-nineteenth century did not produce outstanding dramatists but it did produce great actors and much enthusiasm for classical theatre, especially Shakespeare. For 30 years, until her official retirement in 1812, Sarah Siddons (1755–1831) was queen of the London stage. Hazlitt called her Lady Macbeth 'tragedy personified'. The measure of her reputation is attested by statues in Westminster Abbey and at Paddington Green and by portraits by both Reynolds (Dulwich) and Gainsborough (National Portrait Gallery). Her brothers Charles and John Kemble, and her niece Fanny, were all to achieve theatrical eminence as well. Drury Lane saw John Kemble's debut as Hamlet in 1783; in 1788 he took over the management. Declared unsafe in 1791 Drury Lane was rebuilt by Henry Holland only to burn down in 1809 and be replaced by an even larger house to the designs of Benjamin Wyatt at the stupendous cost of £151,672. Edmund Kean's sensational debut as Shylock occurred there in 1814, as did the farewell benefit in 1818 for the great clown Grimaldi. The tragedian, William Charles Macready, took over in 1841 and did much to improve both standards of acting and the accuracy of texts.

If the theatre was popular that did not necessarily make it respectable. Much cultural life still revolved around the salons of the great and none was more glittering than that at Holland House. The Irish poet Tom Moore advised 'a dose of Lady Holland now and then' as a certain remedy for vanity, but the smooth-tongued Sydney Smith assured the queenly hostess that 'I do not believe all Europe can produce as much knowledge, wit and worth as passes in and out of your door.' Guests at Holland House included the prime ministers Canning, Grey, Melbourne and Palmerston as well as Scott, Dickens, Macaulay and Talleyrand.

Gentlemen's Clubs

If the salon represented a time-honoured mode of social intercourse among the élite the proliferation of gentlemen's clubs represented something novel. They were not in themselves new but the growth in their number certainly was. White's, opened in 1693, had been established as a chocolate house by an Italian, Francesco Bianco (hence White's) and was the oldest and grandest, numbering among its members every prime minister from Walpole to Peel. Hogarth depicted gambling at White's in *The Rake's Progress*. Boodle's, founded in 1762 on the original site of White's, was established to provide a London base for country gentlemen. Its varied membership encompassed such diverse characters as Edward Gibbon, the historian of

Rome, William Wilberforce, the anti-slavery campaigner, Beau Brummel, the dandy, and the duke of Wellington himself. Brooks's (1764) was for the Whigs. There the radical Charles James Fox lost so heavily at the gaming-table that he had to borrow from the waiters.

By 1814 White's had 500 members and an even longer waiting-list. A rash of new clubs appeared to meet pent-up demand, much no doubt fuelled by the nostalgia of discharged officers for the life of the mess. The United Services was appropriately founded in the year of Waterloo, Smirke, himself a militia officer, designing its purpose-built premises in Lower Regent Street. In 1826 Wilkin's University Club opened, to be followed by Crockford's, a club exclusively for gambling, the Carlton, for Conservatives, the Oriental, for East India Company men, the Army and Navy, the Oxford and Cambridge, the Travellers and the Reform. The buildings for the last two, both by Barry, the architect of the new Houses of Parliament, were both in the style of an Italian palazzo and were to serve as the models for much institutional architecture in the middle years of the century.

Most of these clubs were clustered around Pall Mall, within easy reach of suppliers of gentlemen's requisites such as hats (Lock & Coy), wine (Berry Bros and Rudd), both in St James's Street or cheese (Paxton and Whitfield) and cologne (Floris) in Jermyn Street, all of which have been in existence since the eighteenth century. The London club was long to remain in the words of novelist Arnold Bennett 'the most perfectly organised mechanism of comfort that was ever devised. ... In comparison the most select hotels and restaurants are a hurly-burly of crude socialism.'

Sport and Leisure

Leisured persons seeking other diversions than clubland afforded could find many new opportunities. In 1787 a Yorkshireman, Thomas Lord, had opened a cricket ground on the site of what is now Dorset Square and formed the Marylebone Cricket Club, which was eventually to establish itself as the supreme authority on the rules and conduct of the game. In 1805 the first Eton *v* Harrow match was played (Lord Byron was on the losing Harrow side) and the first Gentleman *v* Players match the following year. In 1814 'Lord's' moved to its present site on St John's Wood Road. Thirty years later it provided temporary accommodation for an encampment of Red Indians who gave displays of dancing and archery.

After 1828 a short stroll from Lord's could take the idly curious to the new Zoological Gardens laid out in Regent's Park by Decimus Burton for the newly-founded Zoological Society of London, itself the brainchild of Sir Stamford Raffles, founder of Singapore and Sir Humphrey Davy, inventor of the miner's safety-lamp. By 1834 the zoo had been augmented by the transfer of animals from royal menageries at Windsor and the Tower of London. In 1835 it acquired its first chimpanzee, in 1836 four giraffes (sparking a fashion fad for dappled cloth) and in 1840 a lioness, which tripped over and died, leaving her mate to pine away of grief. In 1843 the zoo opened the world's first reptile house, to be followed by the world's first aquarium a decade later.

Regent's Park's most popular attraction was, however, the Colosseum (1829–75), an immense rotunda, designed by Decimus Burton, which began by displaying panoramic painted views of London and then introduced such novelties as a Hall of Mirrors, an aviary, mockcaves and roller-skating.

From 1835 onwards the curious tourist could head from the Colosseum to Baker Street to visit that other long-standing attraction – Madame Tussaud's Waxworks. A refugee from revolutionary France, Mme Tussaud had arrived in England in 1802 and toured her 35 wax figures extensively throughout the country before settling on a permanent site and offering the public a quality product, hailed by Dickens as 'something more than an exhibition ... an institution, with celebrities ... strictly up-to-date ... continuously added to ...'. The duke of Wellington himself was a keen patron of the Chamber of Horrors.

Other London diversions included, in Spring Gardens, 'Toby, the Sapient Pig' (which could allegedly spell, play cards, tell the time and mind-read), at Leicester Square, Miss Linwood's display of needlework pictures, and, in Piccadilly, the Egyptian Hall, which presented before the curious and the credulous a mermaid (half-fish, half-monkey), a family of Laplanders, with their reindeer, genuine Siamese twins from Siam and the 25-inch 'General' Tom Thumb from America.

A University for London

With its ancient Inns of Court and its teaching hospitals, learned societies and museums, London could claim to be a great centre of higher learning, but, unlike Edinburgh, or even Glasgow or St Andrews, it lacked a university. Oxford and Cambridge were already six centuries old when the nineteenth century opened; sunk in port and torpor they excluded all those who were not of the Anglican communion.

What became University College, London was the creation of a group of Dissenters led by the poet Thomas Campbell, the philosophers, Jeremy Bentham and James Mill, and legal reformers Brougham and Romilly. Admitting all, regardless of religion, the 'godless college', as its critics called it, opened in 1826 and by 1829 was housed in a handsome classical building by William Wilkins.

Medicine early formed a part of UC's programme of study and a separate teaching hospital soon developed. In 1846 a surgeon at UCH performed the first operation in Europe using ether as an anaesthetic. As the amputated leg was removed he pronounced delightedly to his student audience 'Gentlemen, this Yankee dodge beats Mesmerism.' In 1867 another UCH man, Joseph Lister, a quaker refused entry by Oxford and Cambridge, was to pioneer the use of antiseptics in surgery.

Opponents of University College, led by the bishops of the Church of England, established King's College as an Anglican rival in 1828. Students were not required to be Anglicans but governors and professors – with the exception of linguists – were. By 1831 King's, too, had its own building, in effect an extension of Somerset House, designed by Smirke.

In 1836 an umbrella institution, the University of London, was established by parliament to administer examinations to students from both colleges. This federal arrangement has continued to the present day, enabling the university to grow by foundation and absorption until it embraces some 30 semi-autonomous schools, colleges and hospitals, spread over a hundred miles, with out-stations in Scotland and Paris. It remains Britain's largest university and trains more than a third of the doctors entering the National Health Service.

CHAPTER SEVEN

Inequalities and Improvements,
1837–1889

Railway Revolution

The world's first railway proper – using locomotive engines to offer regular services to fare-paying passengers – was opened in 1830. It ran for 30 miles between Liverpool, a major port, and Manchester, a major manufacturing centre, and was trumpeted by its creators as the greatest feat of engineering since the pyramids. The railway soon proved itself to be not only a technological triumph but also a commercial bonanza. All Britain was gripped by a 'railway mania' which led to the construction of lines linking all the major cities by 1850. Railways were to revolutionise not merely the speed, costs and efficiency of transportation but the very perception of time and space. For the first time in human history the horse no longer set the limit to how fast a man could travel. By the middle years of the nineteenth century trains were travelling at twice the speed of the swiftest thoroughbred and offering a service with standards of punctuality and reliability not to be exceeded until the general adoption of electrification.

LONDON TIME

Railways exerted a profound influence on London in two ways. By making the capital more accessible to the rest of the nation than ever before railways strengthened the metropolitan grip on the nation's cultural and economic life as well as its politics. This dominance was symbolised by the nationwide adoption after 1852 of London time as standard. Previously local time in Somerset, for example, would have been 15 minutes different. A stage-coach traveller, bowling along at eight miles an hour or so, would have reset his watch periodically on the journey. But the imposition of a single standard time was essential if railway timetables were to mean anything; so for 30 years, until the uniform adoption of Greenwich Mean Time, most stations ran two clocks, one showing local time, the other London time, by which the train services were regulated.

Without the railway to handle a vastly increased volume of mail the national pre-paid 'penny post' introduced in 1840 would have been inconceivable. Railways also made it possible to distribute London newspapers throughout the nation overnight, confirming the hegemony of the metropolitan over the regional press. And as the building of railway lines was accompanied by the literally parallel construction of telegraph lines, the rapid diffusion of commercial information, such as stock exchange and commodity prices, became possible, enhancing London's role as the integrator and co-ordinator of a national economy which increasingly functioned as a single unit rather than as a confederation of semi-autonomous regions. And what was true for the large-scale operations of big business was true also for the individual consumer.

Fast, punctual services enabled anyone within a hundred miles of London to go shopping there and be back home the same day; by thus enlarging the pool of purchasing-power on which London could potentially draw, the railway greatly hastened the growth of the large department store and made the monthly shopping expedition 'up to town' a regular feature of middle-class life in the home counties.

The second major impact of railways on the capital was to transform the look and lifestyle of the city itself. The construction of major termini (*see p 272*) and bridges led to the demolition of huge areas of slums – and created new ones. Initially railway-promoters concentrated on what would now be called 'inter-city' routes; but they soon came to appreciate the profit there might be in providing commuter services between central London and the villages and small towns of its immediate vicinity. From that it was but a logical, if large, step to building new communities to house new commuters. One such project, involving the construction of 800 'desirable villa residences', was unimaginatively christened 'Railway Town'; today it is called Surbiton.

THE UNDERGROUND

If the north of England had the honour of initiating the world's first railway service, London took the palm in opening the world's first underground railway service. Opened in 1863, it linked Paddington, Euston and King's Cross and terminated just short of Smithfield, from where passengers could stroll to their City offices. The Circle line today still follows this same stretch of track and platform 6 at Baker Street station has been preserved to show what the station would more or less have looked like in its original condition.

Travelling by train cost money and therefore meant that access to transport varied with income, thus accentuating the residential segregation of different social groups. The affluent middle-class could move ten or 15 miles from the city centre to spacious and gracious commuter suburbs, while the poor had to stay within walking distance of the docks, markets and building sites which were the main sources of employment for the casual labourer. The introduction of cheap early morning workmen's fares in east London during the 1860s, and more generally after an Act of Parliament in 1883 obliged all railway companies to offer them, enabled an intermediate group of clerks, shop-assistants and skilled craftsmen to follow their 'betters' out of the inner city, creating what were in effect working-class suburbs in areas such as Deptford, Walthamstow and West Ham.

TRAMS

From the 1870s onwards suburban railway services were further augmented by the horse-drawn tram which was technically more efficient than the horse-bus and could therefore carry more passengers at lower fares. Banned from the City and West End where their inability to manoeuvre out of their fixed tracks would have obstructed the already chaotic flow of horse-drawn traffic, they were eventually to develop into a sprawling but by no means continuous suburban network, complementing the railways, from Richmond in the west to Plumstead in the east and from Ponders End in the north to Streatham in the south.

The Great Exhibition

'The Great Exhibition of the Works of Industry of All Nations' was the first-ever 'world fair'. Conceived by Queen Victoria's high-minded consort, Prince Albert, and carried through by the hyperactive Henry Cole, a leading light of the Royal Society of Arts, it was intended as a celebration of the progress of civilisation, of the fruits of peace, rather than of war. Opponents of the scheme voiced fears that it might somehow expose London to untold dangers, ranging from missionising Catholics to plague-bearing rats. Such nonsense proved ineffectual but what did nearly stop the entire enterprise in its tracks was the lack of a suitable building in which to hold it. A design competition attracted almost 250 entries. The prince's organising committee, manned by such luminaries as Peel, Gladstone, Cubitt, Barry and the duke of Devonshire, rejected them all.

JOSEPH PAXTON

A solution was provided in the nick of time by Joseph Paxton, a man whose extraordinary career was to take him from being a garden boy on the duke of Devonshire's estate to a seat in parliament and the honour of designing a truly revolutionary building which Queen Victoria herself was to describe 'one of the wonders of the world which we English may be proud of.'

Paxton had already designed a glass hothouse to accommodate some huge tropical water-lilies the duke had acquired. What he proposed was to reproduce such a structure on a scale never before attempted. The exhibition hall, covering 19 acres on the south side of Hyde Park,

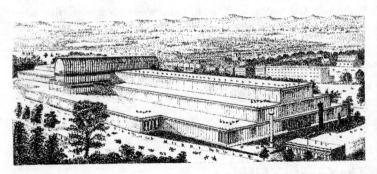

The Great Exhibition of 1851

was erected by 2,000 men in just four months. Foundries usually engaged in making castings for railways were commissioned to mass-produce girders and columns which could be combined on a modular basis to provide the framework for 900,000 square feet of glass, manufactured in standard sheets of 4 foot by 1 foot. The finished structure was, in the queen's own words, 'light and graceful in spite of its immense size.' It was 108-feet high at its highest point, sufficient to accommodate three great elm trees which could thus be left undisturbed, and at 1,848-feet long it was more than three times the length of St Paul's. *Punch* magazine chirpily christened the sparkling apparition the 'Crystal Palace' and the name stuck.

The opening of the Great Exhibition in May 1851 left the queen herself exhilarated – 'one of the greatest, most glorious days of our lives.' Over the next five months some two million visitors made six million visits to view the 100,000 exhibits submitted by 13,937 exhibitors. The items on show embraced the fine arts and natural products as well as mechanical contrivances and ranged from the Koh-i-noor diamond to unpickable locks and a mechanical reaping machine.

When the exhibition closed the Crystal Palace was bought by the Brighton Railway Company who re-erected it at Sydenham as a permanent leisure and exhibition centre, where it survived until it was burnt down in 1936. Prince Albert's own pet contribution, a 'model dwelling' for the working-classes, was rebuilt in Kennington Park and the handsome bronze statue of Richard the Lionheart cast by Baron Marochetti was resited in Old Palace Yard, just outside the nearly-completed Houses of Parliament.

FINANCIAL SURPLUS

To the utter stupefaction of the jeremiahs who had predicted both physical and financial disaster the exhibition actually ended up with a surplus of £186,000 on its hands. This was used to establish a permanent complex of institutions which would further the ideals of technical and artistic excellence which the event had been designed to foster. Bounded by the Cromwell Road to the south and Kensington Road to the north, Exhibition Road to the east and Queen's Gate (then Prince Albert Road) to the west, a site of 87 acres was secured 'safe for future years amidst the growth of the metropolis.' Some of the buildings which appeared in 'Albertopolis' over the next half-century have now gone but what remains is more than sufficient to ensure that the prince's vision has been fulfilled. The South Kensington Museum has become the Victoria and Albert Museum (*see p 286*). The Imperial Institute has given way to the Imperial College of Science, Technology and Medicine, a constituent college of the University of London. The Natural History Museum survives in its Romanesque glory, abutted by specialist museums of Science and Geology. Around the Royal Albert Hall, named in the prince's honour, cluster the Royal Colleges of Organists, Music and Art, the School of Mines and the Royal Geographical Society. Brooding over them, ensconced in the ornate Gothic memorial which won Sir George Gilbert Scott his knighthood, sits the statue of 'Albert the Good' himself, thoughtfully clutching a fat bound volume – the catalogue of the Great Exhibition.

Manufacturing and Money

In the year of the Great Exhibition, which flaunted Britain's industrial supremacy, 86 per cent of the capital's manufacturers employed ten workers or less and only 17 had a labour force of 250 or more. Some of the largest were breweries; in 1830 Adolphe de Custine had been astonished by the sheer size of Barclay Perkins' establishment in Southwark: 'A few centuries from now it will be difficult for people looking at the extent of its remains to guess the purpose for which such a monument was erected. It is the Colosseum of London.'

Ship-building and iron-founding were also large-scale industries, though they diminished substantially in the face of competition from the Tyne and the Clyde, which had better access to supplies of iron and coal and lower costs for both land and labour. Brunel's immense *Great Eastern*, at its launching the largest ship ever built, was the last really big commercial vessel to be built on the Thames, though work on naval bottoms continued into the twentieth century and marine repairs for both types of shipping also flourished.

Some craft industries also suffered severe decline. Competition from Norwich and Paisley eroded the Spitalfields silk-weaving industry but, ironically in view of the Huguenot origins of the business, it was French imports which delivered the *coup de grâce*. In the case of pewter it was not competition but change in consumer tastes which did the damage. As tea and coffee, rather than ale, 'small beer' or milk, became the habitual daily drink of the Londoner, so demand for china cups rose and sales of pewter tankards plummeted.

SWEAT SHOPS

In the case of the garment and shoe-making industries technology proved to be the driving-force of change. The invention of the sewing-machine in the 1860s enabled its operator to sew 30 times faster than the most accomplished and diligent hand-worker. This made possible both the employment of less skilled hands, the development of a more complex division of labour and the mass-production of cheaper garments and footwear to meet the demands of a working-class market which, from the 1850s onwards, began to acquire its share of the prosperity generated by the British economy's unprecedented, if uneven, expansion. The centre of gravity of these industries tended to shift eastwards into the slums of Tower Hamlets where workers, usually females or male youths, were paid rock-bottom piece-rates in sweat shops or as out-workers in their own homes. There were, of course, even more exploitative 'sweated' industries paying a pittance to housebound housewives for such repetitive tasks as assembling matchboxes – at twopence per gross.

Quality furniture-making remained concentrated north of Oxford Street, while Shoreditch catered for the lower end of the market. Piano-making centred on Camden and Lambeth, the latter also being the home of Doulton's pottery which turned out glazed pipes and sanitary-ware, the basic munitions in the mid-Victorian battle for better hygiene. The leather trades centred in the Bermondsey area, while out at Stratford a major metal-working complex grew up around the locomotive and rolling-stock works established by the Eastern Counties Railway in 1847. Not far away, in Bow, Bryant and May's giant match factory loomed like a red-brick Gothic castle beside the railway line. Along the nearby Lea valley clustered plants processing the fruits of imperial commerce, such as sugar, rubber and guano.

Finance and Commerce

If manufacturing was becoming relatively less important in the economic life of the capital, finance and commerce were expanding to redress the balance. Bankers and brokers built imposing new offices in the environs of the Bank of England and the Royal Exchange. The number of Lloyd's underwriters more than doubled between 1850 and 1870 as the expansion of world trade, still largely conducted in British merchant ships, fuelled demand for marine insurance. On the domestic front the Prudential Mutual Assurance, Investment and Loan Association discovered a mass-market for life policies among the 'respectable' lower middle-classes and the skilled 'aristocracy of labour'. On the strength of this business the 'Pru' was able to build a head office in Holborn of an extravagance to put a Loire château to shame.

The Growth of Retailing

Major developments in retailing included the gradual emergence of the department store and the 'multiple'. On Oxford Street Peter Robinson, linen draper, expanded from his one original shop of 1833 to take over five adjacent ones by 1860. By the 1840s Maple's and Heal's were already established on Tottenham Court Road as comprehensive furniture retailers on a grand scale. Harrod's, originally a tea-dealer's in Eastcheap, took over a Knightsbridge grocer's in 1849 and diversified into stationery, perfumes and patent medicines. Between 1870 and 1880 the number of assistants at Harrods rose from 16 to nearly a hundred. Liberty's, established in 1875, soon established a specialised reputation for fine textiles and oriental goods. But Whiteley's, established in 1863, continued to outshine all rivals until the end of the century.

W.H. Smith's chain of bookstalls grew with the expansion of the railways. Sainsbury's grocery stores started from a dairy in Drury Lane in 1869; a turning-point in the firm's history came with the opening of its Croydon branch in the 1880s. This was followed by a rapid expansion throughout the suburbs, matched by the similar expansion of its keen rivals the Home and Colonial stores. What Smith's did for newsagency and Sainsbury's for foodstuffs, Boot's was to achieve for pharmacy. By the 1880s the modern suburban high street was visibly beginning to take shape.

Dickens

Charles Dickens was not a Londoner by birth but few writers have made the city more their own. As his journalistic contemporary Walter Bagehot, editor of *The Economist*, put it 'Dickens describes London like a special correspondent for posterity.' Dickens' portrayal of the city, though many-sided, had certain recurrent motifs – night and fog, wretched hovels and vile courtyards, prisons and poorhouses and, always, the brooding presence of the river. Of extreme poverty he has much to say, of high society a little, of the intellectual life of the metropolis almost nothing. Legal and criminal circles he knew well from first-hand experience and drew upon them for many of his finest creations; the theatre was another of his passions; political London he also knew, but it fascinated him far less.

Dickens' adult years coincided with the advent of the railway, which transformed the metropolis for ever. Yet, despite having been personally involved in aiding the victims of a train wreck, he scarcely mentions the railway at all. Dickens' London is still a pedestrian's city. An inveterate, almost obsessive, walker, Dickens knew the streets – and side-streets – as intimately as any of the new breed of policemen or the old breed of ne'er-do-wells. Much of his authority as a writer came from his ability to expose an unknown London to Londoners themselves, to show those inhabitants who read habitually, the lives led by those who could scarcely read at all.

SLUMS AND ALLEYS

The London Dickens wrote about, as opposed to the London he knew, is surprisingly compact. He was interested in the slums, not the suburbs, the alleys, not the avenues. Few characters or incidents are to be found east of the Tower or west of St James's. King's Cross more or less marks the northern frontier of a London whose heart clearly lies in the labyrinth of turnings around Fleet Street and St Paul's. When Dickens wants to banish a character from the action of one of his novels he exiles him to distant Islington – or Suffolk – it is much the same.

Charles Dickens was born in Portsmouth, Hampshire, home of the British navy, where his father worked in a naval accounts office. The boy's happiest childhood years were spent on the Medway, after his father was transferred to the Chatham dockyard. North Kent is an important setting for incidents in *Pickwick* and *Great Expectations* and remained Dickens' favourite country area. Indeed, he even chose a patch of ground between the castle and the cathedral at Rochester for his grave; but, in defiance of his known wishes, and at the express command of Queen Victoria, he was to be interred in Poets' Corner. His prohibition of a statue has been respected, though the Prudential building in Holborn houses a bust of him to mark the fact that he once lived in Furnivall's Inn which stood on that site.

When Dickens' father was transferred up to London his income proved too slim for his family's needs and at the age of 12 the sensitive boy was sent to work at Warren's blacking warehouse at Hungerford Stairs, where Charing Cross station now stands and from which spot the Micawbers would emigrate to Australia. Dickens loathed the dirty and soul-destroying work and likewise loathed his supervisor, a youth called Bob Fagin. The boy's misery was compounded when his father was imprisoned for debt in the Marshalsea, Southwark. A heaven-sent legacy lifted the clouds after a few months and the boy returned to school; but these bitter and humiliating personal experiences left Dickens with a lifelong hatred of child exploitation and a warm sympathy for the victims of the crass materialism of his day. Somehow, perhaps because he was in advance of public opinion, but never very far in advance, Dickens was to manage to champion the causes of social reform and urban improvement without jeopardising his huge popularity. As George Orwell was to put it 'Dickens seems to have succeeded in attacking everybody and antagonising nobody.'

FAME AND FORTUNE

Leaving school at 15, Dickens became first a solicitor's clerk in Gray's Inn and Chancery Lane and then a gifted parliamentary reporter working out of an office at Bell Yard, Carter Lane. His professional career as an author began with a miscellany about London life *Sketches by Boz* which brought immediate fame and fortune. Having married Catherine Hogarth at the new Gothic-revival church of St Luke's, Chelsea, Dickens took advantage of his success to move into a neat terrace house at 48 Doughty Street which was then sufficiently prestigious to merit gates and a porter with a gold-laced hat to keep out casual traffic. This is the only one of Dickens' 15 London homes to survive and is now a museum dedicated to his memory. Here his two daughters were born, here his beloved sister-in-law Mary (the model for Little Nell) died in his arms. Here he wrote *Pickwick Papers, Oliver Twist* and *Nicholas Nickleby*. Apart from containing many of Dickens' personal possessions, and an unrivalled library of Dickensiana, the house also has a basement fitted out like the kitchen at Dingley Dell and, in summer, sports window-boxes with his favourite flowers, red geraniums.

Plaques mark the sites of Dickens' other homes at 1 Devonshire Terrace, Regent's Park (1839–51) and at Tavistock Square (1851–60) where he conducted amateur theatricals in a first-floor back room. The Marshalsea prison closed a few years after John Dickens' discharge but a stretch of its wall now provides a boundary for a frowzy open space next to the church of St George the Martyr, at the bottom of Borough High Street, where Little Dorritt was married. At the other end of the High Street a plaque in White Hart Yard marks the site of the rambling coaching-inn where Mr Pickwick first met Sam Weller. The nearby 'George', mentioned in *Little Dorritt*, survives as London's last galleried inn. New London Bridge is not the one from which David Copperfield contemplated 'the golden Monument' but some of 'Nancy's Steps' remain to remind us of where the luckless heroine was overheard betraying the whereabouts of Oliver Twist and thus sealing her fate at the hands of Bill Sikes.

A plaque also marks the site of the long-demolished blacking factory, just off the Strand, but one of Dickens' favourite eating-places, Rule's restaurant is still only a few steps away in Maiden Lane, where the original playbills he presented can still be seen on the walls. Other hostelries patronised by Dickens include the Horn Tavern in Knight-rider Street, the George and Vulture, off Cornhill, the Grapes at Limehouse, the Spaniard's Inn and Jack Straw's Castle at Hampstead and the Trafalgar, at Greenwich, long famed for its whitebait suppers.

THE OLD CURIOSITY SHOP

The 'Old Curiosity Shop' at 13 Portsmouth Street, at the south-west corner of Lincoln's Inn Fields, dates from 1567 and is claimed to be the oldest shop in London. It would certainly have been known to Dickens but, contrary to the claim emblazoned on its wall, the fictional home of Little Nell was almost certainly located at the southern end of Charing Cross Road. The attractive timbered 'Dickens Inn' at St Katharine's Dock, just east of Tower Bridge, includes as part of its decor the pronouncements of various of Dickens' characters on the subjects of beer, wine, taverns etc.; but in Dickens' day it stood several hundred yards from its present site and was part of a warehouse complex, not a pub. The author did, however, know the area well and wrote of it with a sort of detached disgust: 'Down by the Docks they consume the slimiest of shellfish, which seem to have been scraped off the copper bottoms of ships.... Down by the Docks, you may buy polonies, saveloys and sausage preparations various, if you are not too particular what they are made of beside seasoning.... Down by the Docks, the shabby undertaker's shop will bury you for next to nothing, after the Malay or Chinaman has stabbed you for nothing at all ...'.

On the opposite side of the river was derelict Jacob's Island (now Jacob Street), bordered by the polluted Neckinger river, 'the very capital of cholera' (now a dock) where Bill Sikes met his end. A local housing estate is named in Dickens' honour. The compliment may seem a back-handed one, until one remembers that, in 1850, a City alderman denounced the place as a pure fiction, provoking Dickens to re-affirm its actual existence in the preface to a new edition of his novel. There can be few greater tributes to the power of fiction than for its factual basis to be dismissed – as a fiction.

Prestige Projects

Victoria's reign saw Britain become increasingly assured of both its technological leadership and its imperial destiny. This self-confidence found expression in the undertaking of projects requiring unprecedented engineering skills or the invocation of architectural imagination on a bravura scale. Typical of the first type of venture was the construction by the Anglo-French Brunels, father and son, of the first tunnel under the Thames. It took almost 20 years to complete and proved to be both a technical triumph and a commercial disaster. It opened in the same year as the raising of Nelson's column, 1843, but lack of funds meant that the proposed approach ramps for carriages were never built, so it was reduced to the role of a short-cut for pedestrians, an attraction for tourists and a bizarre setting for bazaars. The American writer Nathaniel Hawthorne thought it would make a good prison. It was eventually converted for railway traffic and now carries the Underground line between Whitechapel and Rotherhithe, where the pumping house for its ventilation system can still be inspected.

BARRY AND PUGIN

In 1834 the Houses of Parliament burned down. Its replacement was designed by Charles Barry and Augustus Pugin but before it was fully finished both of them would be dead. Barry's taste was for something classical, Pugin was a fanatic for the Gothic. Parliament itself demanded Gothic to emphasise its medieval origins, its sense of six centuries of continuity and to avoid a jarring contrast with its great neighbour, Westminster Abbey. What parliament got was a building which was classical in concept and organisation but exuberantly Gothic in decoration and detail. Barry was faced with, and overcame, a formidable series of practical problems – to double the size of the previous parliament, to harmonise his new building with venerable Westminster Hall and to make the best he could of a low-lying riverside site. Like Wren with St Paul's he was bedevilled with interference and false economies. When he began he hoped to finish it in six years at a cost of £80,000. In the end it took 25 and cost £2,000,000. Workaholic Barry slaved on without slackening, even when the Treasury arbitrarily cut his fee. Pugin went to the madhouse, where he died, aged 40.

COURTS OF JUSTICE

The reconstruction of parliament necessarily had a disruptive effect on the law courts, which for over five centuries had been crowded together in Westminster Hall. After considerable wrangling it was finally decided that they should be relocated near the Inns of Court. The grandiose Royal Courts of Justice were, when completed in 1882, hailed as a triumph of the Gothic, but, as with the new Palace of Westminster, appearances are deceptive. Their romantically asymmetrical disposition of columns, arches and turrets should not obscure the fact that internally the arrangement of courts and corridors is a masterpiece of rational planning, imposing a subtle system of human traffic management which discreetly separates judges, lawyers, plaintiffs and public. The architect, G.E. Street, like Barry and Pugin, was brought to a premature death through the strain imposed by the commission which both crowned and curtailed his professional life. The unsinkable Sir George Gilbert Scott proved more resilient in the matter of the 'New Government Offices' to be erected on the south side of Downing Street to house the Foreign, Colonial, India and Home departments. Scott, and many MPs, wanted a design in the Gothic style to complement the new Houses of Parliament. But the aristocratic, ebullient prime minister, Palmerston, would have none of it and demanded an Italianate building. His obduracy carried the day and Scott, loathe to forego a commission to which he believed his eminence entitled him, treated himself to some big books and 'mugged up' on the classical tradition to produce the effect required.

Disease, Drains and Demolition

Despite the establishment of a police force, London in the 1830s remained a dangerous place in which death lurked, not on the streets, but beneath them. The great majority of the capital's quarter-of-a-million houses still had cesspits rather than water-closets, and far more people relied on street pumps for their water than on supplies laid on to their houses. In either case they usually drank what the water companies siphoned off from the Thames and its tributaries – into which the sewage generated by two million people was regularly discharged.

CHOLERA

In 1832 cholera, a water-borne disease, struck the capital. Parts of north London, served by the New River Company, which piped its water in from Hertfordshire, were far less badly hit than south London, where the Southwark Waterworks Company drew its supplies from the Thames just opposite a sewer outfall near London Bridge. When a second outbreak occurred in 1848–9 an inadequate understanding of the nature of the disease led to remedial measures which made it literally twice as deadly as it had been the first time. Prevailing medical theory suggested that cholera was caused by the inhalation of poisonous 'miasma', foul vapours given off by rotting garbage and excrement. Much effort was therefore directed into watering streets and flushing sewers to clear away stagnant waste, a procedure which only spread the epidemic more widely. The connection between cholera and the quality of the water-supply was finally established by the painstaking detective work of Dr John Snow who analysed and mapped the distribution of deaths in the outbreaks of 1848–9 and 1853–4. One particular case-study focused on the Soho area where he was able to demonstrate conclusively that a single pump in Broadwick Street was the prime cause of infection. Snow's *On the communication of cholera* was published in 1855 but it took another 20 years for the medical profession as a whole to accept his hypothesis.

One of London's poor – a Sewer scavenger

The greatest campaigner for 'sanitary reform' was undoubtedly Edwin Chadwick. Lawyer by training, bureaucrat by inclination and publicist of necessity, Chadwick was by turns an investigator of child labour in factories, an administrator of poor relief and a tireless investigator and chronicler of the manifest deficiencies of London's drainage system. Indifferent to the unpopularity provoked by his bulldog determination to confront the comfortable classes with uncomfortable facts, he published a *Sanitary Report* in 1842, which sold more copies than any government publication ever previously issued, and followed it with a *Report on Interment in Towns* (1843) and a *Report on the Supply of Water to the Metropolis* (1850). Chadwick was instrumental in forcing the passage of a pioneering, if ineffectual, Public Health Act in 1848 and in the rationalisation of a disparate number of separate boards into a united Metropolitan Commission of Sewers. His crusade was given a boost by the environment itself when the long, hot summer of 1858 reduced the Thames to a level so low that a 'Great Stink' threatened to close down parliament itself. Public gratitude was late in coming to a man who fearlessly antagonised the vested interests of water companies and cemetery-owners. Chadwick was knighted shortly before his death at the age of 90. The *Daily News* observed in its obituary that 'had he killed in battle as many as he saved by sanitation, he would have had equestrian statues by the dozen put up to his memory.' As it is he is appropriately memorialised by the makers of urinals and other sanitary-ware by whom the name 'Chadwick' has often been adopted to mark their products as being of the highest quality.

SIR JOSEPH BAZALGETTE

Chadwick's vision waited for its implementation on the establishment in 1855 of the Metropolitan Board of Works which superceded a muddle of parish vestries and miscellaneous boards and commissions and was given the brief, if not adequate powers and resources, to tackle the environmental problems of the city as a whole. The board's greatest enterprise was supervised by its engineer, Sir Joseph Bazalgette, who simultaneously embanked the Thames and installed five new main sewers running east-west across the capital, three north of the river and two to the south. These were linked with processing plants far to the east where the sewage was treated before discharge or, later, being dumped into the North Sea. Bazalgette's monument, appropriately mounted on the river wall by Embankment station, carries the Latin tribute *Flumen ad vincula posuit* – he put chains on the river. In doing so he eliminated its vile mud-flats, speeded its flow and, by reclaiming 37 acres for gardens and a roadway, beautified its shoreline.

Bazalgette's promenade was subsequently adorned by the erection of Cleopatra's Needle, a 3,400-year-old Egyptian obelisk from outside Cleopatra's palace in Alexandria. The project to bring it to Britain was dogged by disaster and took over 60 years to accomplish – and then the contractor put the guardian sphinxes the wrong way round, facing inwards. A wag of the day caught the irreverent reaction of Londoners:

> This monument, as some supposes,
> Was looked upon of old by Moses.
> It passed in time from Greeks to Turks,
> And was stuck up here by the Board of Works.

If the construction of an efficient sewage system was the greatest achievement of the Metropolitan Board of Works its creation of major new thoroughfares for the metropolis was also to prove an enduring legacy. Its first essay, Northumberland Avenue, to link Trafalgar Square to the new Embankment, was vilified as an act of vandalism because it necessitated the demolition of Northumberland House, the very last of the great early Jacobean town-houses; with it went an Inigo Jones' façade and an Adam interior. Charing Cross Road and Shaftesbury Avenue, by contrast, amounted to constructive demolition, striking through the heart of the worst of all the 'rookeries', the slums of St Giles and Seven Dials. A knock-on effect of this project was the reshaping of Piccadilly Circus to give it its present outline. Victoria Street in Westminster and the Clerkenwell Road-Old Street-Commercial Street-Great Eastern Street route linking Holborn to Shoreditch likewise required much slum clearance.

The City Corporation, too, undertook its own improvements, widening Eastcheap, laying out Queen Victoria Street to link Blackfriars Bridge with Bank Junction, and replacing Wren's Temple Bar ('the bone in the throat of Fleet Street) with an ornate column surmounted by a haughty heraldic dragon to mark the western boundary of the 'Square Mile'. Vast new market buildings were put up at Smithfield, Leadenhall and Billingsgate, making striking use of elaborate decorative ironwork. At Holborn viaduct the world's first 'fly-over' was constructed to bridge the valley of the Fleet river, thus linking Cheapside to Oxford Street to create a major east-west through route for the capital. Another city venture with far-reaching implications was the acquisition of Epping Forest in 1878 as a conservation area and recreational facility. In 1885 Highgate Woods were similarly purchased.

Accompanying these local authority efforts to upgrade the urban environment were others undertaken by parliament and private groups and individuals. In 1853 a Smoke Abatement Act was passed, in 1857 a Thames Conservancy Act and in 1860 an Act to regulate London's gas supply. In 1859 a Metropolitan Drinking Fountain Association was established; dedication of a public drinking fountain, for use by humans or horses, became a fashionable way of memorialising local worthies. Many of these structures, expensively decorated or faced with granite or marble can still be seen on the streets, though most are now defunct. 1866 saw the passage of a Sanitation Act, consolidating previous legislation. In the same year the capital suffered its last major cholera outbreak, whose impact was almost entirely confined to the East End, nearly 6,000 dying in Poplar alone.

Worship and Welfare

Although Victoria's reign saw the building of thousands of churches and chapels it was not an era of uniform popular piety. A religious census in 1851 showed that less than one Londoner in four attended an act of worship; allowing for those who went morning and evening brings the overall figure down to one in five. Different parts of the capital varied greatly; in wealthy suburbs as much as half the population may have been active members of a congregation, while in the East End the figure could fall as low as one in ten or even 20. Working-class areas themselves showed considerable variation. North-east London, which drew many in-migrants from nonconformist East Anglia, had numerous well-attended chapels. South of the river the baptists were strong, a tribute to the zeal of Charles Spurgeon, a charismatic preacher who at the age of 23 addressed a crowd of over 20,000 in the Crystal Palace. His 'Metropolitan Tabernacle' at Elephant and Castle could hold a congregation of 6,000 and continues to this day as a centre of evangelism.

THE SALVATION ARMY

Another preacher determined to take his message to the masses was William Booth who stood outside pubs in the Whitechapel area to rail against the evils of drink. His 'Christian Mission to the Heathen of our own Country' became the 'Salvation Army' whose 'citadels' served as beacons of fervour and caring in the darkest of slum areas. Booth's brilliant tactic of attracting crowds and converts by adopting the uniforms and instruments of a military band capitalised on popular patriotism and curiosity and showed that he had flair as well as fire; in his own words – 'Why should the devil have all the best tunes?' By 1881 the 'Sally' had established its international headquarters in Queen Victoria Street, where it is today. In 1905 Booth was presented with the 'Freedom of the City' at Guildhall. His funeral in 1912 reduced London's traffic to chaos so great was the number of mourners.

THOMAS BARNARDO

The East End attracted others burning to bear witness to a social gospel. Thomas Barnardo came from Dublin to train as a medical missionary at the London Hospital in Whitechapel. The plight of local street-urchins led him to forego dreams of China to establish a 'Home for Destitute Boys'. From this developed a nationwide network of refuges, hostels, schools and training-centres which, by the time of his death in 1905, had cared for almost 60,000 children.

CANON BARNETT

Canon Samuel Barnett deliberately chose to go to St Jude's, Whitechapel just because it was reputed to be the most deprived and depraved parish in the entire diocese of London. His priority was the depravity, not the deprivation – 'the principle of our work is that we aim at decreasing not suffering, but sin!' His achievements included the establishment of a

Children's Country Holiday Fund, to give local youngsters a glimpse of green fields; the founding of Toynbee Hall as an educational and social centre for adults; and the organisation of the East London Dwellings Company to build decent tenement blocks to house poor families. Barnett also skilfully used the 'Ripper' murders in 1888 to draw public attention to the much wider problems of the area in which they had taken place. In a letter to *The Times* he argued presciently that: 'Whitechapel horrors will not be in vain, if "at last" the public conscience awakes to consider the life which these horrors reveal.'

Roman Catholics

London's Catholic population was greatly enlarged in the 1840s by the influx of tens of thousands of Irish refugees fleeing the effects of the terrible potato blight which brought devastating famine to their homeland in 1845–6. In 1850 therefore the papacy decided to elevate the senior English catholic bishop to the rank of cardinal and archbishop of Westminster, with authority over 12 dioceses.

The restoration of a Roman hierarchy three centuries after its abolition provoked protests from Bethnal Green, where Cardinal Wiseman was burned in effigy, to Guildhall, where solemn resolutions were passed inside while the old cry of 'No Popery' was bawled outside. Wiseman's hastily-printed *Appeal to the English People* explained the purely spiritual pretensions of his status and enabled his enthronement in St George's, Southwark to pass off without incident. By the 1870s protestant zealotry had abated sufficiently for the City to elect its first Roman Catholic lord mayor and for the catholic community to complete the Brompton Oratory in Kensington in a flamboyantly Italianate style. This remained London's leading catholic church until it was superceded by Westminster Cathedral. Designed in an unusual Byzantine style to look as unlike its near neighbour, Westminster Abbey, as possible, it was built in less than a decade, opening in 1903.

An Englishman's Home

Just as many Victorian social reformers made a connection between physical and moral health, arguing that cleanliness was indeed next to godliness, so others saw that decent housing was a prerequisite for decent family life. The Rev. Andrew Mearns' sensational tract *The Bitter Cry of Outcast London* made a direct linkage between over-crowding, irreligion and incest.

Prince Albert's 'model dwelling', designed for the Great Exhibition, was a well-intentioned but largely irrelevant gesture. The problem was, and remained, at bottom an economic one. The sort of rents that the very poor could afford to pay simply could not give an adequate return on the outlay involved in providing them with acceptable accom-modation. Most philanthropically-funded dwelling schemes ended up by actually worsening the problem for the very poorest. By knocking down slums to build new homes on the same sites they deprived them of the only type of home that they could afford and made available in its place housing which was only affordable by the regularly employed, who could just as easily have been served by the commercial sector.

GEORGE PEABODY

One of the most enduring projects was sponsored by George Peabody, an American banker who had come to Britain in the aftermath of a major financial crisis in the 1830s which had all but wrecked American credit-worthiness. Peabody's industry and probity ensured the rehabilitation of his country's mercantile honour and made him a highly-respected figure in the City. It was his far-sighted generosity which ensured that the United States put on a decent show at the Great Exhibition, and it was his imaginative gesture in hosting an annual Fourth of July dinner which confirmed a new closeness in Anglo-American relations. The fact that the Duke of Wellington accepted Peabody's invitation to be guest of honour at the inaugural dinner set the seal of approval on all his efforts to improve bilateral relations.

When Peabody retired he announced his wish to put something back into the city which he had come to love – and which had enabled him to make a great personal fortune. The result was the Peabody Donation Fund, whose trustees decided to devote its £500,000 endowment to the construction of 'cheap, cleanly, well-drained and healthful dwellings for the poor.' The resulting blocks strike the modern eye as distinctly barrack-like but most still stand and are so well-managed that tenancies are eagerly sought. Peabody was honoured in his own lifetime with a statue, which stands behind the Royal Exchange. When he died he had the most unusual honour of temporary interment in Westminster Abbey before his body was transferred by warship for burial in his home state of Massachusetts.

ETHICAL INVESTMENT

A different but highly-imaginative approach to the housing problem was taken by Sidney Waterlow, stationer, printer, lord mayor and Liberal MP. His 'Improved Industrial Dwellings Company' was an early example of 'ethical investment', offering shareholders the possibility of a return guaranteed to be not more than 5 per cent. His example was followed by Lord Rothschild's 'Four Per Cent Industrial Dwellings Company' which provided accommodation for the influx of Jewish refugees who settled in London's East End after fleeing the Russian pogroms of the 1880s.

The redoubtable Octavia Hill took yet another tack, buying out slum landlords and refurbishing their properties rather than demolishing them to build new ones in their place. She also experimented with using lady rent collectors to give free housekeeping advice to tenants whenever they made their weekly visits.

Despite these worthy efforts and the recommendations of the 1884–5 Royal Commission on the Housing of the Working Classes, provision lagged woefully behind need. As late as 1900 the seven largest housing trusts and companies accommodated fewer than 80,000 people – at a time when London's population was growing by more than that every single year.

If experiments with working-class housing proved largely ineffectual two new trends emerged among the middle-classes which were to have far-reaching effects in the following century – the planned suburb and the apartment block. Both are associated with the avant-garde architect Norman Shaw, who also designed the polychromic Scottish-baronial style New Scotland Yard headquarters of the Metropolitan Police. At Bedford Park, Turnham Green, Shaw laid out London's first 'garden suburb', with its own church, tennis-courts and pseudo-medieval

'Tabard Inn'; it attracted 'arty' types and much mockery. 'Flats', known for centuries in Edinburgh and Paris, were slow to catch on in London, the first being built along Victoria Street as it was developed in the 1850s. Shaw's six-storey 'Albert Hall Mansions' pioneered a widely-imitated 'Dutch' style. Their state-of-the-art facilities included lifts, bathrooms and wine-cellars.

Riot, not Revolution

Karl Marx, living in impoverished exile in Soho, predicted that the collapse of capitalism would come in the most advanced capitalist country – Britain. It never did. But there were more than a few occasions when it began to look distinctly threatened. When the 1832 Reform Act extended the vote to only a small proportion of the property-owning middle-class, radicals of all stripes turned to the so-called Chartist movement which demanded fundamental changes in the parliamentary system as a prelude to wholesale social and economic restructuring. The movement organised several monster petitions and demonstrations but its largest-ever effort in 1848 turned into a fiasco. The authorities were so alarmed by the anticipated scale of the event that the army was put on stand-by, special constables were sworn in by the thousand and the aged Duke of Wellington placed in charge of the overall arrangements for the security of the capital in the event of a mass uprising. As it happened a vast crowd milled around inconsequentially on Kennington Common, the leaders funked decisive action, it rained and everyone drifted off home – end of Chartists.

In 1855 a crowd estimated at more than 100,000 gathered at the north-eastern corner of Hyde Park to protest against a proposed Sunday Trading Bill. In 1866 a rally on behalf of further democratisation of the franchise broke up in disorder as long stretches of railings around the park were pulled down. In 1872 the right of public assembly at the park was at last acknowledged, leading to the development of the world-famous Speaker's Corner.

BLOODY SUNDAY

Violence again alarmed the inhabitants of the West End in February

1886 when the country was in the grip of a severe depression. After a mass-meeting in Trafalgar Square a column of unemployed marched through St James's 'Clubland', smashing windows and looting shops. In November the following year a crowd estimated at 100,000 marched from Clerkenwell to Trafalgar Square. Its members included the artist-poet William Morris, the free-thinker Annie Besant, Eleanor Marx, daughter of Karl, and a then-unknown Irishman with literary aspirations – George Bernard Shaw. 'Bloody Sunday' ended with their dispersal by police and soldiers with fixed bayonets.

Perhaps by highlighting so forcefully the futility of violent tactics the failures of 1886–7 unwittingly prepared the way for spectacular successes on the London industrial front soon afterwards. In the spring of 1888 Annie Besant led the exploited girls at Bryant and May's Bow match factory to form their own union and strike successfully against victimisation and for protection from industrial disease. In the spring of 1889 gasworkers at nearby Canning Town, inspired by their example

Rioters in St James Street, 1886

and guided by Eleanor Marx, likewise successfully formed a union and won an eight-hour day. The most dramatic triumph for newly-organised unskilled labour came in August 1889, when 60,000 'casuals' paralysed Thames shipping by demanding the 'docker's tanner' – a basic wage of sixpence an hour. Thanks to a crucial subvention of £30,000 from sympathetic dockers in Australia the strikers were able to stand firm – and win a famous victory.

French Impressions and an American Butterfly

By the time he arrived in London for the first time in 1868 the reputation of Gustave Doré had already preceded him. In 1869 a permanent 'Doré Gallery' opened at 35 New Bond Street, where Sotheby's now stands; by the time it closed in 1892 an estimated two-and-a-half million visitors had paid its shilling entrance fee. Over that period Doré came to London almost every year, dined with the lord mayor and the prince of Wales – but never learned to speak English and declined the offer of a studio. It is perhaps ironic that the artist's most enduring tribute to the city which lionised him was to depict it as a Babylonian horror. *London: A Pilgrimage* was based on field-work conducted in 1869 in the company of his friend, Blanchard Jerrold, who wrote the text and 'led Doré through the shadows and the sun-light.' The book, published in 1872, was intended to shock and it did. Doré readily mixed realism with fantasy, portraying vagrants sleeping rough on London Bridge being watched over by a guardian angel. The *Athenaeum* dismissed the entire work as 'utterly unlike London.' Undeterred Doré published a French version in 1876, with a new text whose preface proclaimed its purpose: 'It is not a single city that we have to show and make come alive for our readers; it is twenty cities in one, or, more exactly, it is a whole world – a world in which all extremes and excesses meet; where you are dazzled by the wonders of an extraordinary civilisation and appalled by misery of a depth and poignancy unknown in any other nation.'

MONET AND PISSARRO

If Doré came as virtually a conquering hero, Monet and Pissarro arrived as refugees, fleeing the chaos of the Franco-Prussian war of 1870–1. Their paintings of the river, of parks and suburbs, show a clear continuity with their interest in similar subjects in France, but stand in contrast to those of British artists who regarded views of the city as falling within the lowly province of illustrators of cheap magazines.

Monet's depiction of the Houses of Parliament, now in the National Gallery, reveals that his concern was no precise topographical rendering but an evocation of misty grandeur. *The Times* critic hit the point squarely in reviewing an exhibition of contemporary French work put on by the refugee art-dealer Durand-Ruel in New Bond Street – 'always the broadest possible expression of some dominant sentiment, this seems the aim of the French landscape painter.' *The Saturday Review* concluded, in the light of a second Durand Ruel show that French artists' 'ideas about nature are all but unintelligible to the average run of Englishmen.'

Monet returned to London, in very different circumstances, for extended spells in 1899, 1900 and 1901, staying at the Savoy Hotel and painting the view from a fifth-floor balcony. He concentrated totally on three subjects – the Thames, looking east over Waterloo Bridge, the Thames, looking west over Charing Cross Bridge, and the Houses of Parliament, viewed from St Thomas's Hospital. He always came over in winter – to be sure of the fog, which to him constituted a unique artistic challenge: '. . . there are black, brown, yellow, green, purple fogs, and the interest in painting is to get the objects as seen through all these fogs . . . objects change in appearance in a London fog more and quicker than in any other atmosphere, and the difficulty is to get every change down on canvas.' In his pursuit of the shifting effects of light and vapour Monet kept up to a hundred separate canvases on the go at once.

Whereas Monet focused from the first on well-known Westminster, Pissarro painted the obscure new south London railway suburb of Upper Norwood where he found lodgings. His *Lordship Lane Station*, now in the Courtauld Institute, shows rows of modest villas and the actual railway line slicing through still open country. English connoisseurs might well have been puzzled by this almost eccentrically unremarkable subject-matter but Pissarro was painting with an eye on the French market, where tastes were different.

From 1883 onwards Pissarro's son, Lucien, was mainly based in

London and, from 1890 onwards, in the course of family visits, Pissarro *pére* resumed painting London subjects, widening his scope to take in the river, Hyde Park, Kew Gardens and the fashionable planned suburb of Bedford Park, where Lucien lived. Lucien was to become an influential member of the Camden Town Group and the London Group and to play a leading role in developing British understanding of both Impressionism and Post-Impressionism. He became a naturalised Briton in 1916 and continued to paint the same sort of down-beat, unspectacular scenes as his father had, including many of railways.

TISSOT

Unlike Monet and Pissarro, Tissot actually saw action in France before fleeing to London and, unlike them, he stayed on after the war ended, living in St John's Wood with his beautiful Irish mistress, Kathleen Newton, who figured in many of his works. Tissot's paintings of London were of people rather than places and often have an air of sly innuendo which contemporaries found unsettling. Ruskin dismissed them as 'mere coloured photographs of vulgar society,' which was at least a back-handed acknowledgement of Tissot's technical virtuosity. A picture, innocently entitled *The Thames*, exhibited at the Royal Academy in 1876 shows a sailor taking two girls for a pleasure-boat ride through the docks. The lounging postures of the principal figures, their flashy clothes, their champagne bottles, and, glimpsed behind them, a bare-bosomed ship's figurehead, all hint at implications which *The Graphic* thought 'hardly nice in its suggestions. More French, shall we say, than English?'

ALMA-TADEMA

Kathleen Newton's death from consumption at 28 shattered Tissot and forced him back to France and the piety of his early years. His elegant house at Grove End Road was taken over by the hugely successful Lawrence Alma-Tadema, a naturalised Dutchman, of whom the *Oxford Companion to Art* notes severely 'His remarkable social and financial success has yet to be endorsed by posterity as an artistic one. He painted scenes from Greek and Roman life, vapid in content but with skilful imitation of the surface textures of statuesque women.'

LORD LEIGHTON

Alma–Tadema's barely-disguised (and often barely-clothed) pin-ups won him a knighthood, but Frederic Leighton went one better, becoming not only president of the Royal Academy but also the first British artist to be elevated to the House of Lords, even if he did receive the honour on his death-bed. Trained in Florence, Frankfurt and Paris, he had achieved instant fame at the age of 25 when his accomplished pastiche in quattrocento style of *Cimabué's Madonna carried in procession* was bought by Queen Victoria. The 'House Beautiful' he had built for him at 12 Holland Park Road contains a magnificent 'Arab Hall', which incorporates the superb collection of Islamic tiles and woodwork he gathered from Rhodes, Damascus and Cairo. Leighton's artistic neighbours included William Burges, whose fairy-tale castle, Tower House, still stands at 29 Melbury Road, next to the house designed by Norman Shaw for painter Luke Fildes and a few doors from No.8, another Shaw house, occupied by Marcus Stone, illustrator of Dickens. Sculptor Sir William Thornycroft lived at No.2, at No.6 was portraitist G.F. Watts ('the English Michaelangelo') and at No.18 Holman Hunt, the founding father of Pre-Raphaelitism.

JAMES ABBOTT McNEILL WHISTLER

If Lord Leighton represented the body of the Victorian artistic establishment James Abbott McNeill Whistler was its gadfly – although he took to signing his work with a butterfly, rather than his name. After flunking out of the US military academy at West Point, Whistler trained in Paris before settling in London, where he befriended Dante Gabriel Rossetti, leader of the Pre-Raphaelite Brotherhood, who recorded in doggerel that:

> There's a combative artist named Whistler
> Who is, like his own hog-hairs, a bristler.

When the French poet Baudelaire called on artists to respond to modern city life Whistler produced a series of etchings now generally known as *The Thames Set*, giving a distinctly unromantic view of the river's wharves, warehouses and low-life inhabitants. These were followed by the atmospheric paintings Whistler christened his *Nocturnes*, harmonies of colour which reflected the enthusiasm for Japanese art he had picked up in his Paris days. In 1877 John Ruskin, the leading art critic of the day, denounced the 200-guinea price Whistler demanded for his *Nocturne in Black and Gold: The Falling Rocket* as 'Cockney impudence', being tantamount to 'flinging a pot of paint in the public's face.' Whistler sued, won, was awarded a farthing in damages and was bankrupted by his legal costs. He was forced to sell the house E.W. Godwin had just completed for him at 34 Tite Street, Chelsea.

Obliged to live in Venice for a year to recoup his fortunes Whistler wrote wistfully to his sister: 'I am bored to death after a certain time away from Piccadilly! I pine for Pall Mall and I long for a hansom!'

Whistler remained unsinkable. Stylish and charming, he had a circle of friends which embraced Manet, Degas, Toulouse-Lautrec and Oscar Wilde, who called him 'a miniature Mephistopheles, mocking the majority'; but Whistler's deadly wit made it entirely fitting for his best-known book to be entitled *The Gentle Art of Making Enemies*. The author Max Beerbohm said that Whistler 'made London a half-way house between New York and Paris and wrote rude things in the visitors' book.' Whistler himself admitted that: 'I am such a Cockney do you know, that London under all circumstances and at every season seems to me the one dwelling place possible.'

Whistler settled in Chelsea in 1862 and over the next 41 years lived there at ten different addresses. His vision of London was to remain an intensely personal one, which ignored what many contemporaries might have thought of as the capital's most striking features – St Paul's and the other traditional tourist sights, the new buildings, the expanding suburbs. What fascinated Whistler, and supplied the subject-matter for many of his later works were the neighbourhood features daily disappearing before the onslaught of developers – the riverside 'Adam and Eve' pub, London's oldest wooden bridge, at Putney, Maunder's fish shop, which was replaced by an avant-garde residence by C.R. Ashbee. Whistler sneeringly characterised the house, at 74 Cheyne Walk, as 'a successful example of the disastrous effect of art upon the middle classes.' Fate, with piquant spite, decreed that he was to die there.

CHAPTER EIGHT

Heart of Empire,
1889–1919

A Government for London

In 1889 London acquired for the first time a directly elected government with responsibility for the whole capital – except, of course, the 'square mile' of the City of London, which jealously guarded its privileges and exclusiveness. The new London County Council was given wider powers and responsibilities than the Metropolitan Board of Works which it succeeded and jurisdiction over parts of Middlesex, Surrey and Kent. A decade later the 41 vestries and boards which the LCC had inherited as junior partners in the task of government were rationalised into 28 metropolitan boroughs. The area of the new 'County of London' was only 117 square miles, less than one-fifth of the area governed by the Greater London Council in the 1960s, but it was, from the outset, bold and imaginative in its approach to urban problems.

The 1890 Housing of the Working Classes Act empowered the new local authority to provide public housing for London's poor. The result was two handsome estates of red-brick five-storey apartment blocks in the 'Queen Anne' style – one at Boundary Street, Shoreditch, on the site of the appalling slum known as the 'Jago' and the other at Millbank, behind the newly-endowed Tate Gallery.

CONSERVATION

Another progressive initiative was the implementation of what would nowadays be called a conservation policy. When the Corporation of Trinity House petitioned the charity commissioners for permission to demolish its charming group of seventeenth-century almshouses in the Mile End Road, the LCC led the successful protests against the proposal. In 1896 the architect C.R. Ashbee published, as the first report of the Committee for the Survey of the Memorials of Greater London, *The Trinity Hospital in Mile End: An object Lesson in National History*. The fact that Ashbee's optimistic claim that the almshouses were the 'joint creation' of Wren and Evelyn may have 'gone beyond the evidence' is less important than the fact that it was made in a publication which grew into the invaluable *Survey of London* series. The council followed up this early effort at restraining would-be demolitionists by promoting (at the third attempt) the London Squares and Enclosures Preservation Act to forestall predatory developers.

Other LCC innovations included the acquisition, integration and electrification of London's tramways; the elimination of duplicate street names; the improvement of sewers and the provision of technical education.

NEW HEADQUARTERS

As befitted a new authority the LCC commissioned a new headquarters building. A wharf called Pedlar's Acre, diagonally opposite the Houses of Parliament, was chosen as the site in 1905 and Ralph Knott's design for a sweeping neo-classical palace selected in 1908. The Great War brought a halt to building operations, however, and it was not completed until the 1920s. After the demise of the GLC in 1986 it stood empty for almost a decade before being partially converted into apartments.

Interestingly it was three of the poorest of the new London boroughs – Battersea, Woolwich and Deptford – which followed their parent council's example and built themselves elaborate neo-baroque town halls to mark their incarnation.

Expressions of Empire

London's unique status as the chief city of the largest empire the world had ever known was symbolised by the grandeur of the buildings and public works with which it was embellished. Tower Bridge (*see p 271*) became a London landmark as soon as it opened in 1894, but the Blackwall (1897), Greenwich (1902) and Rotherhithe (1908) tunnels (all built by the LCC) did far more to relieve north-south travel congestion on the ship-choked eastern side of the city. A further major traffic improvement was the opening of the Kingsway-Aldwych scheme in 1905 (another LCC venture), followed by Kingsway tram tunnel in 1908. (This now puzzling void found an unexpected role during the 1939–45 war as a – hopefully – bomb-proof shelter for the British Museum's priceless 'Elgin Marbles'.)

Major public building projects included substantial government offices in Whitehall, to accommodate the guardians of empire; the replacement of Newgate prison with a new Central Criminal Court ('the Old Bailey') and the creation of a grand processional route leading through an imposing 'Admiralty Arch', along the Mall to an elaborate Queen Victoria Memorial in front of a re-faced Buckingham Palace. (*see p 263*.)

MEMORIALS

Flanking the Mall new memorials were erected to commemorate the exploits of the Royal Marines and Royal Artillery in the South African War of 1899–1902. Near them a statue was unveiled to honour Captain James Cook, the eighteenth-century Pacific explorer and mapmaker. A stone's throw from him, to the north, another empirebuilder, 'Clive of India', threatened to stride boldly off his plinth, while in the opposite direction, at Waterloo Place, was located a fine bronze (sculpted by his widow) to Captain Robert Falcon Scott whose entire expedition to the South Pole perished in the snowy wastes of the Antarctic in 1912.

Pride of place, the very centre of Trafalgar Square, was given to a statue of a pensive General Gordon, who had been 'martyred' in Khartoum in 1885 and comprehensively 'avenged' by Kitchener at Omdurman in 1898. Gordon has since been demoted to the Embankment, not far from the now unremembered Sir Bartle Frere, an outstanding colonial administrator. A couple of hundred yards in the other direction the chariot of ancient Queen Boadicea looms over the approach to Westminster Bridge and carries on its plinth yet another proclamation of Britain's imperial mission in a quotation from the eighteenth-century poet William Cowper:

> Regions Caesar never knew
> Thy posterity shall sway.

As the heart of the empire London was naturally the setting for imperial celebrations and none was more self-consciously imperial than the immense procession organised to mark Queen Victoria's Diamond Jubilee in 1897. The socialist Beatrice Webb noted sourly in her diary 'Imperialism in the air, all classes drunk with sightseeing and hysterical loyalty.' The unashamedly jingoistic *Daily Mail* did all it could to ram home the message of official propaganda:

> In the carriages we saw the square, strong, invincibly sensible faces of the men who are building up great nations, new big Englands, on the other side of the world. Between the carriages rode and tramped the men who guard the building and who carry British peace and British law into the wildest places of the earth.... Up they came, more and more, new types, new realms at every couple of yards, an anthropological museum – a living gazetteer of the British Empire.... And you began to understand, as never before, what the Empire amounts to. Not only that we possess all these remote outlandish places and can bring men from every end of the earth to join us in honouring our Queen, but also that all these people are working, not simply under us, but with us.... And each one of us ... is a working part of this world-shaping force. How small you must feel in the face of the stupendous whole, and yet how great to be a unit in it!

In the autumn of that year an impoverished Japanese artist arrived in London to find it a haven of cosmopolitan tolerance. Over a decade later Yoshio Markino was to record with awed affection his earliest encounter with the benevolent side of imperial self-confidence:

> At this time I went to a little newspaper shop to buy a box of cigarettes. The shopkeeper treated me quite the same way with his countrymen. I asked him if he has seen Japanese before. He said 'No'. Then I asked him again if he was not curious of me? He said 'No, sir. You see, sir, we 'ave our colonies all hover the world, sir – white men, yellow men, brown men and black men are forming parts of the British nation, so I am not curious of a Japanese gentleman at all.' What a broad mind he had! He was only a little shop-

keeper, but he was worthy of being called one of the most civilised of the nations. I made a friendship with him at once, and I told him how I was treated in California. He said 'Thut ain't fair, sir! Indeed, thut ain't fair!' How sweet this word was to me! I carried this sweet 'thut ain't fair' in my head, and slept with it all night so comfortably.

MAFEKING NIGHT

Rabid patriotism found its next outlet on 'Mafeking Night' – 17 May 1900 – when drunken crowds thronged Trafalgar Square and the surrounding streets to celebrate the relief of the Boer-besieged garrison of the South African town of Mafeking and to cheer the likeness of its heroic commander, Robert Baden-Powell. (The frenzy of the mood of a public desperate for military success after a string of humiliating defeats can be judged from the fact that, even after subsequent rationalisation, there are still six streets named after Mafeking in the Greater London area.)

After the war Baden-Powell, a modest and far-sighted man, capitalised on both his experience and reputation to set up a new organisation to offer city-bred boys a healthy alternative to smoking, drinking and gambling – the Boy Scouts. The first experimental camp was held in 1907–20 boys took part. Within two years it was followed by the first ever scout rally, at Crystal Palace – 11,000 took part.

Warehouse of the World

The continuing expansion of Britain's overseas commerce put such pressure on London's port facilities that a new phase of dock construction became essential. In 1855 the Royal Victoria was opened, three miles downstream of the existing docks, in what had been Plaistow Marshes – the excavated soil having been taken upstream to consolidate the soggy acreage which became Battersea Park. The Royal Victoria was the first dock designed to handle the new iron steamships, the first to be equipped with hydraulic cranes and the first to be properly linked in with the railways, an advantage which all but cancelled out its distance from the traditional centre of cargo-handling operations. Millwall Dock, on the Isle of Dogs, opened in 1868. In

1876 the arrival of the first refrigerator ship led to the need to install cold-storage equipment at the quays handling what was to become a rapidly-growing trade, as distant suppliers such as Argentina and New Zealand could at last send their produce direct to the London market without first canning or otherwise preserving it. (The further extension of Smithfield meat market in 1899 was another indirect consequence of this development.) In 1880 the Royal Victoria was extended to form the even larger Royal Albert, three-quarters-of-a-mile long, with three miles of quays and lit throughout by electricity. When it was opened it was held to be the most advanced port facility in the world. In 1886 a further dock complex was opened downriver at Tilbury; this came to specialise in passenger liners and non-urgent non-perishables such as coal and grain. These new facilities were required not merely because the volume of cargo handled tripled between the 1860s and 1890s but also because it came in ever bigger ships which, if they could not be efficiently accommodated in London, might go where they could be.

THE DOCKERS

By the 1880s between 50 and 100,000 men depended on the docks for their employment. To attempt greater precision would be misleading, for it would be impossible to draw a dividing-line between those, like the ship-repairers, whose livelihood was quite directly related to sea-borne trade and others, like local carters or shopkeepers, whose businesses prospered or perished with fluctuations in the overall level of port activity. Few of the actual 'dockers' moreover were liable to be assured of regular employment. Most were 'casuals' and on any one morning half the crowd milling outside a dock gate might be turned away and be glad to take whatever they could get elsewhere in the way of labouring or coal-heaving.

Intense rivalry between the competing dock companies aggravated the instability of the riverside labour market and provoked retaliatory and destructive strikes from a workforce emboldened by its success in 1889 (*see p 159*). In 1902 a royal commission warned that the complex administrative structure, which had emerged haphazardly over the years, was imposing on port-users avoidable costs and inefficiencies which would inevitably force them to consider going elsewhere. In

1909, over a century after the first enclosed docks had been built, a single body, the Port of London Authority, finally took on overall responsibility for the management of the river and its cargo-handling work. Docking charges were hastily reviewed, reduced and regularised. Long-overdue dredging was undertaken to enable deep-draught modern ships to come upriver more easily. Reorganisation gave London another half-century of useful life as a port. The PLA's imposing headquarters, an unrestrained essay in what might be called brash Baroque, still dominates Trinity Square by Tower Hill. But its muscular guardian deity, King Neptune, now welcomes each morning the staff of an accounting firm whose occupancy of the building epitomises London's transition from a commerce based on trade in physical commodities to one based almost entirely on 'invisibles'.

The expansion of London's docks to accommodate the expansion of the nation's commerce was an unambiguous indicator of a general rise in living standards among the labouring and clerical classes. This was partly their long-delayed share of the benefits of industrialisation but more immediately the result of the importation of cheap food from far-off countries, thanks to British-built railways which opened up prairies and pampas for cultivation, and British-built steamers which brought their produce cheaply and efficiently to Britain, the hub of world trade and of the financial services which lubricated it. The so-called 'breakfast wharves' lining the south side of the Pool of London along Tooley Street were a visible manifestation of these changes. Spending a smaller proportion of a rising income on food, the average London family could spare more for travel, the home and entertainment. The many beneficiaries of this trend embraced tram companies, high street shops, music-halls, public houses and football grounds. But, undeniable though this overall improvement in the quality of life of the modest masses may have been, what continued to strike contemporaries was the grotesque gulf between the lives of London's richest and poorest.

Glitter...

On the second day of 1908 the novelist, Arnold Bennett, wrote in his personal journal: 'Chief observation in London: that it is a city of very rich and very poor. The vastness of this rich quarter is astonishing. In Bond St. this morning the main thing to be seen was the well-groomed, physically fit male animal. . . . The idlers in this hotel make an imposing array.'

NEW HOTELS

Few institutions can have been more expressive of the opulent side of imperial London than the luxury hotel; visitors were poorly served before the 1860s. Morley's, built in 1831 on the site of what is now South Africa House, overlooking Trafalgar Square, was a favourite haunt of Americans, who were used to far better than they could find in London; and even Morley's had only a hundred bedrooms.

In 1860 the Westminster Palace Hotel opened – the first large hotel not to be built by a railway company or at a railway terminus. It had 300 bedrooms but only 14 bathrooms. Its convenient location on Victoria Street and plain English food made it a favourite with members of parliament. The 600-bedroom Langham opened in Portland Place in 1864 in the presence of the prince of Wales, who was to find this new facility a convenient sort of place for the assignations which enlivened his domestic life. The international clientele of the Langham was to include Napoleon III, Ouida, Dvorak and Mark Twain; it derived much business from nearby embassies and offered them the use of a special ambassador's audience room. In the 1880s Frederick Gordon opened no less than three hotels on newly-constructed Northumberland Avenue – the Grand (which daringly allowed non-residents in to dine), the Metropole, and the Victoria, which could take 500 guests, providing they were prepared to share four bathrooms.

Down by the river at Blackfriars, on the edge of the City, a former Belgian waiter, Polydor de Keyser, opened a 400-bedroom hotel on the site of the old Bridewell Palace (now occupied by Unilever House). The proprietor subsequently became a knight and lord mayor of London. The Swiss Cesar Ritz was perhaps less successful socially but even more impressive professionally. He was the first manager of the Savoy Hotel, which impresario Richard D'Oyly Carte, deeply impressed with American hotels, had built next to his new Savoy Theatre. The chef was the legendary Escoffier, creator of the 'Peach Melba'. At the Savoy, Ritz pioneered the practice of meticulously recording on a card index the whims of every individual guest. He then departed, with Escoffier, for the Carlton Hotel, Haymarket (demolished 1957–8 to make way for the tower block of New Zealand House). Here he created a palm-lined 'Winter Garden', imitated but never bettered in lesser establishments throughout the country. He also introduced the after-theatre supper. Ritz's monument – 'the small house to which I am very proud to see my name attached' – opened in 1906. Its delicate Louis XVI architecture disguised London's first steel-frame building. Over the years the Ritz was to become a byword for stylish perfection. The perfectionist Ritz himself may have found some comfort in this; the postponement of Edward VII's coronation in 1902 so disrupted Ritz's complex plans for the glittering 'season' that was to follow that he had a nervous breakdown from which he never really recovered.

Other great hotels built in the quarter-century before the outbreak of the Great War included the Russell, the Piccadilly, the Waldorf and the 700-bedroom Hotel Great Central, by Marylebone station, financed and furnished by the furniture tycoon Sir Blundell Maple (who celebrated his knighthood by rebuilding University College Hospital at his own expense). Claridge's was taken over and refurbished by the Savoy. The Connaught was likewise upgraded. (It was then known as the Coburg but changed its name as a concession to anti-German sentiment during the Great War. During the Second World War it served as General de Gaulle's headquarters.) The Cavendish became the province of the eccentric Rosa Lewis, the 'Duchess of Jermyn St.' and confidante of Edward VII. Her success proved that there was a market for a luxury hotel whose relatively small size gave it an air of exclusiveness. Brown's, tucked away in Dover Street, was such a one. Its regular clients included Cecil Rhodes and Rudyard Kipling. Theodore Roosevelt walked from Brown's to his wedding at St George's, Hanover Square, in 1886. In 1905 Franklin and Eleanor Roosevelt passed their honeymoon there.

LUXURY RESTAURANTS

As well as luxury hotels there were luxury restaurants. The Holborn, down near the city, had 15 private dining-rooms where businessmen could plot together discreetly. The Criterion on Piccadilly Circus was a riot of vulgarity in its decor, with gilded ceilings and yards of ornamental tiles; it boasted that it could serve 2,000 at a sitting. The Café Royal on Regent Street was the creation of a bankrupt Parisian wine merchant and attracted an arty clientele which numbered Beardsley, Wilde and Whistler among its members. (Whistler signed his bills as well as his paintings with a butterfly.) The restaurant of the Adelphi Theatre was in the supremely competent hands of the Gatti brothers, who lived in some style in Bedford Square, where their neighbours included a Chinese merchant, the actor Sir Johnston Forbes-Robertson, Beatrix Potter's publisher and William Butterfield, the architect of fabulously over-decorated All Saints, Margaret Street.

Those who could not contemplate even the table d'hôte at one of the first-class establishments had, after 1894, the option of a snack or light meal at Messrs. J. Lyons teashop at 213 Piccadilly. By 1910 there were 97 more branches of Lyons to choose from – plus the firm's first-ever 'corner house' in Coventry Street, which aimed to offer 'luxury catering for the little man.'

The very idea of luxury for the lower classes could be distinctly unnerving for a frugal foreigner. In his memoirs the novelist Ford Madox Ford recalled an incident involving a great French man of letters:

> . . . I had come upon Zola seated on a public bench in Hyde Park. He had been gazing gloomily at the ground and poking the sand with the end of his cane. . . . He said wearily: 'What was one to think of a country where nursemaids dressed their hair so carelessly that he had found as many as eighteen hairpins on one morning in front of one park bench? A city so improvident must be doomed.'

DEPARTMENT STORES

The retail equivalent of the luxury hotel was the luxury store. Harrod's present building was largely constructed between 1901 and 1905. Whiteley's by 1906 had 159 separate departments which between them offered customers a range of services running from estate agency to dry cleaning and asserted that it could supply 'anything from a pin to an elephant.' Both these giants found themselves boldly challenged in

1909 by a new arrival from America – Selfridges. Chicago millionaire, Gordon Selfridge, proclaimed that his Oxford Street store would be 'dedicated to the service of women.' It exemplified the notion of shopping as a 'total experience' and flaunted its unrivalled facilities under the slogan 'Why not spend a day at Selfridge's?' Customers could not only shop but also lunch and have their hair done; by 1914 the store was employing 3,500 staff. Perhaps all these grand establishments would have been advised to take notice of yet another arrival in the capital. In 1912 Marks and Spencer's of Leeds opened their first London branch in the Edgware Road; by 1914 they had some 30 branches throughout the capital.

. . . *and Grime*

Dickens exposed the misery of the poor through words and Doré through pictures. Charles Booth used maps and statistics. Sceptical of the claims of radicals about the extent of poverty in London, he discovered and documented how much worse it was than even they had claimed. His 17-volume *Life and Labour of the People of London* chronicles and categorises in painstaking detail the incidence and distribution of destitution throughout the metropolis. Booth calculated – and the word is precise – that over 30 per cent of the inhabitants of the capital of the world's greatest empire were living in poverty so dire that they could not feed, warm, clothe and shelter themselves and their families adequately enough to maintain minimum 'physical efficiency'. An even higher proportion of the population would at least pass through phases of such poverty if burdened with large numbers of small children or if they reached old age without adult offspring to support or subsidise them.

Booth was no sentimentalist and recognised that 'the poor' embraced 'loafers' and others whose plight could be laid at their own door. But most poverty, he discerned and demonstrated to be the outcome of low and irregular earnings, which were in turn the outcome of weak bargaining-power on the part of casual labourers and the seasonality of much of the employment offered to them. This basic structural problem was aggravated by inefficient budgeting, which indebted families to the pawnbroker and moneylender, and by the temptation of drink, all too freely available in the East End where there was a pub for every 400 residents.

'THE UNFIT AND THE UNNEEDED'

Booth's detached clinical analysis supplemented but did not supercede more personal accounts. Two from the turn of the century are of real literary merit, one by an 'insider', the other by a complete 'outsider'. The insider was Poplar-born clerk-turned-journalist Arthur Morrison who, in 1894, published a volume of short stories *Tales of Mean Streets* and a novel *A Child of the Jago*, based on his personal knowledge of the worst slums of the East End. The world Morrison revealed was a jungle of brutality and hopelessness whose inhabitants struggled, often vainly, to maintain a veneer of decency to their lives. Unlike many writers of his day, and especially those dealing with the world of the degraded and sub-criminal, Morrison reported in a flat, terse style which neither excused nor condemned.

Morrison never gained the reputation that the quality of his writing might have justified; not so Jack London who arrived in his namesake city in 1902 already famous. Having been a vagrant, a convict and a goldminer the 26-year-old American was used to roughing it and could easily pass himself off as a sailor while he haunted the docklands to gather material for *The People of the Abyss*, an unrestrained tirade against social injustice:

> 1,800,000 people in London live on the poverty line and below it, and another 1,000,000 live with one week's wages between them and pauperism. . . . One in every four in London dies on public charity. . . . The average age at death among the people of the West End is 55 years; the average age of death among the people of the East End is 30 years. . . . In the West End 18 per cent of the children die before five years of age; in the East End 55 per cent of the children die before five years of age. . . .

What London saw around him were the victims of what he termed 'the industrial battlefield' for even those who could find work ran daily risks of maiming, disease or even death from the conditions in which they worked, the tasks they were called upon to perform. As for the mal-nourished, drink-sodden residue:

The unfit and the unneeded! Industry does not clamour for them. There are no jobs going begging. ... The dockers crowd at the entrance gate and curse and turn away when the foreman does not give them a call. ... Women, and plenty to spare, are found to toil under the sweat-shop masters for tenpence a day of fourteen hours. Alfred Freeman crawls to a muddy death because he loses his job. Ellen Hughes Hunt prefers Regent's Canal to Islington Workhouse. Frank Cavilla cuts the throats of his wife and children because he cannot find work enough to give them food and shelter.

The unfit and the unneeded! The miserable and despised and forgotten, dying in the social shambles. The progeny of prostitution – of the prostitution of flesh and blood, and sparkle and spirit; in brief, the prostitution of labour. If this is the best that civilization can do for the human, then give us howling and naked savagery. Far better to be a people of the wilderness and desert ... than to be a people of the machine and the Abyss.

During the South African War of 1899–1902 the government called for volunteers for the army. Of every nine young men who offered to serve their country only two were judged fully fit to do so. Little wonder.

RESPECTABILITY

People wrote about the very rich and the very poor because both were shocking. But who was shocked by what was written? – the respectable inhabitants of the new suburbia which stretched endlessly away all round the metropolis. The novelist Arnold Bennett knew them well: '... hidden away behind sunblinds in quiet squares and crescents, there dwells another vast population ... an army of the Ignorantly Innocent, in whose sheltered seclusion a bus-ride is an event, and a day spent amongst the traffic of the West End an occasion long to be remembered.'

The pettifogging lifestyle and snobbish pretensions of imaginary bank clerk, Henry Pooter, the archetypal lower middle-class resident of such places as Hornsey or Camberwell, was mercilessly lampooned in George and Weedon Grossmith's hilarious *Diary of a Nobody*. But it was a foreign observer, Hermann Muthesius, who perceived the deeper significance of the new suburbs in his magisterial work *The English House*: 'The Englishman sees the whole of life embodied in his house.

Here, in the heart of his family, self-sufficient and feeling no great urge for sociability, pursuing his own interests in virtual isolation, he finds his happiness and his real spiritual comfort.'

Other foreign observers pondered what sort of comfort of any kind a sensitive being could find in row upon row, mile upon mile, of near-identical terrace houses.

Occasionally, however, even a suburb could rise to an altogether more elevated plane. One such was Hampstead Garden Suburb, developed after 1906 as the brainchild of Henrietta, wife of Canon Barnett of Whitechapel fame (*see p 153*). Her vision was to create a socially-mixed community in which the culturally-deprived could be uplifted by living cheek-by-jowl with their betters. Unwin and Parker, designers of avant-garde Letchworth, were responsible for the overall lay-out. Lutyens contributed a striking, pitch-roofed church, named St Jude's after the Barnett's old parish. As a truly mixed community it never came off. Pleasant, indeed posh, it remains. And in one respect at least its high-minded aspirations have been realised. It still has no pubs.

A World of Entertainment

In the 1880s and 1890s London's theatrical life was revolutionised by a brilliant band of impresarios and actor-managers. At the Lyceum Henry Irving, the first actor ever to be honoured with a knighthood, played opposite the electric Ellen Terry – though electric lighting was an innovation he doggedly resisted. At the Theatre Royal, Haymarket, Squire Bancroft replaced the standing-only 'pit' with 'stalls' and introduced the 'picture-frame stage'. His successor, Beerbohm Tree, made so much money that he built his own theatre, Her Majesty's, opposite. Charles Wyndham went one better and named his new theatre in Charing Cross Road after himself. Other new theatres built in this period include the Shaftesbury, Coliseum, Strand, Aldwych, Queen's, Palace, Lyric and Apollo. Serving these and 30 other establishments were the dramaturgical skills of Oscar Wilde, Arthur Wing Pinero, J.M. Barrie, Henry James, George Bernard Shaw and W.S. Gilbert and the thespian talents of Sarah Bernhardt and Mrs Patrick Campbell.

The theatrical boom had its downmarket parallel in the transformation of music-hall from public house side-show to full-blown 'palace of varieties'. The seal of establishment approval was set on this transformation by the first Royal Command Performance in 1912, when 142 artists appeared in a variety pageant, whose elements ranged from the drolleries of George Robey to the ethereal elegance of ballerina Anna Pavlova.

SPORTS

The advent of the five-and-a-half day week both diminished Londoners' exhaustion from work and gave them more time to let off their surplus energy. Tennis invaded the suburban lawn in the 1880s; bicycling was the craze of the '90s. Spectator sports began to draw large crowds on a regular basis. In 1844 a ten-acre market garden at Kennington had been overlaid with turf from Tooting Common to become a cricket ground – the Oval. In 1871 it was to be the venue for the first soccer cup final; of the 15 sides which competed to produce a winner no less than 13 were from London. In 1872 the first international rugby match was also played at the Oval and according to *The Times* 'excited more interest than any previous match in the metropolis'. In 1880 the Oval attracted a crowd of 20,000 to see Dr W.G. Grace score 152 and, aided by two of his brothers, narrowly beat Australia in cricket's first-ever 'Test Match'. Over the following quarter-century sport became ever more significant as an expression of the nation's life. All of London's dozen professional teams were founded between 1881 and 1905. In 1908 rugby acquired a new national home at Twickenham stadium. In the same year London hosted the revived Olympics at the White City and the capital's inhabitants had the satisfaction of watching their countrymen take 56 of the medals to America's 22.

All Lit Up

A century ago the advent of electricity may have caught the imagination of writers of science fiction, but it was neither a cheap nor a reliable source of power, and the full range of its possible applications was only gradually appreciated. Lighting was the first main use for the new power source. The West India Docks installed arc lamps in 1876 – the year in which Alexander Graham Bell used his new invention to make London's first 'long-distance' telephone call, five miles from Brown's Hotel to Ravenscourt Park. In 1878 electric lights were used to illuminate the street outside the Gaiety Theatre in the Strand. A year after that the nearby Embankment became the first London thoroughfare to be electrically lit throughout. In 1881 the brand-new Savoy Theatre thrilled audiences with twinkling lights of magical brilliance. The Langham Hotel and the Reform Club were the first residential institutions to adopt the new technology of illumination.

Each of these installations, however, required its own separate generating facilities. Not until 1882 was the world's first electrical 'power station' established, at Holborn Viaduct, by the American Thomas Edison. In 1888 the first really large-scale power station, designed by Ferranti, came onstream at Deptford. The Deptford power station set a precedent and a model for huge power plants that would be required when the London Underground switched over to electricity as its source of motive power (*see p 279*). Before that time passengers on the Underground had to suffer a poor air supply, as in 1887, R.D. Blumenfeld recorded crossly in his diary his 'first experience of Hades': 'The atmosphere was a mixture of sulphur, coal dust and foul fumes ... so that by the time we reached Moorgate Street I was near dead of asphyxiation and heat. I should think these Underground Railways must soon be discontinued, for they are a menace to health.'

Within a few years such experiences would be a thing of the past thanks to Yankee know-how and the slightly shady speculations of the American entrepreneur Charles Tyson Yerkes. What is now the Northern line, the first true 'Tube', began operation in 1891 and was joined by the Bakerloo in 1906.

In 1898 Harrod's installed London's first escalator and prudently positioned a member of staff at the top with brandy and smelling-salts to revive customers unduly alarmed by this novel mode of travel. By 1900 eight local authorities and 15 private companies were in the business of generating electrical power. And new customers just kept on appearing. Between 1901 and 1910 some 200 miles of electric tramways were laid down. In 1911 the census office at Millbank installed electrically-powered machines to sort the millions of punch-cards which stored the data generated by that year's national survey. Meanwhile some 250 cinemas sprang up throughout the capital to exploit electricity's potential in yet another way. Electric lighting and appliances in the home, however, remained a luxury affordable only by the well-to-do.

THE ADVENT OF TELEPHONE

The diffusion of electricity was paralleled by the spread of the telephone, which was also initially adopted for commercial rather than residential use. The first exchange opened in 1879; by 1882 there were 15. (George Bernard Shaw's first attempt at paid employment in London was to solicit for subscribers to the new-fangled invention. He was not good at it.) Not until 1884, however, could Londoners phone even as far as Brighton and it took another six years to connect them with Birmingham, though Paris became accessible only a year after that. The first telephone box appeared on the capital's streets in 1905.

'Street of Shame'

The expansion of the franchise throughout the nineteenth century meant that the 'political nation' could no longer be confined to the denizens of clubland; public debate could no longer be conducted face to face and by word of mouth. The position of the press as the 'fourth estate' was thereby assured. In the 1830s, the decade of the reform, the number of London newspapers had doubled. The 1840s saw the emergence of such long-lived features of the journalistic landscape as *Punch*, the *Illustrated London News* and the *News of the World*. In 1851 the German immigrant Julius Reuter created the world's first modern press agency. In 1854–5 W.H. Russell's sensational despatches from the Crimea demonstrated the power of a single gifted journalist, if not to topple a government, at least to shake it.

Under the editorship of the legendary Delane *The Times* could indeed claim to the 'The Thunderer', but its rumblings, like those of its rivals, still reached a relatively restricted readership among the educated and propertied classes. And 'readership' was what, indeed, was required of the newspaper-buying public, who were supplied with acres of information and closely-argued opinion in packed columns of dense print.

A generation later the preconditions for what was to be called 'the New Journalism' were emerging. On the demand side there was the effect of mass-education as schooling, free and compulsory by the 1880s, created a potential new market of millions of semi-literates. On the supply side the linotype machine and the telephone drastically reduced the time gap between the occurrence of an event and its reportage in print. The stage was set for the birth of 'sensationalism' and its prophet saw himself as just that.

W.T. Stead arrived in London as a man with a mission, who referred to God as his 'senior partner', believed that 'the editor is the uncrowned king of an educated democracy' and saw it as his task to usher in the age of 'Government by Journalism'. As editor of the *Pall Mall Gazette* he astounded the nation in 1885 with his revelations of juvenile prostitution in the capital, recounting, under the headline 'Maiden Tribute of Modern Babylon', how he bought a 13-year-old girl for £5. Stead's campaign was instrumental in raising the legal age of consent from 12 to 16. The youthful George Bernard Shaw wrote to him in fervent admiration – 'I venture to predict that the future is with journals like the Gazette, which will dare to tell polite society that it lives by the robbery and murder of the poor. . . .'

Lord Northcliffe

It was a false dawn. The future belonged not to the fearless 'muckraker for God' but to Alfred Harmsworth who, as Lord Northcliffe, 'sold news like soap and distributed mad views like stardust.' There were already a dozen London evening newspapers when he started the *Evening News* in 1894, but his demonic drive and uninhibited exploitation of the 'scoop' (real or created), the banner headline and bold pictorial treatment of dramatic incidents enabled him to follow it up with a whole series of new titles. 'Home Chat' was aimed at the housewives' market, 'Comic Cuts' at children and 'Union Jack' at teenagers. The *Daily Mail* was launched as 'a penny newspaper for a ha'penny' and was the first to carry a woman's page. A journalist of the old school described it as having been 'written by office boys for office boys' and by 1901 the young Liberal historian G.M. Trevelyan was bemoaning the fact that 'The Philistines have captured the Ark of the Covenant'. But Harmsworth was unstoppable. In 1904 he created the *Daily Mirror* and in 1905 was created Lord Northcliffe (he also managed the acquisition of titles for four of his seven brothers). In 1908 he gained control of *The Times* and proceeded to boost its circulation from 38,000 to 318,000. An imaginative pioneer of both 'stunts' and cheque-book journalism, he also put up the £1,000 prize which tempted Louis Blériot to become the first man to fly the English Channel in 1909. A striking bronze bust of this doyen of press barons now stands before the church of St Dunstan in the west on Fleet Street. W.T. Stead is commemorated by a scarcely legible metal wall-plate down on the Embankment.

Votes for Women!

As the prime focus of the nation's political life, London was almost inevitably the setting for the dramatic decade of struggle for female suffrage inaugurated by the formation of the Women's Social and Political Union in 1903. The 'Suffragettes' (a term invented by the *Daily Mail*) themselves conceded the importance of London to their strategy by moving their headquarters from Manchester to the capital in 1906.

As they became increasingly convinced that constitutional methods alone would prove futile, the leadership of the movement resorted to a two-pronged campaign which combined peaceful agitation with tactics of direct action. So conventional activities such as launching a newspaper, *Votes for Women*, and holding mass-meetings in the Caxton Hall and Albert Hall, were backed up by headline-grabbing stunts which the new popular press could scarcely refrain from covering. In January 1908 five protesters chained themselves to the railings of Downing Street during a cabinet meeting. In June, after a march on parliament, WSPU members indulged in their first window-smashing spree.

In October 1908, prior to a march on parliament, three suffragette leaders were arrested and held on remand. A sympathetic Liberal MP arranged for the Savoy Hotel to send in dinner and three comfortable beds, a service for which the hotel chivalrously refused payment. Chivalry did not last long. In 1909 the first imprisoned suffragette went on hunger strike in Holloway prison. In 1910 police used violence to break up a deputation heading for Downing Street. In 1911 and 1912 suffragettes organised co-ordinated window-smashing raids throughout the fashionable shopping districts of the West End. The climax came in 1914. A Velazquez nude – the *Rokeby Venus* – was slashed in the National Gallery (you can still see the stitch-marks in the canvas if you catch it at the right angle to the light); the king was 'petitioned' by megaphone during a Covent Garden performance of, fittingly, *Jeanne d' Arc*; and Mrs Emmeline Pankhurst, moving spirit of the WSPU, was carried off bodily by the police (and immortalised by the photographers of the popular press) for chaining herself to the railings of Buckingham Palace. Then came the war. Agitation was suspended and the suffragettes set themselves to prove that they were patriots, fully deserving of the vote. They succeeded: in 1918 women over 30 were enfranchised. In 1928 they got the vote on the same terms as men. Mrs Pankhurst died that same year. Two years later a statue in her honour was unveiled in the gardens beside the Victoria Tower of the Houses of Parliament.

London at War

In August 1914 the streets of the capital were thronged with crowds cheering the declaration of war against Germany. For weeks afterwards recruiting stations were besieged by young men eager not to miss out on a great adventure which combined the attractions of a crusade and a shooting-party and would, they were sure, be 'over by Christmas'. It wasn't and London gradually assumed the character of a base-camp for a war-effort concentrated on northern France. Familiar places acquired unfamiliar functions. Alexandra Palace became an internment camp for German POWs. St Dunstan's, a specialist hospital for the blind, set up a rehabilitation centre in Regent's Park. The main railway termini servicing the south-coast ports, Waterloo and Victoria, carried an endless traffic of departing volunteers and returning wounded, relieved by the occasional leave-party.

As the true character of modern warfare became apparent, popular anger vented itself on enemy aliens. German and Austrian butchers and bakers, musicians and waiters, were rounded up and interned. Shops whose owners had foreign-sounding names were attacked and looted. Many innocent Russian and Polish Jews suffered in this way; other victims, by a supreme irony, even included Belgian refugees, whose plight had fired so many volunteers to join the colours to punish their oppressor.

Music-halls were kept busy by troops on leave seeking diversion and by civilians flush with wages from the booming armaments industry, which by 1918 was employing almost 120,000 people in the capital alone. Half of these were women, who took on a whole range of unaccustomed roles as the slaughter in the trenches drained Britain of its manpower. In March 1916 the first girl ever was taken on as a bus conductor; by the end of the year there were over 1,700 'clippies'.

AIR RAIDS

The greatest change of all, however, was the simple fact that aerial warfare brought 'over there' to over here. In September 1915 the first ever air raid on London left 39 dead. For the first time in more than eight centuries the Channel no longer presented an enemy with an impassable barrier. German aeroplanes and Zeppelins put Londoners in the front line. In all about 650 were killed by enemy action, about half the national total. But the psychological blow was out of all proportion to the actual damage inflicted. It was a limited but bitter foretaste of the ordeal to come a generation later.

CHAPTER NINE

Expansion and Experiment,
1919–1939

The single most important fact about London in the inter-war period was its sustained physical expansion, which quadrupled the extent of the built-up area. Higher birth-rates than elsewhere in recession-hit Britain, plus the long-established attractive power of the metropolis to migrants seeking employment or excitement, raised the population of Greater London from 7.5 million in 1921 to 8.7 million in 1939, at which time it represented a higher proportion of the national population than ever before or since. On the eve of the Second World War a fifth of all Britons lived within 15 miles of Charing Cross.

Growth of the Suburbs

This process of expansion was essentially one of suburbanisation, with the population of the inner city falling by over 400,000. Some moved to new publicly-sponsored housing developments, like the Beacontree Estate at Dagenham in the east, where the population rose 800 per cent in a single decade; but most headed for the swathes of uncontrolled semi-detached houses built to the north and west, where overground extensions to the Underground system thrust into open fields to create 'Metroland', an environment which allegedly combined the convenience of the town with the charm of the countryside and was assiduously idealised and promoted by a metropolitan railway eager to expand its commuter traffic.

The movement of resident population from the inner city was accompanied by a growth of new industrial concentrations along the Lea valley in the east, from the Isle of Dogs north to Enfield, and in west Middlesex, along the axis of the newly-constructed Western Avenue, whose dual carriageway underlined the impact of motorised transport in enhancing the mobility of both labour and goods.

ELECTRICAL POWER

The Hoover factory at Perivale (now used as offices) could stand as a fitting symbol of the emerging new London. Its power-source was not coal but electricity, whose growing industrial value was acknowledged by the construction of Sir Giles Gilbert Scott's monumental and controversial Battersea Power Station (1932–4). Contemporary writers as diverse as George Orwell and J.B. Priestley recognised that electrification was, in itself, transforming both the nature of industrial employment and its context, as workers enjoyed the benefits of an atmosphere which was both literally and figuratively cleaner. The Hoover building itself boldly illustrated the transformation of factory work, its façade consisting not of smoke-begrimed brick but of sparkling green-and-white tiles enlivened with jazzy motifs in the avant-garde Art Deco style. No less symbolic in its significance was the fact that Hoover (like the nearby and equally modernistic Gillette and Firestone factories) was American-owned and that its product was a

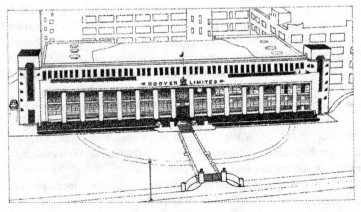

The Hoover Factory in Perivale

response to new market opportunities created by the electrification of the ordinary household and the decline in the servant labour force available for domestic drudgery.

Thanks largely to the industrial experience gained in munitions works during the Great War young women were turning eagerly from 'service' to employment in the emerging industries, above all the assembly of electrical goods, radios and telephones, which valued their nimble fingers above the traditional skills of the male-dominated engineering sector.

HOME COUNTIES

The extent to which these inter-related changes encroached on the surrounding Home Counties can be seen in an account of the period written by Molly Hughes, a widow and schools inspector, who lived in Cuffley, almost exactly 15 miles due north of King's Cross. Cuffley was a satellite community from which, on a clear day, it was said that one could see St Paul's. When Mrs Hughes arrived at the end of the Great War it was still a village, where one could wander through unfenced fields to pick berries or mushrooms and buy milk fresh from the cow at a farm. There were no shops and between them the inhabitants possessed only one car and one telephone. But what the author disdainfully refers to as 'civilisation' crept inexorably in, until the tide of jerry-built bungalows drove the community's most distinguished residents into genteel exile on the south coast and brought with it not only shops, street-lighting and pavements but even a bank, a café and a telephone exchange. Without a trace of irony this chronicle of what the author clearly saw as a degeneration in the quality of her life is entitled 'A London Family Between the Wars.'

Economic Structure

London's economic structure, like its politics and cultural life, remained distinctive and by no means representative of that of the nation as a whole. The 'New Survey of London Life and Labour' revealed that the largest single occupational category was still domestic service (418,000). Transport (316,000) came second, reflecting the capital's position at the hub of the national road and rail network, as well as its status as the main point of entry to Britain for both international travellers and freight, whether by sea, or increasingly, by air. Food and catering (272,000) ranked third, an indicator of higher than average incomes and of the concentration of tourism and entertainment and the large proportion of the population whose work or temporary residence obliged them to eat away from home. Fourth came the 'rag trade' (264,000) which spanned everything from Savile Row bespoke tailoring to the sweatshops of the East End and confirmed the capital's role as style-setter to the nation. Commercial occupations (227,000) ranked fifth, and sixth came building (165,000), a reflection of the construction boom transforming the city's fringe. The large number in professional occupations (153,000) was a consequence of London's dominance in such fields as law, medicine, science and higher education. The metal and machinery trades (150,000) ranged from long-established basic foundry work, marine repairs and silversmithing to rapidly growing newcomers like vehicle and aircraft manufacture. Printing and paper (102,000) meant not only Fleet Street papers but posters and packaging too. Tenth came government (86,000), just ahead of the wood and furniture trades. If London was mainly a service economy it also contained a diverse range of manufacturers.

Grief, Progress and Tension

Despite the shock of the Zeppelin raids, the scars that the Great War left on London were less physical than psychological. The solemn dedication of war memorials in the immediate aftermath of the conflict represented the expression of collective grief on an unprecedented scale. The Cenotaph (1920), in the middle of Whitehall, is the national war memorial and remains to this day the focus of ceremonial on Remembrance Sunday each November and the site for wreath-laying by members of the royal family, leaders of political parties, veterans' organisations and representatives of foreign governments. Designed by Sir Edwin Lutyens, it is a plain obelisk of Portland stone, unadorned except for simple inscriptions. Professor Pevsner praises it as 'an original conception, subtly proportioned' and explains that 'the apparent horizontals are convex to a common centre c.900 feet below ground, the vertical converge towards a point ca 1,000 feet above ground.'

THE UNKNOWN WARRIOR

In Westminster Abbey lies the Tomb of the Unknown Warrior, where, in the nave, a body identified only as being of British nationality, was interred in a coffin of English oak, surrounded by French soil, under a slab of Belgian marble, in the presence of heads of state and an honour guard of a hundred holders of the Victoria Cross. Perpetually garlanded with red poppies, it is the one grave on which no one ever treads. Nearby hangs the American Congressional Medal of Honor conferred at the hands of General Pershing.

Of the many outdoor war memorials, perhaps the most outstanding is that of the Royal Artillery at Hyde Park Corner. The base, by Lionel Pearson, is decorated with bas-reliefs of gunners in action and surmounted by a howitzer ranged to fire in the direction of the battlefield of the Somme. The monumental bronze figures are by Charles Sargeant Jagger and the inscription from Shakespeare's *Henry V* – 'here was a royal fellowship of death.' The nearby memorial to the Machine Gun Corps supports a sinuous, youthful bronze nude and bears a chilling quotation from the Old Testament – 'Saul hath slain his thousands, but David his tens of thousands.'

Other significant memorials include those of the Guards Division, cast from captured German guns, which stands at the southern end of St James's Park; of the Royal Fusiliers, which lost 22,000 men, in High Holborn; of the Submariners and of the Royal Air, on the Victoria Embankment; and of the mercantile marine which stands at Trinity Square, in the shadow of the Tower, and consists of a pavilion by Lutyens, inscribed with the names of all those lost at sea. The more unusual memorials include one to the Imperial Camel Corps, in Victoria Embankment Gardens and another, opposite Cleopatra's Needle, which shows a fleeing woman and children and expresses the gratitude of the 100,000 Belgian refugees who found shelter in Britain when their country was invaded.

BRITISH EMPIRE EXHIBITION

As the immediate shock of loss faded the nation's desire to reassert its self-confidence grew stronger. The British Empire Exhibition, staged at Wembley in 1924–5, was intended to impress visitors with the continuing wealth, might and variety of the world's largest empire. It certainly pulled in the crowds, achieving an attendance of 27,000,000, more than four times as many as the Great Exhibition of 1851. But its success could scarcely obscure the deep tensions arising within the very capital of that empire as the brief post-war restocking boom disintegrated into a deepening and prolonged slump. The effects of depression in the old staple industries – steel, engineering, ship-building and textiles – were certainly worst in Scotland, Wales and the north; but London too, and particularly the East End, knew the misery and hopelessness which accompanied unemployment. When the borough of Poplar diverted local 'rates' – revenue raised from property-holders to finance public services – to the purposes of relieving distress, its mayor, George Lansbury, was gaoled and 'Poplarism' entered the political vocabulary of the decade.

The General Strike

Far more dramatic were the events which accompanied the 'General Strike' of 1926, when what began as a wage-confrontation between mine-owners and unions in the coal industry escalated into a national face-off between the Conservative government and the organised labour movement as a whole. The government, having anticipated the crisis and prepared its position with emergency powers and a volunteer organisation to maintain essential services, abruptly broke off cliff-hanging negotiations at 10 Downing Street and proclaimed that the nation was being faced with a challenge to the constitution itself.

For nine days in May London was reduced to a state of near anarchy which, on the whole, remained remarkably good-natured. Buses, festooned with barbed wire, driven by volunteers and guarded by soldiers with fixed bayonets, careered haphazardly round the streets; the novelist Arnold Bennett counted 22 in Sloane Street in five minutes. Student efforts to run the Underground proved even less useful and consequently roads were choked with bicycles and private cars crammed with hitchhikers as the non-unionised clerical and shop-keeping classes struggled to make their way to whatever work awaited them. Cricket continued at the Oval, while Special Constables, mounted on polo ponies, were manoeuvred into harmless 'patrolling' by a police force as anxious as the trade union leadership to avoid violence. There were baton-charges and mass-arrests, but there were no fatalities before the strike leaders, fearful of a situation clearly beyond their control and lacking agreed objectives to negotiate for, simply caved in and surrendered. Bennett had noted in his diary on the second day of the strike 'General opinion that the fight would be short but violent. Bloodshed anticipated next week.' A week later he summarised the fiasco, 'The general strike now seems pitiful – a pathetic attempt of underdogs who hadn't a chance when the over-dogs really set themselves to win. Everybody, nearly, among the over-dogs seems to have joined in with grim enthusiasm to beat the strike.'

THE LABOUR PARTY

These events proved a grave blow to the prestige of both the labour movement as a whole and, to a lesser extent, the Labour Party as well. But London's politics sometimes lead rather than follow the national mood; support for Labour remained strong in the capital where control of some boroughs gave hope that political action could improve the condition of ordinary lives. From a national point of view Labour's electoral strength may have rested largely in the ravaged industrial regions rather than in the south, but London was an exception, returning not only a clutch of Labour members of parliament but two successive party leaders – George Lansbury and Clement Attlee – as well. Labour politics within London were dominated, however, by Herbert Morrison, who really came into his own after 1934, when Labour won outright control of the London County Council (LCC) for the first time – and kept it until it was replaced by the Greater London Council (GLC) in 1965.

Local Government

London's local government in the inter-war period was often vigorous and imaginative. Operating from palatial County Hall

(1922), right opposite the Houses of Parliament, the LCC constantly aggrandised its powers to become almost a state within the state. It undertook major programmes of slum-clearance and house-building, bought out private operators to establish an integrated tramway service, doubled the acreage of parks and open spaces, introduced planning control throughout the whole of its area and in 1938 initiated the concept of a 'Green Belt' to preserve surrounding countryside from the disfiguring effects of unplanned ribbon development and speculative estate-building – an idea first mooted by Octavia Hill, Victorian pioneer of housing reform and founder of the National Trust. Already functioning as the manager of the nation's largest education service, it added, thanks to the 1929 Local Government Act, oversight of 76 hospitals and clinics; all this, plus drains, libraries, building inspection and the fire-service, too. Despite its achievements, London's local government seemed to some critics still to be doing too little too late, simply because the capital was growing faster than it could be controlled.

Writing in 1937 the socialist G.D.H. Cole observed: 'Fully half the people of London live nowadays outside the area administered by the LCC ... Moreover, the bigger London grows, the more evident become the disadvantages of its growing without any sort of comprehensive plan. It is costing millions to establish some sort of green belt of open land around Greater London; and, even so, in face of the chaotic development of the past, this belt is bound to be broken by many stretches of built-up land. This might have been avoided if, at an earlier stage, London had possessed any sort of unified governing authority with power to plan its development on rational lines. But no such Greater London authority has ever existed; and unhappily none exists today, or seems likely to exist in the near future ... This is London's tragedy – never to have had a government and to seem today further off than ever from acquiring one.'

Fascist Movement

If the LCC was rather self-consciously 'progressive' it was scarcely extremist. But the capital spawned extremist elements, both of the left and the right. The disastrous contraction of the world economy between 1929 and 1932 challenged 'moderates' in every industrial democracy. In London the crisis threw up the British Union of Fascists, led by Sir Oswald Mosley, an energetic, mercurial figure of striking physical presence and limited political judgment. A war veteran and former Labour cabinet minister, Mosley attracted to his ranks a mixed bag of disillusioned ex-servicemen and plain bully-boys, eager to don the 'Blackshirt' uniform and join in a proclaimed crusade to set the nation on a new course to glory. How this was to be achieved was never quite clear and the lurch from pet nostrums such as public works programmes or free trade within the empire to scarcely-veiled anti-Semitism, probably passed most members almost unnoticed.

The BUF never had more than a few thousand active members and never won a seat in parliament, but it did win up to 19 per cent of the vote in some East End local elections and certainly hit the newspaper headlines. Taking his cue from his Italian paymasters Mosley stage-managed mass-rallies at such prestigious London venues as the Albert Hall, Olympia and Earl's Court. Many of these meetings were marred by vicious thuggery as fascist stewards 'escorted out' hecklers.

BATTLE OF CABLE STREET

Mosley's decisive hour came, however, not on the podium but on the pavement, when, on 5 October 1936, he attempted to lead columns of Blackshirts from the Tower (a highly-charged symbolic assembly point) through those areas of the East End which had the highest proportion of Jewish inhabitants. The contingent of police gathered to protect his right to demonstrate was, in the face of overwhelming local opposition, unable to do so, as barricades and showers of missiles barred the way. A mural (just by the Britannia pub) commemorates the 'Battle of Cable Street'. A week later the fascists wrought a spiteful but futile revenge, smashing the windows of Jewish-owned shops along the Mile End Road. A hastily-passed Public Order Act, which enhanced police powers to ban marches which might endanger public order and pro-hibited the wearing of political uniforms marked the beginning of the end for what Orwell called 'Mosley's pimpled followers.'

The most active opponents of the fascists were the communists, whose national membership rose ten-fold in the 1930s to 15,000. The fascists may have out-numbered them but had not one-tenth of their influence on other organised groups such as trade unions or tenants' associations.

Royal Traditions

As far as ordinary Londoners were concerned however the prevalence of street-parties which celebrated the jubilee of George V (1935) and the anxious street-corner gossip which agonised over the abdication of Edward VIII (1936) suggested that neither far left nor far right offered a serious threat to the popular attachment to traditional institutions. A sensitive French observer, Pierre Maillaud, analysed the significance of these phenomena with acute perception: 'Among those who have witnessed a few of the ceremonies, melancholy or joyous, which illustrate the continuity of the monarchy, its power to communicate a sense of national permanence cannot be disputed ... all have left on my mind a single impression ... The sensation was not that the clock had been put back some hundreds of years because the rites performed, the scenes enacted and garments worn had not changed for centuries; it was that what I saw and heard did exist irrespective of time and present circumstances, and that both were transcended. Here was a national symbol of permanence beyond the reach of contingency.'

THE HUNGER MARCH

In the year of the Battle of Cable Street London also received the men of the Jarrow Crusade. Jarrow, a ship-building town in the north-east had two-thirds of its labour force out of work and sought to attract attention to its plight with a 'Hunger March' to the capital, led by its MP, 'Red Ellen' Wilkinson. Carefully-selected and warmly-supported en route the Jarrow men ended their 300-mile odyssey with a rally in Trafalgar Square. They were by no means the only ones to do this but they are the ones the history books remember, just as the same books seem to overlook the equally imaginative and attention-grabbing tactics of Communist Wal Hannington's National Unemployed Workers' Movement who reduced Oxford Street to chaos by staging orchestrated 'lie-downs' among the traffic, reducing the confused police to despair. The fact that so many of the protesters wore their Great War medals showed how far the gesture of national solidarity represented by the Cenotaph had been betrayed. Or perhaps, like the Cenotaph, the parameters which defined the fundamental oneness of the nation lay invisible or far beneath the surface?

Homes for Heroes

War prime minister, David Lloyd George, in a typically rhetorical flourish, proclaimed that post-war Britain would be 'a land fit for heroes to live in.' Some public housing initiatives were substantial. The Beacontree Estate at Dagenham enabled thousands of families to exchange damp, dilapidated and overcrowded squalor in Stepney and Bethnal Green for homes that had electricity, indoor lavatories, bathrooms and gardens. The estate offered some 90 different designs of dwelling and street-lines which varied from broad tree-lined avenues to sweeping crescents. The fact that the houses were almost all built of the same brick and to the same height, however, gave an overall impression of monotony, reinforced by the relative absence of pubs, shops and other amenities for the casual encounters which gave East End street-life its variety and vitality. A giant Ford factory, attracted by a site which combined availability of labour and deep-water access, opened in 1932, providing much-needed employment. Ironically workers on the new estate lived in houses without garages; no one envisaged the day when they might themselves be able to afford one of the cars they made.

What the new inhabitants of Dagenham were escaping was described with disgust by the Czech writer Karel Capek in 1925: 'The horrible thing in East London is not what can be seen and smelt, but its unbounded and unredeemable extent ... miles and miles of grimy houses, hopeless streets, Jewish shops, a superfluity of children, gin palaces and Christian shelters. Miles and miles ... everything equally dull, grimy, bare and unending, intersected by dirty channels of deafening traffic and the whole way equally cheerless. . . . And that is just the distressing thing about the East End – there is too much of it; and it cannot be reshaped. . . . But man can live there i.e. sleep, eat repulsive food and beget children.'

PRIVATE HOUSING

Private housing projects, although sometimes small in themselves, were cumulatively on a far larger scale than public ones, which faltered with the uncertainties of government confusion in the face of depression. The relative lack of attractive investment opportunities made both land and money cheap in the 1930s, affording strong encouragement to the speculative builder to develop areas served by new railway or Underground extensions, such as the Northern line from Golders Green to Edgware (1923–4) or along new arterial roads and bypasses. From Upminster in the east to Uxbridge in the west, from Barnet in the north to Epsom in the south relentless miles of 12-to-the-acre semis were built, adding almost a million new homes to the overall stock of housing in the capital's immediate commuting area. The basic design was much the same everywhere but variety of styling was evident in the detailing of windows, porches and the tiling of roofs and walls, though 'mock Tudor' decorative half-timbering and the Art Deco sun-ray motif were recurrent favoured themes. The poet John Betjeman might rage:

> Come, friendly bombs and fall on Slough,
> It isn't fit for humans now ...

But for millions the suburban idyll represented a major up-grading in the quality of their lives.

The new private estates represented significant concentrations of purchasing-power and were therefore attractive to companies looking to tap the mass-market for consumer goods and services. The more successful developments, soon boasted shopping 'parades' and their own cinemas and 'road-house' pubs, looking like over-neat, over-sized farmhouses to make them as different as possible from the garish gin-palace of the inner city.

Architecture

The public buildings of the inter-war period were predominantly in a traditional mode which drew on baroque or Georgian motifs. The leading practitioners were Sir Edwin Lutyens and Sir Herbert Baker. Lutyens' work included the petite 'Wrenaissance' bank, designed to blend with its neighbour, St James's, Piccadilly, the Reuter's office on Fleet Street, the grand Britannic House (now Lutyens House) on Finsbury Circus and the massive Midland Bank headquarters on Poultry, characterised as 'banker's classicism at its best.' Baker's most important projects included India House, at Aldwych, South Africa House on Trafalgar Square, Church House, next to Westminster Abbey, and the rebuilding of the Bank of England within Sir John Soane's retained curtain of windowless outer walls.

Charles Holden, by contrast, worked in a more severely modern manner. His Senate House building for the University of London in Bloomsbury is a spectacular example of the Aztec-style stepped-pyramid shape which, in the 1930s, inspired the design of items as various as fireplaces and radio-sets. Holden's major employer was the London Underground, for whom he designed futuristic stations for the extensions of the Piccadilly and Northern lines and his masterpiece, the towering headquarters building above St James's Park station, which incorporates sculptures by Eric Gill and Jacob Epstein.

Buildings in even bolder modern styles were the province of commerce and include the Fleet Street offices of the *Daily Express*, with their striking black glass façade, Simpson's not dissimilar menswear store on Piccadilly, the cream-tiled Dorchester Hotel on Park Lane and, most daring of all, Peter Jones department store on Sloane Square, with its sensational curved glass wall.

VANDALISM

If there were some architectural gains there were also two spectacular losses, one accidental and one deliberate. In 1936 Paxton's Crystal Palace, relocated at Sydenham after the Great Exhibition of 1851, went up in flames. In the same year the Adam brothers' Adelphi block, just off the Strand, was demolished in an act of almost unparalleled architectural vandalism.

The satirist, Max Beerbohm, regarded the overall impact of these changes with undiluted horror: 'To an intelligent foreigner, visiting London for the first time, what would you hasten to show? ... London has been cosmopolitanized, democratized, commercialized, mechanized, standardized, vulgarized, so extensively that one's pride in showing it to a foreigner is changed to a wholesome humility ... I could not ask them to accompany me along Piccadilly or up Park Lane to admire the vast excesses of contemporary architecture.... Think how inspiring to the historic imagination it will all be, a century or so hence! I couldn't speak thus, for I cannot imagine any history being made in these appallingly bleak yet garish tenements ... when one thinks of the significant houses, the old habitable homes, that were demolished to make way for them ... then one's heart sickens and one's tongue curses the age into which one has survived.'

High Brow, Low Brow

'Bloomsbury' was past its heyday by the 1920s and the centre of gravity of avant-garde intellectual life had moved a few hundred yards west across Tottenham Court Road to 'Fitzrovia', where garrets could still be rented for a few shillings a week, inexpensive restaurants sold cheap, filling food and the British Museum reading room was still within easy walking distance. Here the archetypal Bohemian artist, Augustus John, introduced the archetypal Bohemian poet, Dylan Thomas, to his future wife, Caitlin, and George Orwell drank in the same pub as Thornton Wilder and Cyril Connolly. Half-a-mile or so to the south, in a room above a restaurant in Soho's Greek Street, an intense young Scot, John Logie Baird, gave the world's first public demonstration of his single-handed invention – television. A couple of miles to the west another Scot, Alexander Fleming, a research immunologist at St Mary's hospital, Paddington discovered penicillin more or less by accident. Throughout London intellectual and cultural life was greatly enriched by an influx of refugee talent fleeing European fascism to bring such innovative minds as those of the architect Walter Gropius and the photo-journalist Stefan Lorant, founder of *Picture Post*, Britain's only successful photo-illustrated weekly.

POPULAR CULTURE

None of these developments would have struck the casual visitor half so forcefully as the positive explosion of what came to be called 'popular culture', much of which had a distinctly American flavour. The Mayfair smart set took to drinking cocktails while the less adventurous patronised milk bars or shopped at Woolworth's. Enthusiasm for jazz, the Charleston and American slang were common to the young of all classes and irritating to the old of all classes, a trend which was intensified by the coming of the 'talkies'. Film-going was already a firmly-established habit, with over 250 cinemas in the LCC area alone by 1929. But the thirties saw the movies enter a golden age. On Leicester Square three theatres – Daly's, the Empire and the Alhambra – all made way for cinemas.

Although it could scarcely compete with Hollywood, Britain's film industry benefited from the movie boom. It was almost exclusively concentrated in and around London, with studios at Elstree, Denham, Pinewood and Islington. The Hungarian Alexander Korda scored a major success with a rollicking portrayal of *The Private Life of Henry VIII* (1933) which made Charles Laughton a star. *The Thirty-Nine Steps* (1935) and *The Lady Vanishes* (1937) heralded the advent of a major native talent – Alfred Hitchcock.

THEATRE

The London stage also sparkled in the thirties. New theatres included the Whitehall, which came to specialise in farce, the Windmill, which became notorious for risqué burlesque, and an Open Air Theatre in Regent's Park, which made *A Midsummer Night's Dream* its standard offering. Serious devotees of Shakespeare or Shaw, Ibsen or Chekhov, could make their way to the Old Vic which, under the redoubtable Lilian Baylis, functioned as the national theatre London still had not got, bringing on such young talents as Laurence Olivier, John Gielgud and Peggy Ashcroft. Lilian Baylis also undertook the rebuilding of Sadler's Wells (1931) in Islington, where a ballet company was established under Ninette de Valois, in rivalry to the revived Russian ballet at Covent Garden. Those seeking less demanding fare could find plenty in the West End, where Noël Coward was offering his crackling comedies *Private Lives* and *Bitter Sweet* and Ivor Novello and C.B. Cochran were presenting a succession of elegant musicals and extravagant revues.

MUSIC

Music-lovers of the day found encouragement in the re-establishment of the London Symphony Orchestra in 1929 and Sir Thomas

Beecham's founding of the London Philharmonic in 1932. From 1927 onwards the BBC took over sponsorship of Sir Henry Wood's annual 'Promenade' concerts, which took place then at the Queen's Hall. Popular music was dominated by American imports, imitations of American imports and the dance craze. London made a rare but original contribution to the latter with the 'Lambeth Walk', based on a hit number from Lupino Lane's smash musical of 1937 *Me and My Girl*.

SPORTING LIFE

London remained the focus of England's sporting life, just as soccer began to rival cricket as the national game. In 1923 the FA Cup Final was played for the first time in the brand-new Wembley stadium. With a planned capacity of 125,000 it was besieged by almost twice as many fans. Once those who could get inside did so they surged onto the pitch, threatening disorder and even possible disaster; only the belated efforts of startled police, inspired by a single constable on a white horse, managed to turn a potential tragedy into a friendly farce. The match eventually started 45 minutes late and Bolton Wanderers went on to beat West Ham United comfortably by 2–0.

If any one team ever ruled English football it was Arsenal in the 1930s, marking its ascendancy by moving from south to north of the river and building a fine new stadium at Highbury (1932) on the ground formerly occupied by their henceforth deadly rivals and neighbours, Tottenham Hotspur. Arsenal won the Cup in 1930 and 1936 and the League in 1931, 1933–5 and 1938 and were runners-up in both in 1931–2. Their presiding genius, manager Herbert Chapman, combined a flair for showmanship with an informed technical knowledge of the game. Offering Charles Buchan a £100-a-goal bonus and persuading the London Passenger Transport Board to change the name of the Gillespie Road tube station to 'Arsenal' showed his skill in public relations, while experiments with a white ball, rubber-studded boots, all-weather pitches and floodlights revealed a progressive attitude to professional innovation. Chapman died in 1934. In the following year Arsenal honoured his inspiration by winning the League for the third successive year, Ted Drake put a never-beaten record seven goals past Aston Villa in a single match and a record 73,000 turned up to see a clash with Sunderland.

GREYHOUND RACING

If cricket at Lord's and the Oval, tennis at Wimbledon and the annual Oxford and Cambridge boat race remained the high-spots of the London and national sporting scene, entirely novel attractions were gaining local support and exploiting new technologies. In 1927 the White City stadium introduced the American sport of greyhound racing; the hare, the floodlights and even the totalisator board showing the betting odds all depended on electricity to give the 'punter' a cheap night out. The 'dog track' soon became the poor man's race-course and by 1932 the annual attendance in the London area alone had risen to 6.5 million, about a third of the national total.

Motor-cycle racing, with competitions between locally-based teams, was another newcomer, attracting keen fans from among the young, relatively affluent and technically-minded who made up the ranks of skilled labour in the new technology-based industries.

GOLF IN THE SUBURBS

The complex relationship between sport and society in this period has yet to be explored in depth, but Richard Holt hints at its significance in a passage of characteristic insight, with reference to the quintessential suburban game:

> ... golf fostered a new kind of community life in the suburbs ... the golf club helped consolidate the new routines of suburban life. Its trees, fairways and greens epitomized *rus in urbe*. Calling in at "the club" for tea or a drink after the shopping or a drive in the car was part of a new middle-class style of life ... Tennis and golf clubs were worlds within worlds, business contacts and mutual reassurance for the reasonably well-off, islands of sociability within the unfathomable seas of domestic privacy.... In golf family membership and male sociability were not incompatible. The oft-derided lady golfer ... may have been an embarrassment on the course but she quietly built and maintained the links between middle-class families that lay at the heart of the community life. (*Sport and the British* pp 133–4)

JACK HOBBS

Unlike golf or tennis, a passion for cricket transcended social class. Its outstanding figure, Jack Hobbs, was the first working-class sportsman to receive a knighthood. In a career spanning almost 40 years he scored over

60,000 runs and 197 centuries. In 1926, aged 45, he made 16 hundreds in a single season. Combining grace and power on the pitch with dignity and quiet humour off it, he was a hero that every London boy with the fare to the Oval could worship in person. His Fleet Street sports shop brought him a prosperity which was modest beside his fame. Perhaps it was his curiously ambiguous social background as the son of a Cambridge college servant that enabled Hobbs to negotiate the uncertainties of his status so deftly. A dedicated professional, he never aspired to the captaincy of his county, Surrey, or of England, which were the traditional prerogative of the gentleman amateur. Even if cricket could rise above social class it could not entirely detach itself from it.

The BBC

A new national institution which likewise apparently aspired to rise above class, while remaining rooted in it, was the BBC. Established in 1922, it was a securely London-based organisation, with facilities at Savoy Hill and Alexandra Palace and an imposing new headquarters, Broadcasting House (1932), at Portland Place. Its first director-general, John (later Lord) Reith brought a high-minded Scottish certainty to his office, determining to bring to the millions 'listening-in' what was good for them rather than what they wanted. If broadcasting had a triple mission to inform, educate and entertain, it was definitely in that order.

During the 1926 General Strike, when there were no regular newspapers, radio, viewed variously by non-enthusiasts as a trivial toy or an infernal irritation, suddenly emerged as a calm and authoritative source of vital news coverage. The BBC, having just about evaded direct governmental manipulation, emerged from the crisis with enhanced status and growing self-confidence.

Reith's Presbyterian conscience made him agonizingly aware of the awesome responsibilities attaching to a medium of communication which, by the end of the 1930s, could reach some 90 per cent of the nation's households. The BBC, with London at its feet, could bring the culture and current affairs of the capital to the nation as a whole, enabling it to be, in Reith's words 'present equally at functions or ceremonials upon which national sentiment is consecrated.'

Thanks to a rapidly-advancing technology which facilitated the feasibility of the 'outside broadcast' listeners might hear the hotel-based 'Savoy Orpheans' as easily as the studio-based BBC Symphony Orchestra. Coverage of royal and state occasions was as extensive as technical limitations permitted, but it was sport that provided the most regular 'great occasions'. In 1939 an audience survey showed that no less than 70 per cent of respondents had listened to the Boat Race, with 50 per cent for soccer, cricket and boxing and over 30 per cent for Wimbledon. In September of that year no doubt the figures were even higher than for the Boat Race when Prime Minister Chamberlain announced Britain's declaration of war – broadcast live from 10 Downing Street.

A bus in a bomb crater at Balham, October 1940

CHAPTER TEN

Phoenix City – from the Blitz to the Eye

Finest Hour?

In 1934 Winston Churchill warned the House of Commons: 'The flying peril is not a peril from which one can fly. We cannot possibly retreat. We cannot move London.'

As the international situation worsened the threat from the skies prompted preparations for the possibility of a 'national emergency' – the word 'war' was still taboo. In 1937 parliament passed an Air Raid Precautions Act which required local authorities to plan how they would keep essential services going and assist the civilian population. The Munich crisis of September 1938 provided a tense opportunity to test these arrangements as 4,000 children were evacuated from nurseries and special schools. The lessons learned in what turned out to be an unnecessary exercise, proved invaluable the following year. 1938 also saw the establishment of the Women's Voluntary Service for Civil Defence (WVS), which was eventually to enrol a million women throughout the country to provide care and comfort for the dazed and dispossessed. A campaign was also begun to recruit volunteers for an Auxiliary Fire Service.

By the late-summer of 1939 trench shelters were being dug in the London parks. Special arrangements were in hand to store and protect the capital's treasures, with 80,000 sandbags used at Westminster Abbey alone. Millions of gas-masks were stacked ready for distribution. The sentries at Buckingham Palace exchanged their scarlet tunics and bearskins for khaki and 'tin hats'. This bustle of activity may have helped to maintain civilian morale, but the confidential forecasts of officialdom were deeply pessimistic. It was estimated that each enemy air raid might cause up to 100,000 casualties, with perhaps half-a-million in all in the first month of the war. Even a tenth of that figure would have totally overwhelmed the capital's emergency and medical services. There were, at most only 16,000 hospital beds available to receive casualties.

EVACUATION

The most effective step taken was the evacuation of London's most vulnerable inhabitants – children of school age, children under five with their mothers, pregnant women and the blind. Even before the actual outbreak of hostilities some 600,000 had been dispersed north-wards and westwards into safer country areas. Their departure released much-needed hospital beds for emergency use and emptied school buildings which could be turned into ARP posts and reception centres to provide a temporary roof and hot food for those who had been 'bombed out'. The expected bombing raids did not, however, materialise and by Christmas about half of the evacuees had drifted back to the capital. Their brief sojourn in the countryside had proved an enlightening experience on both sides as middle-class families with large houses found themselves 'billeted' with bewildered and, in many cases, verminous slum-children. As the official historian of the LCC was later to put it rather coyly: 'The way of life of the slum dwellers was startlingly revealed, giving an added impetus to the movement . . . for a planned reconstruction of London so as to provide better living conditions for its citizens.' Quite.

During the winter of 1939–40 the main danger to civilians came not from the skies but on the roads. Enthusiastic enforcement of the 'blackout' by zealous ARP wardens, coupled with the requirement that vehicles should drive with only one (masked) headlamp, doubled the average peace-time figure for road deaths and serious injuries.

THE BLITZ

For Londoners the war began in earnest at tea-time on the afternoon of Saturday 7 September 1940. Four hundred German bombers attacked what was virtually a defenceless city. That night another wave of 250 followed up with a further raid; 430 civilians were killed and 1,600 seriously injured. For 57 nights consecutively, Luftwaffe raids continued. The emergency services were pushed to breaking-point. Preparations had been based on the assumption that raids would be made in daylight using gas; but they were made at night, using high explosives and incendiaries. The authorities had thought they would need mass-graves and quicklime, not shelters, bomb-disposal squads and demolition engineers. London's 2,500 regular firemen, supported by 23,000 volunteers, battled desperately not only against danger but also against despair as the raids blocked roads, destroyed communications and shattered water and gas mains. The first week of the raids brought London to the brink of chaos. Then a special force of 14,000 army pioneers and civilian technicians was hastily organised into rescue and repair teams. In the nine months of the 'Blitz', which finally ended with one last massive raid on 10 May 1941, the rescue service saved at least 10,000 people from being buried alive in the wreckage of their own homes.

UNDERGROUND SHELTERS

There is a widespread myth that the entire population of London found shelter in the Underground during the blitz. In fact the peak figure was 177,000, rather less than 5 per cent of the population served by 'the Tube'. Many preferred to take their chances in damp, corrugated-steel, earth-banked 'Anderson' shelters at the end of their gardens; but only a quarter of London households had a garden. Sixty per cent simply went to bed, the rest crouched under staircases, in basements or under tables. The government was at first resolved to prevent Londoners from using the Underground as a refuge, ostensibly on the grounds that their presence would interfere with the efficient functioning of an essential service, but also because they feared that if terrified civilians sought the safety of deep shelters they might not come up for weeks at a time (some didn't). As George Orwell sardonically noted after the war, Londoners contested the ban not by storming the barriers but by buying tickets, thus acquiring the legal status of passengers.

The Hungarian artist Joseph Bato thought the atmosphere on the station platforms was almost festive, like people 'sitting in a café on a

Paris boulevard.' The press photographs which passed the censor suggest a hearty cheerfulness. The sculptor Henry Moore's pencil sketches of people sleeping in corridors or on escalators convey a sense of exhausted strength. None of these images are false but they omit the pervasive reality of hopelessly inadequate sanitary arrangements and the consequent stench from tunnels used as substitute lavatories. Rats, fleas and lice flourished. The government fretted over the possibility of an epidemic; fortunately none materialised.

Nor were Underground stations necessarily safe. A high explosive bomb could penetrate 50-feet deep or more. At Marble Arch a direct hit ripped ceramic tiles from the walls, lacerating shelterers with appalling results. At Balham 600 casualties were caused by a bomb which drove through pipes and conduits to launch a tidal wave of water and sewage along the platforms. At Bank a similar catastrophe killed over a hundred. A simultaneous bombing campaign by the IRA caused further fatalities.

The wealthy at least had the additional option of shelter in the basements of such steel-framed hotels as the Ritz, Savoy and Dorchester. Some carried on dancing, regardless. The subterranean Café de Paris in Coventry Street advertised itself as 'the safest place to dance in town.' On 8 March 1941 it took a direct hit which killed band-leader Ken 'Snakehips' Johnson and 80 other revellers. A simultaneous hit on the Madrid restaurant in nearby Dean Street killed a further 17.

'LONDON CAN TAKE IT'

The proud boast of the day was 'London can take it.' The fact that the hospitals recorded admissions of only 23 neurotic cases attributed to bombing and that millions of Londoners, dazed from lack of sleep, struggled to work each day through and over the previous night's wreckage, suggests that London could, indeed, take it. When the interviewers of Mass Observation asked Londoners what made them most depressed in the winter of 1940–41 more respondents blamed the weather than the bombing. The fire, ambulance and medical services never actually broke down. The port never closed. But road transport was severely disrupted and whole sections of railway closed for months at a time. The sewerage system suffered far more damage than had been expected. The education service, despite valiant improvisation, was a shambles. And, with gas and electricity supplies being so frequently cut off, tens of thousands of Londoners were reduced, for days at a time, to cooking, boiling water and heating their homes with wood looted from the wreckage of their neighbours' houses.

Allies and Aliens

Britain may have 'stood alone' in the summer of 1940, but her capital had never been more cosmopolitan as refugees, royalty and resistance fighters poured in from the defeated states of mainland Europe. In one respect, however, London was less cosmopolitan as German and Austrian citizens, (many of them refugees from Nazism) had been interned on the outbreak of hostilities as suspected spies and saboteurs. On 10 June 1940 Italy declared war on Britain. A round-up of London's old-established Italian community began that night and within four days 1,600 had been imprisoned. Three weeks later the *Arandora Star* left Liverpool bound for Canada where its complement of German and Italian internees would be held long-term. Within three hours of leaving port the liner was torpedoed with the loss of 730 lives.

The American invasion of London began in 1942. In September 300 picked US troops marched through the West End and City to lunch at Guildhall with the Lord Mayor; they were cheered all the way. From November they could relax with coffee and doughnuts at the Rainbow Club. By January 1943 they were already training for combat in the bombed-out streets of Battersea. Meanwhile 3,000 American sappers were receiving instruction from the LCC's Heavy Rescue Service in the techniques of demolishing and repairing bomb-damaged buildings. On the eve of D-Day there were so many Americans around the US embassy and military offices in Grosvenor Square that it was nicknamed 'Eisenhowerplatz'. Appropriately today it is the setting for statues of Franklin Delano Roosevelt and Eisenhower and a memorial to the pilots of the Eagle squadrons, American volunteers who flew with the RAF before the United States entered the war.

War gave London new lifestyles and new landscapes. Parks became quarries for the filling of sandbags and dumps for the stock-piling of coal and building materials. In the City and East End acres of rubble were piled up into heaps where wild flowers sprouted and the Home Guard fought mock battles against imaginary parachutists. Harkening to the government's exhortation to 'Dig for Victory' Londoners turned their gardens into allotments. Even royal parks and the moat of the Tower of London were turned over for the cultivation of vegetables. Society photographer Cecil Beaton recorded whimsically that: 'While the buses roar along Oxford Street the gentler sounds of hens and ducks can be heard among the ruins of nearby Berners Street. The vicar of St James's, Piccadilly counted 23 different varieties of wild plant behind his bombed altar.'

WARTIME ENTERTAINMENT

The West End afforded other entertainments than the contemplation of unexpectedly rural delights. At the Windmill Theatre troops on leave could gaze upon statuesque young ladies whose nudity was permitted by the censor, provided it was displayed only in rigidly immobile tableaux. A few streets away the more high-minded could attend lunchtime concerts at the National Gallery given by the celebrated pianist, Dame Myra Hess. Cinemas showed a new breed of British feature films, more rugged and realistic than Hollywood could produce, created by young British talents like Noël Coward, David Lean, John Mills, David Niven and Deborah Kerr. But *Gone with the Wind*, which played continuously at Leicester Square for four years, outshone them all.

Pubs did good business, even if the Scotch was scarce and the beer was watery. The French resistance took over the York Minster so completely that it became known as 'the French' (and changed its name in due course). On the other side of Shaftesbury Avenue, in Macclesfield Street, De Hems became the unofficial headquarters of the Dutch – and still serves Dutch food and beer to this day.

Writing in the summer of 1944 Francis Marshall, a former fashion artist, observed that:

London has become more cosmopolitan than ever in its long history and occupies the position that Paris did in the last war. Revisiting it recently on leave, one even got the impression that Londoners were in the minority! The escalator at Piccadilly Circus was a pageant of all the nations; one saw Americans – both men and women – French, Dutch, Poles, Czechs, Belgians, all in the few minutes it took to ascend. Coming out in the black-out American voices were all around.

While the West End and Westminster were seemingly given over to pleasure-seekers and the ranks of a bureaucracy hugely swollen by war, in the East End and the suburbs industry worked seven days a week to churn out the material of war. An unfinished extension of the Central Line was turned into a factory for making aircraft components. A few miles away in Bow a former furniture-maker was turning out propellers. Along the river workers assembled huge pre-fabricated sections of the artificial harbours which were to be installed at the invasion beach-heads. Further downstream at the Ford works in Dagenham the production of family saloon cars had given way to the manufacture of trucks and tanks. Despite its vulnerability to aerial bombardment London contained too many vital skills and was too near the invasion base-areas not to serve as a crucial centre of war-production.

V–Bombs and Victory

As General Eisenhower and his aides organised the liberation of Europe from a newly-excavated tunnel deep beneath Goodge Street station, Londoners faced a fresh ordeal with the onslaught of the first of the *Verwaltungswaffen* ('revenge weapons') with which Hitler hoped to turn the tide of war. Known as the V–I (or more popularly 'doodlebug') it was a pilotless plane whose engine cut out over its target, leading its high-explosive load to explode on impact. Daring pilots could sometimes shoot them down in flight or even knock them off course by flying alongside and flipping over their wings to send their gyro guidance system haywire. Allied counter-intelligence also managed to feed back to the German control centres false information that the missiles were over-shooting their targets. This caused them to re-target the V–Is so that in fact they fell short, striking the less densely-populated suburbs of south-east London, rather than the close-packed city centre. Nevertheless between June and August 1944, 13,000 casualties were sustained in the capital. In September 1944 the V-I was superceded by the V-2, a full-scale rocket which was simply unstoppable. Only the capture of its launch-sites by the advancing Allied armies brought an end to its brief reign of destruction which, by March 1945, had caused almost another 5,000 casualties.

The last bomb fell on London on 26 March 1945, A third of the 'square mile' of the City had been flattened, including 40 acres where the Barbican complex now stands. Over a dozen Wren churches had been destroyed as had the chamber of the House of Commons. Almost 30,000 Londoners had been killed and 50,000 injured. Hundreds of thousands had been made homeless as only a fraction of the city's housing-stock had escaped unscathed and 130,000 houses had been damaged beyond hope of repair. On 8 May – VE Day – the streets were filled with revellers. Then the long task of reconstruction began.

New Beginnings

George Orwell's dystopian novel *1984* reflected the realities of London life in 1948, when it was written – an over-organised, under-nourished city of battered buildings, rationing and regulations. In that same year beloved 'Eros' was reinstated in Piccadilly Circus; in nearby Soho Ronnie Scott and John Dankworth opened London's first jazz club; and at Wembley Stadium the capital hosted the Olympics in conditions still so austere that the Americans brought their own food and distributed the surplus to local hospitals. Despite all privations, the wartime dispersion of London's population was reversed, the population of the LCC area rising by 800,000 between 1945 and 1950.

1951 was marked by a 'Festival of Britain' on the south bank of the Thames, partly to mark the centenary of the Great Exhibition but mainly as a 'tonic to the nation' after a decade of death and deprivation. Displays of British achievement in science and technology raised hopes of higher living standards for the eight million who visited them. Well-intentioned but tepid in comparison with Albert's visionary enterprise of 1851, the Festival left the Royal Festival Hall as its legacy and the nucleus of today's South Bank arts complex. Londoners might have been forgiven for thinking there were more urgent matters to address.

In 1951 44 per cent of London households had no bath and another 18 per cent had to share one, while 35 per cent had to share access to a lavatory and 16 per cent even had to share a sink.

The Coronation

A million lined London's streets to watch the coronation of Elizabeth II in June 1953 and another 20 million watched on television. This new branch of the mass media was to become a core element of the creative industries emerging as a dynamic sector in London's post-war economy. In 1955 the BBC moved to a purpose-built Television Centre at White City, just in time to meet the challenge of new rival Independent Television, and the Queen opened the first proper terminal at Heathrow, a former wartime airstrip, destined to become the world's busiest international airport. Less publicity but unsuspected potential attended the opening that same year of Mary Quant's fashion 'boutique' in the King's Road, Chelsea. Coupled with the arrival of the coffee bar (Frith Street, Soho 1953), the comprehensive school (Kidbrooke, Woolwich 1954), the first anti-nuclear protest march (1958) came the widely-reported delinquencies of gangs of style-conscious Teddy Boys (draped, velvet-collared jacket, 'drainpipe' trousers, suede shoes and greased quiff) and 'Mods' (snappy Italian suits, high-collared shirts, felt hats, close-cut, ungreased hair). Together these marked the inchoate origins of a novel 'yoof'culture which had its subsequent metamorphosis as 'swinging London'.

Moving Out and Moving In

Post-war London's housing crisis was dramatised in 1946 when well-organised squatters invaded luxury flats being renovated in Marylebone and Kensington. A limited solution was offered by the hasty erection of 'pre-fabs' on cleared bomb-sites and other derelict areas. Pre-fabricated from asbestos in former aircraft factories, these bungalows could be put up in weeks, rather than the months required for conventional brick homes. Families welcomed them as an escape from in-laws and took pride in the possession of a bathroom, 'fitted' kitchen and separate front door. Intended for a life of five years, some lasted over forty.

Huge housing estates were begun. In Pimlico, where bombs intended for Battersea power station had obliterated whole streets opposite, prize-winning Churchill Gardens integrated shops, school and community facilities into its overall plan. At Poplar, the Lansbury estate, named after the local ex-mayor and Labour leader, was built as an exemplar of excellence to accompany the Festival of Britain. At Roehampton high-rise blocks on an attractive sloping site provided a perhaps misleading model applied elsewhere with much less happy results. Where land was cheap out in Essex and Hertfordshire, the LCC built estates at Debden, Harold Hill, Oxhey and Boreham Wood. Unaccompanied by industry to provide jobs locally, they were criticised for adding to suburban sprawl and worsening the problem of commuting congestion.

NEW TOWNS

The Greater London Plan drawn up by Professor Abercrombie of University College embodied a radical re-think, envisaging the con-trolled dispersal of a million Londoners to a ring of 'New Towns'. These were to be grafted onto existing communities at least twenty miles beyond the 'Green Belt' of farmland, low-density settlement and recreational space encircling the capital. They aimed at a 'balance' of social classes – an idealistic residue of enforced wartime egalitarianism – but the New Towns' lack of amenities and raw sameness made them unattractive to their intended élite, who opted for their surrounding villages. This left the New Town as typically a community of upwardly-mobile technicians employed in the engineering or electrical industries attracted to them by cheap 'greenfield' sites. Wilmott and Young's classic investigation of *Family and Kinship in East London* showed what was being lost by relocating, and thereby dislocating, Cockney communities dependent on inter-generational networks of female solidarity and mutual support.

The first New Town, at Stevenage in Hertfordshire, was vigorously opposed by existing local residents but their imaginative campaign was so brusquely swept aside by government that other designated targets submitted to their fate. Crawley in Surrey would benefit from the growth of Gatwick as London's second airport. Hemel Hempstead and Hatfield in Hertfordshire preserved something of the graciousness of the *rus in urbe* ideal realised nearby in Welwyn Garden City. Basildon in Essex grew to more than twice its intended population size, largely as a dormitory for commuters, contrary to its creator's intentions. Meanwhile at the fringes of the existing metropolitan area Croydon, Kingston, Ealing, Hammersmith and Edgware were redefining themselves as 'office suburbs'.

NEWCOMERS

Londoners abandoning the inner city for New Towns or suburbs were replaced by overseas migrants. Some, like the 30,000 Poles clustered around Chiswick, feared to return to countries under Communist rule. Thousands of former Italian POWs opted for the catering trade in London rather than the uncertain prospects of their shattered homeland. Ex-RAF technicians from the Caribbean returned to 'the Mother Country', whose history and literature had formed the staple of their education. In 1948 the *Evening Standard* greeted Jamaicans arriving aboard the *Empire Windrush* with the headline 'Welcome Home' and the mayor of Brixton laid on a civic tea-party for them. Labour-hungry employers established recruitment offices in the West Indies, with London Transport alone importing 2,000 Barbadians between 1956 and 1961.

The catch-all category 'West Indian' ignored the significance of island identity which the newcomers retained in seeking the support of family, friends and neighbours transplanted to the chilly and bewildering metropolis. Jamaicans became concentrated in Brixton and Stockwell, Trinidadians and Barbadians in Notting Hill, Guyanese around Tottenham. As the annual number of arrivals from the Caribbean passed 20,000 they experienced increasing hostility and discrimination in employment, where they were relegated to low status, low paid work, and in housing, where they were exploited by vicious slum landlords, like Perec (Peter) Rachman. Himself a Polish immigrant, in building his empire of semi-derelict but highly profitable properties he made 'Rachmanism' a by-word for a unique syndrome of squalor and intimidation.

London's first race riots broke out at Notting Hill in 1958, inspiring Colin MacInnes' to write his atmospheric novel *Absolute Beginners* and inspiring magistrates to imprison the white perpetrators held responsible for the beating, stone-throwing and stabbing which exposed the depth of racism amongst young white working-class men. On the other hand when the former Fascist leader Sir Oswald Mosley returned from exile to exploit racial tensions in a by-election in that same area he and his acolytes were annihilated at the poll. Parliament followed through with legislation banning discrimination but also limiting immigration from the 'New Commonwealth' but not from Europe, i.e. by whites. By 1991 there were 250,000 Irish in London, who, with their second generation offspring, made up 5 per cent of the total population. In the same year London's 150,000 Greek Cypriots equalled a fifth of the entire population of Greek Cyprus.

In Notting Hill the Trinidadian tradition of street carnival was re-established, initially for children, but it swiftly grew into an expression of Pan-Caribbean and 'Black British' cultural identity. Within a quarter of a century it had become Europe's largest human gathering, attracting over a million celebrants annually. On the negative side destructive riots at Brixton (1981) and Broadwater Farm, Tottenham (1985) expressed the rage of London-born black youths marginalised in their own city.

ASIAN COMMUNITIES

Discharged or disabled lascar seamen and 'ayah' Indian nannies, discarded by employers after their voyage home could be found throughout Victorian Dockland but they were neither numerous nor coherent enough in terms of language or religion to constitute a community. Later came high-caste students, like the fathers of anti-colonialism Gandhi, Nehru and Jinna, who all qualified as barristers at the Inns of Court. But they were essentially birds of passage. The development of substantial Indian, Pakistani, Bangladeshi and Kashmiri communities, with an entire, complex social infrastructure of mosques, gurdwaras, temples, newspapers and specialist suppliers of ethnic foods, clothing and cultural services is essentially a post-war phenomenon.

Immigrants from the South Asian sub-continent came both directly, following the partition of India in 1947, and indirectly, as a result of their expulsion from Kenya and Uganda. Punjabi Sikhs settled around Southall, near Heathrow, their point of arrival, where many found work. Bengali Muslims concentrated around Brick Lane, Aldgate, opening restaurants and converting the Huguenot chapel of 1743 from a synagogue to a mosque. Gujarati Hindus dominated the electronics businesses of Tottenham Court Road. Many 'Asian' newcomers brought substantial capital or professional skills and set themselves up in catering or textiles or as doctors or accountants. The 'Mr Patel' corner newsagent-cum-grocery, 'open all hours', became a familiar institution throughout the city.

The South Asians' commitment to self-help through education, enterprise and the ownership of homes and businesses was matched by the Hong Kong Chinese, who opened restaurants and take-aways in every High Street and made Gerrard Street, Soho the heart of a new Chinatown. In the 1970s oil wealth enabled Arabs and Iranians to colonise the area between the Edgware Road and Queensway. Japan's post-war economic 'miracle' was mirrored in the emergence of communities of semi-permanent Japanese residents in affluent suburbs such as Finchley and Wimbledon.

'Swinging London'

In 1966 *Time* magazine deemed London 'The Swinging City' – 'a city steeped in tradition, seized by change, liberated by affluence ... In a decade dominated by youth, London has burst into bloom. It swings, it is the scene.' With the ending of rationing and compulsory military service, the post-war 'baby boom' turned into a tidal wave of teenagers. Well over half the capital's population was under thirty – a lively presence, a social challenge and a lucrative market. The vibrant, anarchic atmosphere of London's dozen art-schools attracted many who were to find their talents leading them elsewhere, into acting, fashion or music, like the Who's Pete Townshend, The Kinks' Ray Davies and Keith Richards of the Rolling Stones. The culture-heroes of the sixties established a new range of social types from across the social spectrum. Among photographers David Bailey was an East End lad while Patrick Lichfield was the Queen's cousin and Anthony Armstrong-Jones married the Queen's sister. John Stephen, presiding genius of Carnaby Street dandyism, was a Glasgow grocer's son. Jocelyn Stevens, editor of *Queen* magazine, was an Old Etonian. Hairdresser Vidal Sassoon was a Jewish East Ender raised in a Maida Vale orphanage.

Britain's counter-offensive to American musical dominance was spearheaded by the 'Mersey Sound' but London produced the Rolling Stones (led by ex-LSE student Mick Jagger), Eric Clapton's Yardbirds and The Who and such individual stars as Tommy Steele (ne Hicks), Adam Faith (Terry Nelhams) and Cliff Richard (Harry Webb). The Animals migrated from their native Newcastle to London in 1963 and by 1964 the Beatles had made Abbey Road recording studio peculiarly their own.

Theatre's renaissance was prefigured in 1956 John Osborne's *Look Back in Anger* at the Royal Court Theatre. In 1959 Bernard Miles opened the Mermaid Theatre at Blackfriars, the first new theatre in the City since the Great Fire. The Royal College of Art moved to new buildings at Kensington Gore in 1961-2 and the South Bank arts complex added the Queen Elizabeth Hall (1967) and the Hayward Gallery (1968). A new theatre opened at Greenwich in 1969 and the 'Young Vic' theatre company was launched the following year.

Design-based, style-oriented industries grew throughout succeeding decades, if less rapidly. From the opening of his first branch in the Fulham Road in 1964, Terence Conran's 'Habitat' shops did for housewares what Marks and Spencer had once done for clothes, offering variety with value. As Sir Terence, Conran sponsored the Design Museum, opened at Butler's Wharf in 1989, and then, with Mezzo in Soho, turned restaurateur on a spectacular scale. Anita Roddick promoted environmentally-aware beautification through her 'Body Shop' chain. The Saatchi brothers built what was briefly the world's biggest advertising empire. British film was honoured by a Museum of the Moving Image (1988), saw in the rise of video and television's Channel Four outlets for its underemployed talents and exported to Hollywood such London-born stars as Michael Caine, Bob Hoskins and Terence Stamp to follow in the footsteps of their predecessors, Charlie Chaplin, Bob Hope and Alfred Hitchcock. The capital at long last acquired a National Theatre in 1976, up-graded to 'Royal' in 1991. The Barbican Arts Centre (1982) gave the City a first-class gallery and concert facility, homes for the Guildhall School of Music and Drama and Royal Shakespeare Company and, in the Museum of London, the largest museum in the world devoted to the history of a single city.

Cleaning Up the Capital

Despite the advent of electricity, which cut smoke and soot from coal fires, London's famous fogs persisted, with long-lasting 'pea-soupers' in 1944, 1947 and 1948, culminating in the fog of December 1952 which caused at least 4,000 deaths from respiratory disorders. Seven centuries after it was first suggested, a Clean Air Act was finally passed in 1956 to make central London a 'smokeless zone'. It took time to take effect. A bad fog in 1957 claimed another thousand lives and caused a rail disaster at Lewisham, killing 87. In the absence of comparable fogs since 1962 the capital began a clean-up campaign to scrub the smoke-stains of centuries from its landmark buildings.

Growing awareness of ecological degradation provoked a similar campaign to reverse long-term damage to the environment. A 1957 survey found only eels in the 40 mile stretch of Thames between Richmond and Tilbury. In 1974 a salmon was caught in the river – the first since 1833 – and 82 other species were recorded. A London Wildlife Trust was established in 1981 to oversee the conservation of the capital's flora and fauna and encourage the establishment of 'wildlife reserves' and 'urban farms'. More than ten per cent of Greater London now consists of parks, gardens, sportsfields and woods and even the tiny square mile of the City has over 200 designated open spaces. Burgess Park in the south and Mile End Park in the east were pieced together over decades as decayed housing and commercial premises were demolished to create green corridors more accessible and more suited to a world of joggers and dog-walkers than the conventional rectangular patch of Victorian times. By the 1990s environmental surveys revealed that the metropolis was shaded by some 5,000,000 trees and that the Purple Hairstreak butterfly was recolonising the suburbs. Control of vehicle emissions, however, remained a major problem as did litter and graffiti.

From Trade to Tourism

Debt-burdened post-war Britain undertook an all-out export drive to which London contributed its output of cars from Ford's giant Dagenham works and buses and trucks from AEC in west London. Old-established industries like Tate and Lyle's sugar refineries, employing 8,000, were still important as were traditional Commonwealth markets for London double-deckers and sugar cubes. In return a third of all Commonwealth exports flowed through London which in 1956 handled a record 70,000,000 tons of cargo and employed 30,000 dockers. In the 1960s as countries like Nigeria and Malaya achieved independence they built up their own industries and diversified their trading partners, both trends being to London's disadvantage. As cargo volume shrank technical advances offered ways to cut costs but strongly unionised dockers resisted 'containerisation' bitterly – and to no effect except their own elimination. The East India Dock closed first in 1967, St Katharine's and the London in 1968. The 'Royals' went last, in 1981. Docklands was dead. Tilbury downriver containerised and survived. The rest of London's once mighty traffic diverted to formerly obscure (but ununionised) east coast ports such as Harwich and Felixstowe. Unemployment in the poor riverside boroughs of Tower Hamlets, Newham and Southwark rose from 10,000 in the 1960s to 80,000 in the 1980s.

Manufacturing disappeared with dock work. The London garment industry lost two-thirds of its 150,000 jobs. In the 1970s the engineering and electrical industries of west London were decimated by Japanese and European competition. Employers fled the capital in search of cheaper labour and premises, encouraged by tax and grant incentives to 'decongest' the capital in favour of creating new jobs in traditionally depressed South Wales and Tyneside. Westland, GEC, Lucas, Thorne-Emi and Hoover all decamped. Manufacturing jobs fell from a million in 1973 to just over half that in a decade.

GLOBALIZATION

Tourism, unexpectedly, took up the slack as long-haul jets slashed air fares. Between 1960 and 1965 foreign visitor figures tripled to 3,000,000. By the 1980s of Britain's 14,000,000 visitors 90 per cent passed through London. Two million came from the USA, another million from the 'Old Commonwealth' countries of British settlement and hundreds of thousands from the Middle East and Japan. Many came for business, education or medical treatment but most came to see the sights, shop and buy 40 per cent of the tickets sold by West End theatres. By 1994 over half of tourist spending in Britain was concentrated in London. Hotel building boomed. The skyscraper Hilton on Park Lane led the way in 1963 and later the dilapidated Langham was handsomely refurbished by the same chain. The Tower Thistle disfigured St Katharine's Dock and a line of giant cigarette-packets lowered over the Cromwell Road. St George's Hospital at Hyde Park Corner became the five star Lanesborough. Covent Garden acquired two museums, a covered market, a host of eating-places and a community of street entertainers. By the 1980s tourism became London's best job-creator, accounting for a tenth of the entire labour force. Financial services also grew rapidly, fuelled by new information technology and the 'Big Bang' of deregulation. Employment in this sector tripled from 270,000 in 1964 to 847,000 by 1989, much of it accommodated in the new granite and marble Broadgate Centre on the site of demolished Broad Street station. With 550 foreign banks the City became the world's most internationalised financial centre, with the planet's largest concentration of economic analysts. The presence of speakers of more than three hundred different languages induced Air France to relocate its international call centre to London. By the end of the century it became clear that globalization had two very different sides. The presence of thousands of highly-paid financial technicians from North America, Europe and Japan helped drive the price of the average London property past the £200,000 mark. Meanwhile refugees and asylum-seekers – Somalis, Kurds and Kosovans – attempted to re-establish settled lives in the East End.

Ruin or Revival ?

Radical changes in the structure of London's economy were reflected in its architecture. The City became a city virtually without citizens, its only substantial clusters of residents existing on its periphery – in the Temple, Bart's Hospital, the Barbican, Charterhouse Square and the

The Telecom Tower

Golden Lane estate. What were still in Victorian days at least semi-residential streets became intersecting canyons of offices. From 1710 until World War Two the City's tallest building was St Paul's (365 ft.); from 1980 it was the (now former) National Westminster Bank Tower (600 ft.). Mammon literally towered over all. Labour favoured housing and industry in 1945–51, restricting office development. The Conservatives fulfilled their 1951 pledge to make a 'bonfire of controls'. The resulting tawdry blocks of the 1950s were to be demolished unmourned a generation later. Labour reimposed controls from 1964 and relocated 50,000 government jobs to distant Swansea and Newcastle. The Conservatives took the brakes off again in 1970. Centre Point at the eastern end of Oxford Street was consequently built as the West End's first and last office skyscraper.

TOWER BLOCKS AND TERRACES

Housing provision depended on the haphazard interplay of government policy and market forces. For council tenants tower blocks were much favoured in the 1960s, when four hundred were built, 125 in Newham alone. They promised light, air, breathtaking views and, at ground level, the replacement of narrow alleys with open green spaces. But communities which flourished horizontally perished vertically. All too often the towers bred a social isolation which expressed itself in vandalism and neglect. When the explosion of a domestic cooker caused multiple storeys to collapse at Ronan Point in 1968, killing five, major structural design faults were revealed. Enthusiasm for towers waned as their drawbacks became evident.

In great arcs stretching from Hammersmith to Hackney and Greenwich to Dulwich the Victorian villas and terraces deserted by the new tower-dwellers were snapped up by bourgeois gentrifiers. White walls and wine bars marked the advance of yuppies recolonising what their grandparents had abandoned for the outer suburbs. Their two-car affluence worsened London's congestion, which had already seen vehicle density quadruple between 1945 and 1960. Bus use fell 40 per cent between 1950 and 1970 as car ownership grew. In 1958 yellow lines, parking-meters and traffic wardens were introduced to 'keep the capital moving'. In 1968 came bus lanes. Major road underpasses were built at Euston, Hyde Park Corner and Blackfriars. The orbital M25, 125 miles of motorway, encircling and thus redefining the capital, was completed in 1986 and soon carrying six times its anticipated volume of traffic.

CONCERN FOR CONSERVATION

As new landmarks were established, old ones were erased. Protests failed to save The Grange, where Samuel Richardson wrote *Pamela* and the Pre-Raphaelite painter Sir Edward Burne-Jones had his studio; or the St James's Theatre, King Street, where Wilde's plays were premiered; or the City's majestic iron-framed Coal Exchange of 1849. In 1957 the Civic Trust was established to promote conservation. By 1960 it had thirty affiliated groups in the London area and by 1974 ninety. The wanton destruction of Philip Hardwick's majestic neo-classical station arch at Euston in 1962 served as a clarion call to action. In the 1970s the newly-formed Soho Society successfully resisted Westminster City Council's plans to flatten their urban village, encouraging other reaffirmations of locality. A generation later this impetus would find new incarnations in cyber-neighbourhood websites and TV 'docu-soaps' like *Paddington Green*.

Docklands

The terminal demise of London's inner docks created a new canvas for the creative efforts of architects and developers. In 1981 the London Docklands Development Corporation was set up to rejuvenate eight square miles of commercial dereliction. Capitalising on abandoned berths as 'water features', the LDDC proclaimed its intention to create a space age mini-city which 'Looks like Venice, Works like New York'. With more vigour than vision the erection of high-rise offices and luxury apartments raced ahead of the infrastructure needed to serve them while government and developers wrangled over the bill. The epicentre of the constructional typhoon was the Isle of Dogs peninsula, soon to be immortalised in the opening credit sequence of the TV soap-opera *Eastenders*. Dazzling new office towers were vilified as the architectural embodiment of Thatcherite greed while critics noted that the main benefits to the 14,000 existing 'Islanders', many of them third-generation residents, were low-level jobs in labouring, catering and security and access to a new hypermarket where their offspring stacked the shelves. The predictable outcome was low-intensity class warfare expressed through mugging, burglary and car-theft at the expense of highly-paid incomers. Soaring above all was Cesar Pelli's 800 foot Canada Tower at Canary Wharf, the tallest building in the country. Steel-clad to shimmer in sunlight, ablaze with light at night, it was visible beyond the M25, an ambiguous signpost to an uncertain destination.

Unplanned Planning

Much of post-war London's growth has simply happened, not for lack of planners but for lack of powers. In 1965 the LCC, responsible for 117 square miles, gave way to the Greater London Council, with a jurisdiction of 610 square miles. But the GLC's strategic role was undermined by its frequently adversarial relationship with central government, which whittled away its functions under the guise of administrative reform. New Water and Health Authorities took over drainage, flood control and ambulances in 1974. Supervision of the capital's transport as an integrated system was lost in 1984. In 1986 the GLC itself was abolished. In 1990, like the smile of a bureaucratic Cheshire cat, the vestigial Inner London Education Authority disappeared. Alone among the world's great cities London prepared to face a new millennium bereft of any authority to cherish its past, speak for its present or plan for its future.

Political Tensions

The GLC never did manage to reconcile its own goals with those of the boroughs which were theoretically under its sway. With a territorial jurisdiction five times greater than the old LCC's, it aimed to use the resources of the metropolis as a whole to tackle the problems of the metropolis as a whole. In practice this meant Robin Hood redistribution from the rich boroughs – mostly leafy outer suburbs under

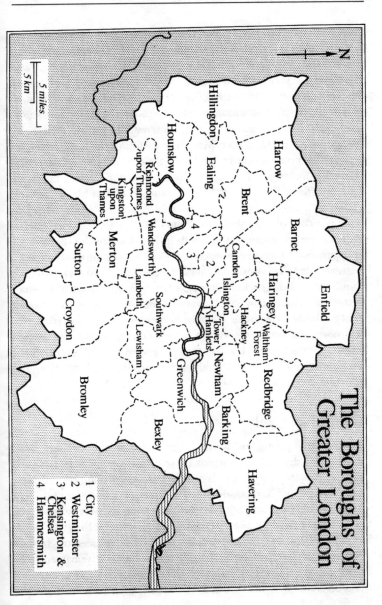

The Boroughs of Greater London

1 City
2 Westminster
3 Kensington & Chelsea
4 Hammersmith

Conservative control – to the run-down inner-city ones run by Labour. Political activists and commentators alike were surprised to find London's local politics becoming political. Received wisdom was that compared with national politics civic affairs were non-ideological, almost conflict-free, apart from the occasional whiff of corruption, a matter of ' what's best administered is best', tepidly endorsed by low voter turn-outs and marginal media interest. In sparky 'Red Ken' Livingstone, the GLC leader, Mrs Thatcher found an antagonist eager to tweak her political nose by subsidising flat-rate Tube fares in defiance of 'market forces' and posting up London's unemployment figures in figures ten feet tall on the balcony of County Hall. But Mrs Thatcher's trump card, control of Parliament, enabled her to destroy what she could not control. The abolition of the GLC was followed by a fierce effort to impose regimes at borough level committed to 'best value' managerialism through privatisation and competitive tendering. Resistance led the boroughs to align themselves into two camps – the Conservative-led London Boroughs Association and the Labour-dominated Association of London Authorities. With no overall strategic body to exercise effective power over planning, transport, environmental protection or the promotion of tourism or inward investment the Greater London Council gave way to Greater London Confusion, epitomised in a toothless London Residuary Body whose very title said it all.

Capital of Cool

In 1995 the prestigious Reith Lectures flayed the Conservatives' abolition of the GLC as a major cause of metropolitan decay. Tube passengers were plagued by daily delays from signalling breakdowns, staff shortages and disruptions caused by attempts to shore up the system while building a massive Jubilee line extension to Greenwich at the same time. Economic analysts warned of growing polarisation in the local labour force as buoyant finance and computing faced crucial skills shortages while the capital's overall unemployment remained stubbornly above the national average. The introduction of educational 'league tables' revealed that inner-London schools combined some of the highest spend per pupil figures in the country with the lowest levels of academic achievement.

The 1997 edition of a bestselling back-packer's guide-book excoriated London as litter-strewn, extortionately over-priced and over-populated with panhandlers and street-sleepers. Still the visitors poured in, passing the 20 million mark. The Eurostar service from Waterloo brought Paris and Brussels within three hours reach of London – and vice versa. London's new attractions ranged from the opening of Buckingham Palace to tours of criminal haunts in the East End. The British Tourist Authority pleaded for the retention of red buses and the daily Changing of the Guard, while Westminster City Council in a user-friendly gesture to changeless foreigners abolished charges in public lavatories. The triumphant reconstruction of the Globe Theatre in Southwark, reinforced by the extension of the Jubilee line, provided a catalyst for the piecemeal regeneration of the south bank of the Thames between Vauxhall and Docklands, stringing together existing visitor attractions with new ones such as a replica of Drake's *Golden Hind*, the Vinopolis wine exhibition, a farmers' market in the Borough and the Tea and Coffee Museum. Over time these would relieve pressure on the peak-loaded Tower and Abbey by offering alternatives to repeat visitors, as well as providing much-needed employment in the capital's less-favoured boroughs. In 1996 *Newsweek* hailed London as 'the world's coolest city'. The Museum of London boasted that there were more artists living in Hackney than in the Left Bank Quarter of Paris. Hackney's standing as the capital's poorest borough gave an ambiguous resonance to this claim.

FACE-LIFTS

London's physical appearance continued to change dramatically. Significant demolitions included unloved Holborn Viaduct station, the graceless Barclays Bank building in Gracechurch Street, windswept Paternoster Square and – delicious irony – the overbearing Marsham Street blocks of the Department of the Environment. The traditional fish market at Billingsgate and the fruit and vegetable market at Spitalfields relocated to new state-of-the-art premises in the east. Smithfield meat market underwent a £60,000,000 updating. The

University of Greenwich took over most of the grandiose buildings of the former Naval Hospital. The Art Deco OXO building was refurbished, affording a fine panorama from its rooftop restaurant. The Albert Memorial was restored to glittering glory. Spencer House, ancestral town-house of Princess Diana's family, was re-opened to the public, a miniature Versailles in a St James's side-street. In Marylebone two rare surviving Adam properties – Chandos House and 20 Portman Square – underwent extensive and expensive re-fits. In Newham inner city tower-blocks were brightened by repainting in bold, asymmetric designs and at Hackney the National Trust rescued a much-abused treasure in a battered but sturdy Tudor mansion, Sutton House. Brand new buildings included the post-modernist MI5 headquarters at Vauxhall, Vintner's Place in stripped-down neo-Classical overlooking Southwark Bridge, Reuter's new headquarters building at Blackwall, the British Library at St Pancras and No. 1 Poultry, overlooking the City's major architectural nexus at Bank. The Prince of Wales may indeed have likened the British Library to a training academy for Communist secret policemen and No. 1 Poultry to a 1930s radio set, but it was less easy to deny that they were buildings of quality.

Past . . .

Widespread building activity brought new archaeological discoveries as a bonus by-product. The Museum of London imaginatively recreated its finds at No. 1 Poultry as 'High Street Londinium'. At Spitalfields, on the site of St Mary Spital, a cemetery used since Roman times yielded 8,000 bodies, including the remains of a Roman yuppie, interred with phials of her favourite perfumes and wrapped in cloth of gold in a stone sarcophagus complete with a shell-patterned lead cover. Other finds proved curious, charming or bizarre – a banana from Tudor Tooley Street, a Roman oil lamp shaped like a human foot, the jetty at Bermondsey where Raleigh famously threw his (or somebody's) gorgeous cloak in the mud for Elizabeth I to walk on, the site of the anatomy theatre where the bodies of the Tyburn hanged were dissected afterwards. Other discoveries were more profound in their implications. In east London sewer engineers uncovered the remains of a six thousand year old forest. Painstaking investigations of Roman rubbish tips suggested Londinium may have flourished for a much briefer period than was once thought. Other investigations provoked hypotheses that Londonium may have begun in Southwark – or around a fort in Mayfair – and that, even when it was flourishing in the second century, large areas were grassy open spaces. Excavations conducted during the refurbishment of the Royal Opera House uncovered a tangled network of Saxon street-lines, confirming that 'Lundenwic' stretched much further inland from the river bank than previously thought.

Londoners were more preoccupied with less remote times than with their city's origins. In 1994 the Bank of England and London cabdrivers both celebrated their three-hundredth anniversary. Bond Street shopkeepers commemorated the same landmark by erecting a quirky statue of Franklin Roosevelt and Winston Churchill sharing a bench – with space for Japanese tourists to squeeze in between them for photographic immortality. Handel's house on Upper Brook Street was converted to a museum – and Jimi Hendrix's residence next door was memorialized with a plaque. Elsewhere the Dead Comics Society placed plaques on their former homes to honour Arthur Lowe, Kenneth Williams and Benny Hill. Statues were erected to memorialize Mozart and Purcell, the Gurkhas, Dr Johnson's cat, Hodge, Oscar Wilde, Swedish diplomat Raoul Wallenberg, General Sikorski and the Royal Tank Regiment. Westminster Abbey installed effigies above its west door representing a global selection of ten 'modern martyrs' including Dr Martin Luther King, Dietrich Bonhoeffer, Archbishop Luwum and Oscar Romero. Alexandra Palace gained listed status. At the south-eastern corner of Hyde Park £1,500,000 was spent on gates dedicated to the Queen Mother – who remained infinitely more popular than the gates.

. . . *and Present*

During the 1980s out-migration from London began to be reversed. One factor may have been the cost of commuting, confirmed by a European Union survey of 1993 as the highest in western Europe. A similar 1995 survey confirmed that London had the highest housing costs – but was the fourth cheapest capital to live in overall. The idea of London as a desirable place to live in heightened incentives for developers to provide accommodation at convenient or fashionable locations – no easy task in a city as densely built-up as London. (98 per cent of new buildings are now estimated to be built on 'brownfield' sites formerly occupied by demolished structures.) Conversion of schools, offices and churches to residential purposes relieved entrepreneurs of many infrastructure costs and offered unusual opportunities for creating 'character' homes. Warehouses along the river and in Docklands gave Londoners a supposed taste of New York style 'loft living'. The former administrative block of County Hall and the old Harrod's Depository at Barnes represented unusual examples of this trend and the former Bryant and May match factory at Bow one of the largest. Other conversions included Shell's redundant headquarters at Waterloo and historic Spitalfields soup-kitchens, one (vintage 1797) in Brick Lane, the other (of 1902) in Brune St. In Mayfair fifty year leases for commercial use, granted by the Grosvenor estate after the war when prestige office space was at a premium, began to terminate, prompting a reversion to residential use. Clerkenwell, too, began to regain a residential character.

Activity at the top end of the housing market was maintained by the super-rich who could ignore the financial constraints and fluctuations governing national trends outside London itself. In Chelsea an Anglophile Japanese set a new record for the price of an existing house by paying £25,000,000 for an old rectory, while in adjacent Pimlico a Kuwaiti prince set a new record for a new property by spending £40,000,000 on a riverside residence. This was eclipsed by another riverside phenomenon at Chelsea where a millionaire recycled £60,000,000 made from TV rentals into constructing a Tudor 'prodigy house'. This involved grafting three wings, built in imitation of three extant Tudor survivals, onto the genuine fifteenth century carcase of Crosby Hall, a merchant's mansion which had once stood in Bishopsgate.

German property speculators, South East Asian investors and Russian *nouveaux-riches* kept up the demand for large, luxurious and historic properties. A survey of the super-rich revealed that they perceived London as a very secure environment with every temptation for consumption and diversion. Being less visible to the casual observer than the cardboard-coated casualties who nightly lined the doorways along the Strand, their endorsement passed largely unnoticed. But by 1998 *for every one* of the four hundred who slept outdoors each night there were over a hundred millionaires who were happy to call London their home – or one of their homes.

London's new-found reputation for gastronomy continued to advance at all levels. At Aldgate, where the City rubs a shiny-suited shoulder with the East End (where the suits were once made) historic Bloom's closed its doors for the last time. Having for decades modestly described itself as 'the most famous kosher restaurant in the world' – it was certainly famed for the legendary rudeness of its venerable waiters – Bloom's finally gave way to a branch of Burger King, though its suburban incarnation lived on at Golders Green. The much-hyped opening of a branch of Planet Hollywood just off Leicester Square suggested that burgers with attitude had indeed supplanted salt beef with a scowl.

There was a proliferation of bars and restaurants 'themed' around sport, fashion or the cuisine of particular countries, including Peru, Poland, Belgium, South Africa and New Zealand. Pseudo-Irish pubs and Seattle-style coffee-bars spread like a rash. Liverpool Street station acquired a sushi bar. Many self-styled 'Indian' restaurants began to confess that they had really been Bangladeshi all along – and now they were proud of it. Brick Lane, heart of London's Bengali community, acquired a triumphal arch informing visitors they were entering 'Banglatown'. At the far end of the Lane London's best and cheapest bagel bakery kept alive an older local culinary tradition.

New Dawn? False Dawn?

Tony Blair's 'New Labour' government in May 1997 pledged that Londoners would be given the chance to vote on whether they wanted an elected Mayor and assembly with city-wide responsibilities – left largely undefined. Londoners voted firmly in favour. Whatever the powers of the mayoralty it soon became evident that it would enjoy (a

Ken Livingstone, the first elected Mayor of London

term that might prove two-edged) a high public profile. Being held responsible for managing London's policing and transport, raising environmental standards and attracting inward investment would prove a mighty task even if matched by adequate budgetary and staff resources. When Ken Livingstone announced his intention to run for mayor the People's Party tried to manipulate the electoral process to keep him out. Londoners exercised their new franchise by voting him in. Although the turn-out was low, the verdict was decisive and a year later four Londoners out of five could correctly identify Ken Livingstone as mayor, a level of name recognition far in excess of all but the top three or four members of the Cabinet.

New Labour also agreed to follow through on the outgoing government's pet prestige project – the construction of a mighty Dome on the (expensively detoxified) site of a former gas-works at Greenwich, site of the meridian, and therefore deemed the most appropriate place to mark the advent of the third Millennium on 31 December 1999 – i.e. one year early as historians measure these things. The Dome, designed by the newly-ennobled Lord Rogers (he of the Lloyd's building), would cost in the region of £800,000,000. Providing access to it by extending the Jubilee line, which would then re-cross the river to terminate at a projected international freight depot at Stratford, would cost some £4,000,000,000. Initial surveys revealed that the general public remained unenthusiastic about the Dome, Londoners no less than others. A Mayor for London – someone to speak in their name and bat on their side – would fill a vacuum which most Londoners had regarded as a nonsense and an insult all along. But the Dome? To what possible question facing the capital was building the Dome an appropriate answer?

As it turned out none. While the actual building was praised its contents, or lack of them, attracted much derision. A creative failure, a managerial nightmare, a commercial disaster and a political embarrassment, the Dome cost more than would have been needed to update the signalling system on the District line six times over. The Millennium Bridge, linking St. Paul's to Bankside, was, at £13,000,000, at least a cheaper embarrassment. Opened by the Queen in June 2000 it was closed within days, having revealed an alarming tendency to wobble when a body of persons larger than a royal entourage attempted to cross it. Engineers grumpily denounced the decision to give the design brief to architects in the first place, in this case the prestigious Arup partnership. Over a year later the bridge had still not been fixed. The new attraction at its southern end, however, proved a triumph. The Tate Modern art gallery in Sir Giles Gilbert Scott's 1963 Bankside power station attracted 5,000,000 visitors in its first year, triple the most optimistic estimate and a snip at £134,000,000. Upriver opposite Parliament the 135 metre high London Eye, the world's tallest observation wheel, was also a huge hit. The British Museum spent £100,000,000 on opening up and roofing over its Great Court to achieve one of the most stunning interior spaces the capital could offer. In the suburbs plans for a super-stadium to replace condemned Wembley collapsed in a fiasco of indecision.

So much for the London visitors' experience. Surveys conducted for

The London Eye

the new Greater London Authority revealed that resident Londoners wanted their new mayor to make transport his number one priority, followed by crime and housing. Livingstone responded by importing as transport supremo Bob Kiley, a former American general who had 'sorted' New York's mass transit system. Kiley's much-trumpeted salary of £500,000 made him Britain's most highly paid public servant. Mayor and mentor then clashed head-on with government plans for partial privatisation of the Underground, a confrontation seemingly doomed to fester in litigation and further delay while Londoners continued to be tormented by overcrowding, breakdowns and gridlock. Entering the twenty-first century London as an economy ranked as the twenty-first country in the world – with seven of the nation's ten most deprived local government areas and 60 per cent of England's most sub-standard public housing.

Chronology of Major Events

A.D.

43	Invasion by Claudius
ca.50	First London Bridge built
61	London burned by Boudicca (Boadicea)
ca 200	City encircled by walls
ca 350	Bastions added to eastern walls – Saxon pirate attacks
410	Roman emperor Honorius advises Londoners to defend themselves
457	Beaten Britons shelter within city walls
604	First St Paul's Cathedral built. Mellitus appointed bishop of London
ca 7/8	Lundenwic develops round Aldwych
886	Alfred the Great retakes London from Vikings
899	First mention of Queenhithe
949	First mention of Billingsgate
1066	William of Normandy crowned in new Westminster Abbey; White Tower begun
1097–9	Westminster Hall built by William II
1123	St Bartholomew's Hospital established
1176–1209	Peter de Colechurch builds first stone London Bridge
1192	Henry FitzAilwin, first Lord Mayor of London
1214	City Charter awarded by King John
1269	Reconsecration of rebuilt Westminster Abbey
1290	Expulsion of Jews (to 1656)
1348–9	'Black Death' – bubonic plague
1381	Peasants' Revolt
1477	Caxton's printing press at Westminster
1500	Population ca 75,000; by 1600 200,000
1513	Establishment of royal dockyards at Woolwich and Deptford
1536	Dissolution of the monasteries
1558	First true map of all London, by Ralph Agas

1577	Burbage builds 'The Theatre' at Shoreditch
1598	John Stow's *Survey of London*
1599	Globe Theatre
1613	New River brings clean water supply from Hertfordshire
1631	Inigo Jones' Covent Garden
1637	Hyde Park opened to the public
1642–60	Civil War and Commonwealth
1649	Execution of Charles I in Whitehall
1665	Great Plague – kills 100,000
1666	Great Fire wipes out four-fifths of City of London
1676–1710	Wren rebuilds St Paul's, the Monument and 51 City churches; also Chelsea Hospital; Greenwich Hospital; Greenwich Observatory; Hampton Court and Kensington Palace
1685	Revocation of the Edict of Nantes; Huguenot refugees develop silk-weaving and silversmithing
1694	Bank of England founded
1698	Burning of Whitehall Palace
1700	Population 575,000 (City 203,000) = 10 per cent national total
1725–31	Grosvenor Square laid out and Mayfair developed
1729	Chiswick House
1739	Capt. Coram establishes Foundling Hospital
1739–53	Mansion House built
1749	Westminster Bridge
1759	British Museum established; Royal Botanic Gardens, Kew established
1761	New Road opened
1768	Royal Academy opened
1780	Gordon riots
1801	First census of population 959,000 (City 128,000)
1802	West India Dock opened
1816–29	Nash's remodelling of Regent's Park, Regent Street
1826	University College founded
1829	Shillibeer's omnibus begins service; Metropolitan police founded
1832	Cholera outbreak
1836	London Bridge – Greenwich Railway
1837	Queen Victoria makes Buckingham Palace the official royal residence
1843	Brunel's Thames Tunnel
1845	Victoria Park opened
1846–7	Influx of Irish fleeing potato blight and famine
1848	Influx of refugees fleeing failed European revolutions

1849	Cholera outbreak
1851	Great Exhibition – South Kensington developed from its profits
1855	Metropolitan Board of Works established
1858	The 'Great Stink'
1862–4	First Peabody Buildings erected
1863	First Underground railway – Paddington–Farringdon
1865	Salvation Army established
1875	Bedford Park – first planned suburb
1877	First Wimbledon tennis tournament
1880s	Russian Jewish influx
1884–9	Savoy Hotel
1888	London County Council established; Whitechapel ('Jack the Ripper') Murders
1889	Great Dock Strike
1890	Northern Line – first electric Tube
1895–1903	Westminster Cathedral built
1901	Population 6,506,000 (City 27,000)
1908	Olympic Games
1909	Port of London Authority established; Selfridges opened
1915	First German air raids on London
1919	Cenotaph unveiled
1922	BBC begins broadcasting from Savoy Hill
1924	British Empire exhibition at Wembley
1927–9	Broadway House built as HQ for London Transport
1930s	Refugee influx fleeing European fascism
1935	'Green Belt' policy formulated to limit urban expansion; Battle of Cable Street; television broadcasting begins from Alexandra Palace
1940–1 and 1944–45	Blitz
1946	New Towns Act
1947–8	New Commonwealth influx
1948	Olympic Games
1951	Festival of Britain
1952	'Killer' smog
1953	Heathrow airport terminal formally opened
1956	Clean Air Act ends smog
1960–5	Post Office Tower built
1961	New US Embassy building, Grosvenor Square
1965	Greater London Council established (to 1986)
1968	Ronan Point tower block disaster; St Katharine's dock closes; Victoria line opened

1974	Covent Garden market moves to Nine Elms
1976	National Theatre opened; Brent Cross shopping centre opened
1978	Central London Mosque, Regent's Park
1979	Jubilee line opened
1981	London Docklands Development Corporation established
1982	Barbican Arts Centre opened; Thames Flood Barrier completed
1987	Docklands Light Railway and City Airport opened
1988	Museum of the Moving Image
1989	Design Museum; storm destroys many London trees
1991	Canada Tower, Canary Wharf opened
1992	IRA bomb St. Mary Axe
1993	Limehouse Link tunnel opened; Spencer House re-opened to the public; major IRA bomb in Bishopsgate; Buckingham Palace opened to the public
1994	Bank of England, Bond Street and London cab-drivers all celebrate their 300th anniversary; Westminster City Councillors charged with gerrymandering and financial impropriety
1996	IRA bomb South Quay in the Docklands; reconstructed Globe Theatre opens
1998	British Library opened; demolition of Marsham Street towers, Holborn Viaduct Station & Paternoster Square; Londoners vote in favour of an elected Mayor and Assembly
1999	Millennium Dome and Jubilee Line extension created
2000	Tate Modern, London Eye and British Museum Great Court opened; Ken Livingstone elected mayor
2001	Closure of Wembley Stadium

Rulers and Monarchs

Anglo-Saxon Kings

Alfred the Great   *871–99*
Edward   *899–924*
Athelstan   *924–39*
Edmund   *939–46*
Edred   *946–55*
Edwy   *955–59*
Edgar   *959–75*
Edward the Martyr   *975–79*
Aethelred the Unready   *979–1016*
Cnut   *1016–35*
Harold I   *1037–40*
Harthacnut   *1040–42*
Edward the Confessor   *1042–66*
Harold II   *1066*

The House of Normandy

William I (the Conqueror)
    1066–87
William II (Rufus)   *1087–1100*
Henry I   *1100–35*
Stephen   *1135–54*

The House of Plantagenet

Henry II   *1154–89*
Richard I (the Lionheart)   *1189–99*

John   *1199–1216*
Henry III   *1216–72*
Edward I   *1272–1307*
Edward II   *1307–27*
Edward III   *1327–77*
Richard II   *1377–99*

The House of Lancaster

Henry IV   *1399–1413*
Henry V   *1413–22*
Henry VI   *1422–61*

The House of York

Edward IV   *1461–83*
Edward V   *1483*
Richard III   *1483–85*

The House of Tudor

Henry VII   *1485–1509*
Henry VIII   *1509–47*
Edward VI   *1547–53*
Mary   *1553–58*
Elizabeth I   *1558–1603*

The House of Stuart

James I   *1603–25*
Charles I   *1625–49*

The Commonwealth and Protectorate

Oliver Cromwell (Protector)
    1653–58
Richard Cromwell   *1658–59*

The House of Stuart (Restored)

Charles II   *1660–85*
James II   *1685–88*
William III and Mary   *1689–94*
William III   *1694–1702*
Anne   *1702–14*

The House of Hanover

George I   *1714–27*
George II   *1727–60*
George III   *1760–1820*
George IV (Regent from 1811)
    1820–30
William IV   *1830–37*

The House of Saxe-Coburg-Gotha

Victoria   *1837–1901*
Edward VII   *1901–10*

The House of Windsor

George V   *1910–36*
Edward VIII   *1936*
George VI   *1936–52*
Elizabeth II   *1952–*

The Tower of London

'A most famous and goodly Citadell, encompassed round with thicke and strong walles, full of loftie and stately Turrets, fensed with a broad and deep ditch, furnished also with an armorie or magazine of warlicke munition, and other buildings besides: so as it resembleth a big towne.' Thus William Camden, author of the first great topography of Britain, in 1610.

'Her Majesty's Fortress and Palace – The Tower of London', to give it its full title, has received Professor Pevsner's supreme accolade as 'the most important work of military architecture in England.' It has been not only a fortress and a palace but also a prison and place of execution; it has housed the Royal Mint, Royal Observatory, Royal Menagerie and Public Records. It still provides high security protection for the Crown jewels and the world-class collections of the Royal Armouries. Covering 18 acres the Tower once housed 1,500 people and is still home to about 150, including the awesome Yeomen Warders.

The Tower of London consists, in fact, of 20 towers, set within two concentric walls, built over the course of two-and-a-half centuries and much altered and extended ever since. The strategic value of the site, immediately downstream from London Bridge, was apparent to the Romans. Their riverfront wall and defensive turret were incorporated into the fortifications of the Tower by later builders.

The White Tower

William I began the construction of the White Tower, partly to protect his new capital, partly to overawe its turbulent citizens. Designed by Gundulf, bishop of Rochester, the massive keep, with walls 90-feet high and 15-feet thick, was built of Kentish rag, strengthened by stone brought by sea and river from Caen in the Conqueror's native Normandy. Visitors to the White Tower still enter by the original door, set 15 feet above ground level and approached via a wooden staircase, which could be burned in case of attack. The four-storey interior was equipped with three wells, three fireplaces, garderobes (lavatories) on the top three floors and a chapel of austere simplicity.

Henry I added a free-standing chapel, appropriately dedicated to St Peter *Ad Vincula* – St Peter in Chains – which was rebuilt by Henry VIII in 1520. During Richard I's reign a curtain wall was begun and the Bell Tower built. The elaboration and completion of the main structure was the work of Henry III and Edward I, who also added a luxurious great hall (now vanished) and a moat, devised by a Flemish technical adviser. Edward II added two portcullises, one of which remains in working order. Henry VIII constructed the attractive half-timbered houses, where Guy Fawkes was interrogated; he also added two artillery bastions, which face inward, towards the City. Sir Christopher Wren built the Grand Storehouse and remodelled the windows of the White Tower. After the terrible fire of 1841 which gutted the Grand Armoury, the Wellington Barracks block was built; it now houses the Crown jewels, Oriental Armouries and Education Centre.

Royal Residence

The Tower was first used as a regular royal residence by Stephen, but it was Henry III who gave it the sort of splendour and comfort befitting a king. He also ordered the White Tower to be whitewashed, thus giving it its name. A reconstruction of what a private royal apartment would have been like during his reign can be seen in St. Thomas's Tower, which at that time gave direct access to the river. It was during Henry's reign also that a royal menagerie was established, thanks to gifts from the Holy Roman Emperor (3 leopards to match those on the royal arms of England), from the king of Norway (a polar bear which, safely chained, swam to catch its supper in the river) and, from the king of France an elephant, now buried somewhere within the precincts of the Tower. The last monarch to use the Tower as a regular royal residence was James I, who took perverse pleasure in staging fights between the lions and bears of the menagerie or tormenting them with mastiffs.

PRISON

The Tower was first used as a prison in 1101 when Ranulf Flambard, bishop of Durham, was arrested for corruption. Having made his guards drunk, he escaped from a window by a rope. The fat Welsh prince Llewellyn was less fortunate in his attempt by the same method; his fall thrust his head right into his rib-cage. In 1303 the abbot of Westminster and 80 other suspects were imprisoned after the theft of items of royal regalia from the abbey. Ever since then the Crown jewels have been kept at the Tower.

Blood and Execution

The bloodiest phase of the Tower's history was under the Tudors, a time when the unity of the nation was threatened as never before by disturbing religious ideas as well as the more traditional problems of dynastic ambitions and foreign hostility. Henry VIII's victims included his father's unpopular tax-collectors, Empson and Dudley, the principled Thomas More (*see p 51*) and the frail Bishop Fisher. Their tormentor, Thomas Cromwell, followed them to the block on Tower Hill. The brief reign of Edward VI brought 'Lord Protector Somerset' and the 'Nine Days Queen', Lady Jane Grey, to the headsman's axe. Queen Elizabeth herself, as a princess, served her time, shrilly protesting her innocence. Under her rule many catholic priests and nobles were to suffer for their faith. The often elaborate inscriptions they carved while awaiting their fate can still be seen in the Beauchamp, Salt and Martin Towers.

Executions normally took place on Tower Hill, outside the precincts of the fortress itself: only seven people have been executed on Tower Green, next to St Peter *Ad Vincula*. Lord Hastings was dragged out of a meeting on the orders of Richard III for refusing to support charges of sorcery levelled against the widow of Edward IV; his head was struck off on a log of wood. Anne Boleyn, second wife of Henry VIII and mother of Elizabeth I, was charged with incest and adultery and executed, at her own request, by a French swordsman and buried in an arrow-box because no one had ordered a coffin. The aged countess of Suffolk, after an unseemly scuffle, suffered the king's venom because her son, a cardinal, was safe in Rome. Catherine Howard, Henry VIII's fifth wife, calmly practised putting her head on the block the night before she lost it, and on the day defiantly declared 'If I had married the man I loved instead of being dazzled with ambition all would have been well.' On that same day Viscountess Rochford, who had also served Anne Boleyn, had to be dragged half-swooning, to her end. The bookish, teenage Lady Jane Grey carried a prayer-book in which she had written 'As the preacher sayeth, there is a time to be born and a time to die.' The last person to expire on this spot was the flamboyant earl of Essex, whose futile revolt Elizabeth could not overlook, even in her dotage. His courtly rival Sir Walter Raleigh had the grim satisfaction of surveying the scene from the roof of the White Tower. Raleigh himself was imprisoned here three times. The first time, briefly, for seducing Elizabeth

Block, axe and executioner's mask at the Tower of London

Throgmorton, one of Elizabeth's ladies-in-waiting, the second time he was found guilty of plotting against the newly-installed James I. Sentenced to death, he was reprieved on the eve of his execution. Visitors today can see a reconstruction of his roomy apartments in the Bloody Tower. Here he experimented with herbal cordials, enjoyed the novel solace of tobacco and composed a vast *History of the World* to instruct the chivalrous Henry, prince of Wales, in the mysteries of statecraft. This gilded youth, the hope of a generation, asked 'Who but my father could keep such a bird in such a cage?' but died tragically of fever after swimming in the Thames. Henry's dazzling armours can still be seen in the White Tower. Raleigh, in despair, abandoned his history, and accepted a poisoned chalice, an invitation to lead an expedition to South America in search of gold. It cost him a son, his health, fortune and reputation. Returning, empty-handed and under sentence of death, he was executed in Old Palace Yard, Westminster.

Of the later executions at Tower Hill two stand out. The handsome and popular James, Duke of Monmouth, bastard son, of Charles II, was condemned for his abortive rising in pursuit of the throne on his father's death. The axe was so blunt that it took five strokes to despatch him and his executioner had to be escorted to safety from the fury of the onlookers. The last person to be beheaded on Tower Hill was the Jacobite Lord Lovat, condemned for his part in the 1745 uprising to restore the Stuart line in the person of 'Bonnie Prince Charlie'. A fat, arthritic 80-year-old, he retained both his dignity and sense of humour, being vastly amused when a temporary stand collapsed, killing 12 onlookers who had come to see him die. The axe and block used for his decapitation can still be seen among the instruments of torture in the Martin Tower. The very last executions to take place at Tower Hill were of two prostitutes and a one-armed soldier identified as ring-leaders in the anti-Catholic Gordon riots of 1780. (*see p 110*). The half-crazed Lord George Gordon himself was held in the Tower at the same time as Henry Laurens, a former president of the revolutionary American Continental Congress, who had been captured at sea on his way to negotiate Dutch support for the American Revolution. His needlessly close confinement left him much embittered.

FIRING SQUADS

The Tower has remained a place of imprisonment and execution into the present century. In 1916 Irish nationalist Sir Roger Casement was held in St Thomas's Tower, over Traitor's Gate, for his part in enlisting German support for the Easter Rising in Dublin. Rudolf Hess, Hitler's deputy, was held in the Lieutenant's House for four days in 1941 during his abortive mission to mediate a peace between Germany and Britain. Executions of spies by firing squad took place at the Tower during both world wars. If the Tower has served as a prison for the monarch's enemies it has also served more than once as a prison for the monarch, too. Henry III, at the nadir of his reign, shut himself up here and summoned a parliament to support him – it refused to attend. His unpopular queen, Eleanor of Provence, was besieged there in 1263; when she tried to escape by water she was pelted with so much rubbish from London Bridge that she had to give up. Henry got his own back in 1265, imprisoning the lord mayor of London and assigning the revenues from the bridge to the queen. During the revolt of 1381 (*see p 38*) the Tower likewise proved to be anything but a safe royal refuge.

During the Wars of the Roses the luckless Henry VI was murdered at his prayers in the Wakefield Tower. On the anniversary of his death lilies and white roses are laid on the spot on behalf of his two scholarly foundations, Eton College and King's College, Cambridge.

THE LITTLE PRINCES

The equally hapless Edward V and his brother, the Duke of York ('the little princes in the Tower') were almost certainly murdered in the Garden (henceforth Bloody) Tower in 1483, probably on the orders of their uncle, the Duke of Gloucester, who took the throne as Richard III – though his partisans passionately deny this charge as a malicious fabrication of Tudor propaganda. The bodies of two boys were uncovered near the White Tower in the reign of Charles II and, on his personal orders, re-interred in Westminster Abbey (*see p 250*).

Today's Visitors

Nowadays the Tower attracts over two-and-a-half million visitors a year. Visitors have been coming to see the armouries and Crown jewels since at least the sixteenth century. In the basement of the White Tower today's visitor can still see exhibits from the wildly unhistorical and propagandist 'Line of Kings' display which was arranged to impress the credible until the nineteenth century when the collections at last came under serious scholarly supervision.

That perceptive and sympathetic American observer Nathaniel Hawthorne noted in 1863 that: 'An Englishman cares nothing about the Tower, which to us is a haunted castle in dream-land.'

Over half-a-century later the irascible and cynical Canadian humourist Stephen Leacock observed that: '. . . when a Londoner says "Have you seen the Tower of London?" the answer is "No, and neither have you." '

Visitors should allow at least half a day to see what the Tower has to offer. Those who have the time may wish to attend the Anglican service held in St Peter *Ad Vincula* every Sunday at 11 a.m. and experience the Tower as few ever see it – without visitors – no prior arrangements are needed. Those who wish to attend the Ceremony of the Keys, the nightly ritual which attends the locking of this mighty fortress, must however apply beforehand in writing. (Allow at least three weeks. Tickets will not be sent to hotels.)

Westminster Abbey

Westminster Abbey – more properly the Collegiate Church of St Peter at Westminster – is one of twelve 'Royal Peculiars', whose dean is answerable directly to the monarch rather than coming under the jurisdiction of a local bishop. This special status reflects the abbey's unique role as the coronation church where every sovereign since 1066 (except Edward V and Edward VIII) has been crowned. Many sharp comments were made about the monarchy following the death of Diana, Princess of Wales. Few, however, criticised the funeral service which the Chapter improvised so brilliantly in a week or questioned that the Abbey was the only fitting place for it. The Abbey also serves as 'the parish church of the Commonwealth' and as such organises many ecumenical services embracing not only different strands of Christianity but non-Christian faiths as well. As if to underline this ecumenism in July 1998 ten statues of 'modern martyrs', including Nobel Peace Prize winners Dr Martin Luther King and Oscar Romero were added to the Abbey above the west doorway.

Legend attributes to Saebehrt (Siebert), king of the East Saxons (*see p 22*), the establishment in 604 of the first church on this site, then the marshy wilderness of Thorney Island in the delta of the River Tyburn. St Dunstan, briefly bishop of London and creator of the basic form of the coronation service in 973, certainly re-established a Benedictine monastery here in line with the best reformed Continental practice. Edward the Confessor's state-of-the-art abbey church (*see p 27*) was replaced by Henry III, an ardent adherent of his cult. Between 1245 and 1269 the present choir, transepts and chapter house were completed, together with parts of the cloisters and one bay of the nave. Henry himself helped to carry the bones of the Confessor to their present resting-place in the chapel behind the high altar. (The present shrine, however, is substantially a restoration dating from the reign of Mary Tudor.)

The overall design of Henry III's abbey, a distinctive blending of French and English elements, was inspired by the Francophile monarch's admiration for the recently completed cathedral at Rheims and the Sainte Chapelle in Paris; its architect was Henry de Reyns (i.e. possibly of Rheims, though he seems to have been English and may therefore have been from Rayne in Essex). A special feature of the lay-out was the provision for a spacious 'theatre', at the junction of the choir and transepts, where the coronation ritual could be performed with maximum solemnity, display and participation. After a break of a century the nave was completed under the direction of Henry Yevele, who modestly ignored the new styles of his own day and faithfully followed through his predecessor's notions in the interests of aesthetic coherence and unity. Further work continued intermittently until the Reformation and the final major project was not completed until 1745. This was the building of the West Towers, designed by Wren and Hawksmoor, which give the Abbey its best-known aspect.

Apart from serving as a monastery the Abbey in medieval times also housed the Pyx, the standard measures against which coins were judged, and the Crown jewels, until 1303, when some of them were stolen (*see p 244*). For over two centuries the House of Commons met in the chapter house. The turbulence of the Reformation brought the dissolution of the monastic house, but the Abbey's royal associations saved its statuary and art treasures from wholesale destruction, though Cromwell's men treated it with scant regard a century later. To compensate for the loss of its traditional revenues, the Abbey from the dissolution onwards allowed those who could pay for the privilege to be buried there. This helps to explain why today it has some 5,000 graves and memorials. According to the poet Alexander Pope the painter Sir Godfrey Kneller vowed on his deathbed 'By God I will not be buried in Westminster . . . they do bury fools there.' His wish was respected but his monument can be seen in the south choir aisle. Designed by Kneller himself, it was sculpted by Rysbrack; Pope confessed that the epitaph he wrote for it were the worst lines he had ever penned. Nelson is said to have proclaimed before his battle at Cape St Vincent 'Westminster Abbey or Victory!' Ironically he was to be buried in St Paul's (*see p 257*).

THE NAVE

Visitors are struck by both the length and height of the nave. The view to the high altar is cut off by Blore's gilded pseudo-medieval screen, but soaring columns lead the eye up over a hundred feet to the ceiling of what Pevsner has called 'the most French of all English Gothic churches.' As the eye travels back down it is caught by the handsome Waterford crystal chandeliers, a gift of the Guinness family to mark the 900th anniversary of the Abbey in 1965. The stained glass windows of the north aisle commemorate other benefactors and builders. Look out for Henry III who cradles in his arm a model of the half-completed church of his dreams.

MEMORIALS

In the centre of the nave lie the Tomb of the Unknown Warrior (*see p 189*), as well as memorials to Churchill, Peabody (*see p 155*) and the missionary-explorer David Livingstone. Architect Charles Barry's (*see p 132*) brass shows the ground-plan of the Houses of Parliament. Clustered around the south side of the nave, near the west door, are memorials to Baden-Powell (*see p 168*), Mountbatten and F.D. Roosevelt, as well as a contemporary portrait of Richard II, usually regarded as the first accurate likeness of an English monarch. On the opposite side, in the north aisle, is 'Radicals' Corner' where the memorials range from Fox (*see p 103*) to Lloyd George and Attlee. At the eastern end of the nave Newton (designed by Kent, sculpted by Rysbrack) presides over a truly international conclave of scientists including the Englishmen Darwin and Lister, the German Herschel, the Scottish Kelvin, the New Zealander Rutherford and the Australian Florey.

Moving towards the Royal Chapels one stands in the shadow of the organ and near memorials which honour two great abbey organists – Orlando Gibbons and Henry Purcell. Floor plaques record the names of such modern British composers as Elgar, Walton and Britten.

The north transept is dominated by Victorian statesmen. Palmerston, Gladstone, Disraeli and Peel, contrastingly robed, gartered and decorated, stare and glare past each other. Note also the nearby huge memorials to General Wolfe, draped with Canadian flags (*see p 260*) and to the brilliant Scottish judge Lord Mansfield – who explicitly said he didn't want one, as the lengthy inscription makes clear.

The visitor then passes a row of side-chapels stuffed with tombs and their attendant tales. Note the Islip rebus, the gargantuan 36-foot monument to Hunsdon, commander of Elizabeth I's personal bodyguard, the slab with a space for a second wife, who declined the honour, and the enigmatic Popham memorial, whose (politically) embarrassing lettering has been turned towards the wall to cover it up. A separate side-chapel beyond these houses the remains of Elizabeth I and her half-sister, Mary Tudor, ironically buried in the same tomb, and a small casket, containing the alleged bones of the 'Princes in the Tower' (*see p 247*).

HENRY VII'S CHAPEL

Henry VII's chapel is undoubtedly the jewel in the Abbey's crown. Originally intended to honour his uncle, the saintly, martyred Henry VI (*see p 247*) it became the resting-place of its builder. A notoriously stingy sovereign, Henry spared no expense for once, lavishing £14,000 on the project, enough to pay for three artillery forts or six battleships. The ceiling, a delicate cobweb of fan-vaulting, was almost certainly the work of the Vertue brothers who were also responsible for the contemporary St George's Chapel at Windsor. As the eye travels downwards it is inevitably arrested by the banners of the Knights of the Bath whose chapel this is. Their intricately carved stalls are festooned with exquisite plates carrying the armorial bearings of former members of the order. The marble chequered floor covers the tombs of Edward VI, James I and

George II, the last monarch to be buried in the Abbey. Behind the altar lie superb effigies of Henry VII and his queen, the work of Torrigiano, who had fled to England after a brawl in which he broke Michelangelo's nose. Behind this a floor slab marks the spot where Cromwell briefly lay. Beyond that, in the impressive RAF chapel, the ashes of Second World War commanders Trenchard and Dowding lie undisturbed. On leaving the chapel the visitor passes a glass case containing George VI's naval sword, with which he conferred the honour of knighthood.

EDWARD THE CONFESSOR'S CHAPEL

Edward the Confessor's chapel contains the tomb of Henry V, victor of Agincourt; his 'Kate' sleeps in her own chapel above him. Around the Confessor's shrine lie the last resting-places of Edward I and Eleanor of Castile, of Richard II and Anne of Bohemia (their intertwined hands long vandalised away) and of Philippa of Hainault and Edward III, the sunken left cheek of whose effigy betrays the effect of the stroke which followed her death and left him the feeble victim of his unscrupulous mistress, Alice Perrers. The most important treasure of this chapel is the Coronation Chair, a sturdy oak throne, once incorporating the legendary Stone of Scone on which medieval Scottish kings were crowned. The stone was finally returned to Scotland in 1997. Every English monarch since Edward II in 1308 has been crowned in this chair.

The side-chapel on the south side of the Henry VII chapel contains the flamboyant tomb of Mary Queen of Scots, the remains of Charles II, William and Mary, Anne and Lady Margaret Beaufort, mother of Henry VII, patron of Caxton and founder of two Cambridge colleges. The face and hands of her effigy are considered to be one of Torrigiano's greatest achievements. Near the entrance are discreet wall-plaques to the memory of imperial administrators such as Milner and Curzon.

The Coronation Chair

POET'S CORNER

Geoffrey Chaucer (*see pp 44–5*) probably found his place in what has become Poet's Corner, not as a tribute to his literary standing but because when he died he was a tenant of the Abbey and had also supervised some of its building work. Near him lie Spenser, Dryden, Johnson, (*see p 102*), Sheridan, Browning and Tennyson, Dickens (*see p 143*) and literally dozens of other novelists and poets. Surveying the scene are Roubiliac's striking monument to Handel (*see p 102*), Epstein's bold bust of William Blake (*see p 128*) and two colourful wall-paintings of saints beside the door leading to the intimate St Faith's chapel (where communion is celebrated at 8 a.m. daily). Before passing into the cloisters visitors should note the new memorials to entertainer Nöel Coward and broadcaster Richard Dimbleby, whose single-handed commentary on the first ever televised coronation (*see p 212*) was a *tour de force*.

The Chapter House and Cloisters

The cloisters give access to the startlingly light chapter house, with its amazingly preserved medieval tile floor and to the museum which houses some of the abbey treasures and a collection of the wax effigies used in royal and state funerals. (Charles II is said to be a particularly good likeness). The cloisters also contain further interesting memorials – to Clementi ('Father of the Piano'), to Halley, of comet fame, to Aphra Behn, Restoration dramatist and spy, to the blind Baron Fraser (with an inscription in Braille) and to the circumnavigators Drake, Cook and Chichester.

Westminster School

The quiet sanctuary of Dean's Yard affords a glimpse of venerable Westminster School whose old boys include Ben Jonson (*see p 61*), Sir Christopher Wren (*see p 78*) Edward Gibbon (*see p 98*) and Lord Lloyd Webber. Outside, on the south side of Parliament Square, stands the late medieval church of St Margaret's, Westminster where John Milton, Samuel Pepys (*see p 72*) and Winston Churchill were all married and where Sir Walter Raleigh (*see p 245*) is probably buried; Caxton (*see p 49*) certainly is. St Margaret's has served as the parish church of the House of Commons since 1614 and were it not metaphorically as well as literally overshadowed by the Abbey would be visited and perused far more often.

St Paul's Cathedral

The present St Paul's is the fifth to stand on the commanding site which is one of the two highest points in the City and which may once have housed a Roman temple dedicated to Diana.

The first cathedral, probably a modest wooden structure, was built in 604 by St Ethelbert, king of Kent, England's first Christian monarch and the patron of St Mellitus, bishop of London. As a key centre for the reconversion of England it was appropriately dedicated to the missionary St Paul, who has ever since been London's patron saint. A sword, emblem of St Paul's martyrdom in Rome, forms part of the City's coat of arms. After the first cathedral burned down it was rebuilt in stone (675–85) by St Erkenwald, fourth bishop of London, whose own tomb became a scene of miracles and a major shrine for medieval pilgrims.

Old St Paul's

The second St Paul's was destroyed by Vikings in 961 and its successor by fire in 1087. The fourth cathedral – 'Old St Paul's' – survived for almost six centuries. Begun by the Normans in Caen stone, it was extended over the centuries to become both longer and higher than today's cathedral which is itself second only to St Peter's in Rome amongst European churches. The west end boasted bell towers so huge they were used as prisons, and the east end a rose window so dazzling it was imitated as a motif on fashionable garments. Walled and gated, the cathedral became the focal point of a complex of religious buildings which included a parish church, the bishop's palace, a school and a campanile, the Jesus bell tower, which three times a year was used to summon Londoners to a 'folk-moot' (town meeting) at Paul's Cross to hear royal and papal proclamations. Thomas Carlyle was to call it 'The Times newspaper of the Middle Ages.' The cross itself served as a pulpit for outdoor services and it was here also that Tyndale's unauthorised English translation of the Bible and the works of Martin Luther were publicly burned.

It was in St Paul's churchyard that Malory set the scene in Morte d'Arthur in which Arthur pulls the sword from the stone to become rightful king. The area around St Paul's churchyard later developed as the home of the London booktrade. John Newbery, the first publisher to specialise in children's books (*Mother Goose* and *Goody Two Shoes* were two of his titles) is commemorated by a plaque set in the wall a few yards west of the Japanese bookshop on the north side of the cathedral today. The turmoils of the Reformation saw a deterioration in both the fabric and the standing of the cathedral. The reredos and high altar were demolished and the nave became a common thoroughfare, 'Paul's Walk', used as both a short-cut and a shopping-mall. In 1561 the roof and spire were destroyed by fire; the roof was replaced but the spire was not. In 1569 the first public lottery in England was drawn at the west door; but the proceeds went to pay for national defence, not the refurbishment of the cathedral.

In 1628 William Laud became bishop of London and Inigo Jones the king's surveyor – a combination of willpower and talent which led to the clearance of nearby slum properties and the construction of an impressive, but to modern eyes incongruous, classical portico along the west façade. Restoration was interrupted by the civil war, when Cromwell's troops used the nave to stall their horses (until the roof fell in again), the porch was let out for workshops and Puritan fervour vented itself by vandalising windows, carvings and effigies and by demolishing the bishop's palace.

Christopher Wren

In 1663 the 31-year-old Christopher Wren was asked to survey the ruinous cathedral and sketch a programme of repairs. His strong advice – demolish and rebuild – was rejected; so he then drew up six different plans, one of which was finally accepted a week before the outbreak of the Great Fire – which did ensure that demolition and rebuilding would, indeed, be the only practical course.

Wren's initial concept of a design in the shape of a Greek cross was turned down flat as too radical and continental. His second design, embodied in a 'Great Model' (which cost three times as much as his annual fee to put together) won the approval of Charles II but was also dismissed by the cathedral authorities, reducing Wren, quite literally, to tears. His third attempt, known as the 'Warrant Design', was authorised in 1675 by a royal warrant which empowered the architect 'to make some variations rather ornamental than essential, as from time to time he should see proper.' These variations were in fact to include shortening the whole nave and dispensing entirely with the planned steeple. It was replaced with a dome, an unprecedented element for an English cathedral. Weighing 64,000 tons it consists, in fact, of two domes, with a brick cone inserted between them to support the 700-ton golden ball and cross which surmounts the whole.

Wren also headed off possible further modifications of his basic design by

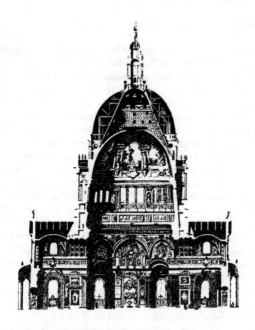

Part of Christopher Wren's original plan for St Paul's, a westerly view from the south transept showing the proposed three domes in cross-section.

organising construction to realise the whole plan, from foundations upwards, layer by layer as it were, rather than, as was usually the case, section by section, starting at the east end and moving westwards in successive stages. This meant that no one could impose cut-backs without visibly sabotaging the entire enterprise; but it also meant that no service could be held in the still uncompleted building until 1697. A supervising parliamentary committee vented its frustration at such slow progress by vengefully holding back half of Wren's annual fee of £200. It took a personal petition to Queen Anne, after completion, to get the arrears paid off.

Wren's masterpiece is a triumph of art, science and organisation, the supreme creation of a man hailed by the hypercritical John Evelyn as a 'miracle of youth'. An Oxford professor (of astronomy) in his twenties and later president of the Royal Society, Wren combined aesthetic, engineering and administrative talents to an unusual degree. He was also able to select, enthuse and control a fine international team of craftsmen.

'RESURGAM'

Thomas Strong and William Kempster, his master-masons, were English but his master wood-carver, Grinling Gibbons, Evelyn's discovery, although English, too, had been born and bred in the Netherlands. St Paul's superlative decorative iron-work was wrought by a Frenchman, Jean Tijou, the organ was by the German, Schmidt, and much of the sculpture by a Dane, Caius Gabriel Cibber. One of Cibber's most interesting pieces is the phoenix in the pediment of the south transept, which soars above the motto '*Resurgam*' (I shall rise again). When Wren called for a workman to bring him a piece of rubble to mark the centre-point of his proposed dome the man turned up a fragment of a grave-stone with that single prophetic word already carved on it. Wren took it as a happy omen. The prominent statues of Saints Paul, Peter and James on the west pediment, and of Queen Anne, outside the west front, are the work of Francis Bird. Anne, during whose reign the work was completed, is surrounded by four figures representing her claimed territories – Britain, Ireland, France and America, the last being an Indian brave with his foot on a severed head.

Wren's St Paul's was, until the present century, the only English cathedral to have been built within his lifetime by a single architect – who was at the same time supervising the construction of over 50 churches, plus half-a-dozen other major projects. The cathedral cost £721,552, most of which was raised by a tax on the coal imported from Newcastle to London to light the capital's fires, which meant that fire restored what fire had destroyed.

Wren was among the first to be honoured with burial in his cathedral. The epitaph, composed by his son, is inscribed both above his modest tomb in the crypt and on the floor of the crossing, beneath the dome and is brilliant in its cryptic simplicity – *Lector, si monumentum requiris, circumspice* (Reader, if you seek his monument, look around you). A generation later a wit was moved to observe:

> No thought arises of the life to come.
> For, tho' superb, not solemn is the place,
> The mind but wanders o'er the distant spece,
> Where, 'stead of thinking on their God, most men
> Forget his presence to remember Wren.

If Wren's master-vision was substantially realised in his lifetime this did not mean that the embellishment of the cathedral ceased. Bells, presented by the City livery companies, were not added until late in Victoria's reign when the cathedral also acquired elaborate mosaic ceilings by G.F. Watts and Salviati, as well as Holman Hunt's celebrated painting *The Light of the World*. Its recent acquisitions include a striking modern sculpture by Henry Moore *Mother and Child*.

To the faithful, St Paul's stands as a place of worship. To all Londoners it is a symbol of civic pride. Over the last two centuries it has acquired further functions, as the last resting-place of Britain's great men and women and as the focus for major national ceremonies.

MEMORIALS

The only significant memorial to have survived the Great Fire was Nicholas Stone's haunting marble statue of the poet and former dean of St Paul's, John Donne (1573–1631). Donne, wearing his own shroud and perched on a funerary urn – which still bears visible scorch-marks from its ordeal – can be seen in the south choir aisle. The first new public memorial to be erected (1795) was a statue of prison reformer John Howard, who is matched at opposite corners of the area beneath the dome by near contemporaries – the painter Sir Joshua Reynolds, lexicographer Dr Samuel Johnson and oriental linguist, Sir William Jones. National heroes whose memorials lie in St Paul's include Nelson, Wellington and Kitchener. Nelson is buried beneath the very centre of the dome in a coffin made from the mast of the French flagship at the Battle of the Nile, which is itself encased in a sarcophagus originally made for Cardinal Wolsey. Wellington's monument is the largest of them all but the effigy of Kitchener, military supremo of the Great War, lies in a separate chapel near the north-west entrance; his body lies beneath the North Sea.

The last person whose actual body was interred in St Paul's was Admiral Earl Beatty (1936) Britain's chief naval commander during the Great War. A neo-classical tablet in the crypt pays unique honour to the memory of Pilot Officer Fiske, an American pilot killed in August 1940, flying as a volunteer with the RAF during the Battle of Britain. The most recent military memorials record the names of the men killed in the 1982 Falklands war and 1992 Gulf war; for the first time these are listed in alphabetical order, without distinction of rank.

Although some men of letters are commemorated in St Paul's (Blake, Bulwer-Lytton, de la Mare) they are heavily outnumbered by artists such as Constable, Lawrence, Millais and Munnings; Turner and Lord Leighton have memorials to rival any general. Nor are the artists only British, for they include the Americans Benjamin West, John Singer Sargent and Edwin Austin Abbey, the Dutch Alma-Tadema and the Swiss Fuseli. Other distinguished figures include the architects Dance and Lutyens, the composers Novello and Sullivan, 'Lawrence of Arabia' and Florence Nightingale, founder of the modern profession of nursing.

Major public ceremonies which have taken place at St Paul's include thanksgivings for the duke of Marlborough's great victory at Blenheim (1704), and, prematurely, for the ending of the Napoleonic wars (1814); the funerals of Nelson (1806), Wellington (1852) and Churchill (1965); the jubilee celebrations of Queen Victoria (1897), George V (1935) and Queen Elizabeth II (1977); and the marriage of the Prince of Wales and Lady Diana Spencer (1981) and the memorial service for the victims of the World Trade Center atrocity (2001).

SECOND WORLD WAR

During the Second World War St Paul's became for the nation a symbol of London's defiance against destruction. Over 160 acres around it were laid waste but, thanks to the devoted efforts of some 100 volunteer fire-watchers, the cathedral itself was protected from incendiary bombs. It did, however, suffer two substantial direct hits from high-explosive devices. One of these damaged the north transept; the original decoration has not been replaced and the scars remain as a deliberate reminder of the past. The other hit smashed the high altar and the Jesus chapel immediately behind it; these were reconstructed (financed by public donations collected on the streets and in cinemas) to incorporate an American Memorial Chapel to mark the nation's gratitude and respect for the 28,000 US citizens killed on active service while based in the UK. The altar and its magnificent baldachino honour the war dead of the Commonwealth.

To the south of the cathedral, on the other side of the road, stands a striking memorial to London's wartime Fire Brigade bearing the names of over a thousand fire fighters killed during the Blitz.

Royal Palaces

Greenwich

The first royal palace to be built separately as such was at Greenwich and was the residence of the scholarly Humphrey, duke of Gloucester and brother of Henry V. Completed around 1427 it was known as Bella Court; moated and fortified, it was still a stronghold as well as a home, and was surrounded by a walled area of 200 acres, which now forms Greenwich Park. Margaret of Anjou, having seen to the disposal of the former owner (who was unwise enough to lend it to her for her honeymoon with the pious and no doubt frustrating Henry VI) renamed it Placentia, the pleasant place, and installed glass windows. Henry VIII was born at Greenwich and it became his favourite residence. He greatly extended the palace complex, adding a tiltyard and a banqueting-hall, with a ceiling painted by Holbein. Nearby he established armouries, staffed by German and Flemish craftsmen. The park afforded him hunting and hawking and at the neighbouring dockyards of Woolwich and Deptford he could supervise the development of his new navy in person.

Mary Tudor and Elizabeth I were both born at Greenwich and Edward VI died there. The first Italian 'masquerade' to be performed in England was organised at Greenwich as part of the Christmas festivities for 1516 and it was at Greenwich that Elizabeth revived the ceremony of the Maundy money in 1573, signed the death-warrant of Mary, Queen of Scots and ostentatiously stepped over a muddy puddle on Sir Walter Raleigh's chivalrously-proffered cloak.

THE QUEEN'S HOUSE

After Elizabeth's death Greenwich passed to Anne of Denmark, James I's consort and it was for her that Inigo Jones began the exquisite 'Queen's House' (1618–35), the first Palladian building in England and the first to use a hall as a reception area in its own right. The Queen's House has now been superbly restored, with facsimile wall-hangings, to look as it would have done when Henrietta Maria was in residence as queen dowager in 1662. The rest of the palace was stripped of valuables by the parliamentarians during the Civil War and used first as a biscuit factory, and then as an internment camp for Dutch prisoners of war, before being demolished to make way for Wren's handsome Royal Naval Hospital, built both as a home for ex-sailors and as a memorial to the five-day battle of La Hogue where the French fleet was annihilated.

GREENWICH PARK

Greenwich Park still shows traces of the formal gardens in the French manner designed by Le Notre, who never actually came to England and seems to have been unaware that the site was on a steep slope; its amenities include a 'snow well', possibly England's first deep-freeze. On the foundations of an old fort, Duke Humphrey's Tower, Wren built the first Royal Observatory, which marks the Greenwich meridian. Nearby stands a massive statue of General Wolfe, conqueror of Quebec (1759), a gift of the Canadian people.

Nonsuch Palace

Like Greenwich, Nonsuch Palace vanished centuries ago. Built by Henry VIII in 1538 as a hunting-lodge and guest-house for foreign visitors, it was intended to be so fabulous that 'Nonesuch' could compare with it. The effect was to be achieved not by its size, but by the splendour of its decorations in the new Renaissance style, the work of a team of Italian craftsmen led by one Nicolas Belin of Modena who produced a series of stucco reliefs framed in elaborately-carved slate. The palace eventually passed to Charles II's extravagant mistress, Barbara Villiers, who sold it on to Lord Berkeley, who demolished it to use the stone to build a mansion at nearby Epsom.

Whitehall Palace

Whitehall Palace has disappeared almost as completely as Nonsuch. Originally York Place, the London residence of the archbishop of York, who ranks second only to Canterbury in the hierarchy of the English church, it was greatly enlarged when Thomas Wolsey held that office. After his fall from favour, Henry VIII took it over, renamed it and added a turreted gateway, new gardens and orchards, a bowling alley and steps leading down to the river. A tiltyard stood on the site of what is now Horse Guards Parade and tennis courts and a cockpit where William Kent's neo-classical Treasury Building (1734) now stands. The thoroughfare now known as Whitehall continued to run right through the entire palace complex, whose two sides were connected by overarching gateways. Henceforth Whitehall became the chief London residence of the court and provided the setting for Henry's weddings to both Anne Boleyn (1533) and Jane Seymour (1536), as well as for his death (1547). By the reign of James I the palace contained some 2,000 rooms and covered more than 20 acres. A discerning French visitor was distinctly unimpressed, judging it to be 'nothing but a heap of Houses, erected at divers times, and of different models.'

BANQUETING HOUSE

Inigo Jones and his son-in-law, John Webb, drew up grandiose plans for further expansion; but only his magnificent Banqueting House was completed (1622). It was the first purely Renaissance building in London and is the only part of Whitehall Palace to have survived. A century after it was built, the ultra-critical Horace Walpole considered it 'the model of the most pure and beautiful taste'. The ceiling, painted by Rubens, celebrates in complex allegory the benefits of wise Stuart rule. With savage irony the victorious parliamentarians chose the Banqueting House as the setting for the execution of Charles I in 1649. His statue, by the Huguenot Hubert Le Sueur, now gazes down upon the site of his scaffold. Lord Protector Cromwell installed himself in the palace in the king's place and sold off his wonderful collection of 460 paintings, which included no less than nine Raphaels and 28 Titians.

Cromwell died at Whitehall in 1658 and it was from Whitehall that James II fled 30 years later; his daughter, Mary, and son-in-law William of Orange, were jointly offered the crown at a ceremony in the Banqueting House, the last great royal occasion to take place there. William found the damp, smokey atmosphere around Whitehall aggravated his asthma and transferred the court to Kensington Palace. In 1698, allegedly through the carelessness of a Dutch laundry-maid hurriedly drying washing before an open fire, the palace was razed to its foundations in a unstoppable conflagration.

St James's

Henry VIII built St James's Palace from scratch, having demolished the hospital for leprous women which stood on its site and pensioned off its inhabitants. The only part of his original construction to survive is the impressive brick gatehouse, with its octagonal turrets, but the buildings subsequently erected are still grouped around four courts, according to the first plan. Here Mary Tudor died, Charles I spent the night before his execution and Charles II walked his spaniels on the way to and from the house of Nell Gwyn, who lived conveniently nearby on Pall Mall. Between the burning of Whitehall and the completion of Buckingham Palace St James's was the principal royal residence in London and technically it remains so to this day.

Ambassadors are credited to the Court of St James's, even though they no longer go there to present their credentials, and the accession of a new monarch is still proclaimed from the balcony in Friary Court. Queen Anne refurbished St James's which still contains carvings by Grinling Gibbons and a stable block by Hawksmoor. In 1712 the three-year-old Samuel Johnson was brought here to be touched by her for 'the King's Evil' (scrofula), Anne being the last monarch to keep up the practice, which dated back to Edward the Confessor. She also kept a court jester but banned smoking and the wearing of spectacles. The stifling respectability of Anne's court was replaced by coarse licence under Hanoverian George I, who refused to learn English and installed his buxom German mistresses in the palace with no attempt at discretion. When he tired of them he looked to his two Turkish attendants, Mustapha and Mahomet, (who had saved his life at the siege of Vienna in 1685), to provide him with other companions for nocturnal diversion.

St James's has been well described as looking like an Oxford college that has somehow got stranded in the West End. In 1776 Sir John Fielding wrote scornfully that 'The buildings that compose this merely nominal palace ... are low, plain and ignoble ... It reflects no honour on the kingdom and is the jest of foreigners.' Nevertheless George III, George IV, Queen Victoria and George V were all married there. Nowadays it houses the offices of the Lord Chamberlain and residences for the officials of the royal household.

Kensington Palace

Kensington Palace, originally a modest gentleman's country residence, was bought by William of Orange in 1689 and hastily upgraded by Wren and Hawksmoor. The route through Hyde Park to the palace, now a fashionable ride known as Rotten Row (i.e. *route du roi*), was illuminated by hanging lanterns as a precaution against robbers and was therefore London's first example of street-lighting. Mary, William's consort, was to die of smallpox at Kensington at the tragically early age of 32, having gallantly ordered out of her new home everyone who had not already had the illness. The elegant orangery was added for Queen Anne, who used it for tea- and supper-parties, with a small orchestra discreetly screened by lemon and gum trees. A keen gardener, Anne also uprooted the newly-planted French flower-beds with their symmetrical hedges and battalions of Dutch tulips and relaid the grounds in a rambling English style. Like her sister Mary, Anne died at Kensington, but, less appealingly, of apoplexy brought on by over-eating, as did George II, also of apoplexy (in his lavatory). George II's wise, cultured and long-suffering wife, Queen Caroline, extended the palace gardens, adding the Broad Walk and Round Pond; but her revolving summer-house has, alas, long since gone.

QUEEN VICTORIA

The future Queen Victoria – 'plump as a partridge' – was born and brought up in Kensington Palace, held her accession council there and celebrated the event by demanding a bedroom of her own, separate from her mother, for the first time in her life. After her departure for Buckingham Palace the state apartments were neglected for half-a-century until restored and opened to the public by the queen herself to mark her eightieth birthday.

Nowadays Kensington Palace provides London apartments for Princess Margaret, Prince and Princess Michael of Kent and the Duke and Duchess of Gloucester. It remains, however, the only working royal palace in London which can be visited by the public. Among its attractions are William Kent's luxuriant painted ceiling and clever *trompe l'oeil* 'illusionist gallery' above the King's Grand Staircase, where two-dimensional courtiers on the walls and ceiling appear to be looking curiously at the figures mounting the stairs towards them. The brilliantly arranged court dress collection reflects the fashions and protocol of two centuries.

Buckingham Palace

The core of Buckingham Palace was built (1702–5) for John Sheffield, Duke of Buckingham and Normanby on land originally planted with 10,000 mulberry trees by James I in the hope of starting an English silk industry. The trees were, however, of the variety which silk-worms won't eat, but, one said to have come from Persia and planted in 1609, still survives in the palace's 45-acre gardens. George III, who disliked nearby St James's Palace, bought the house to serve as a modest private residence. His son, George IV, ordered John Nash to turn it into a palace. The project went three times over budget and was an aesthetic disaster. Friedrich von Raumer, having toured the still uncompleted site in 1835, declared:

> I never saw anything that might be pronounced a more total failure, in every respect ... For my own part, I would not live in it rent-free; I should vex myself all the day long with the fantastic mixture of every style of architecture and decoration – the absence of all pure taste – the total want of feeling of measure and proportion.... In the same apartment, fragments of Egypt, Greece, Etruria, Rome, and the Middle Ages, all confusedly mingled together ... The best thing that could happen would be if Aladdin, with his magic lamp, would come and transport it into an African desert.

After the burning of the Old Palace of Westminster (1834) the half-finished project was considered, and rejected, as a possible home for parliament. When Victoria moved in (1837) the plumbing was still defective and, while some of the doors wouldn't close, many of the windows wouldn't open. It was left to Edward Blore to sort out the shambles. He enclosed the existing three-sided courtyard by adding the east front which looks down the Mall and gives the building its familiar face today. Blore also removed to its present site at the north end of Park Lane, the Marble Arch, modelled by Nash on Rome's Arch of Constantine, which was the ceremonial entrance to the palace from 1827 to 1851. The present Portland stone façade of the east front is the work of Sir Aston Webb (1913), the face-lift being paid for out of surplus funds from the construction of the Queen Victoria Memorial (1911) which stands in front of it.

After the death of Prince Albert in 1861 Victoria retired into deep mourning to become 'the widow of Windsor'. In 1873 the deserted palace was placed at the disposal of the visiting Shah of Persia who ruined the carpets by eating his meals on the floor and shocked his neighbours by watching a prize-fight in the palace grounds. He was also said to have had one of his servants strangled with a bow-string and cremated in the garden.

Buckingham Palace today contains over 600 rooms, though the queen's suite of private apartments (on the first floor of the north wing overlooking Green Park) consists of only a dozen. The facilities available to the royal family when living 'over the shop' as the Duke of Edinburgh puts it, include a swimming-pool, cinema and nuclear fall-out shelter.

THE QUEEN'S GALLERY

Public access to the main Palace is limited to a few weeks in summer, when the Queen holidays in Scotland. But the Queen's Gallery is open year round to exhibit treasures from the royal collection, the world's greatest private holding of Old Masters, Sèvres porcelain, Fabergé jewellery and postage stamps. The gallery stands on the site of the former chapel, wrecked by a lone German bomber on 13 September 1940, an incident which is said to have prompted the then queen (now the Queen Mother) to say 'now I can look the East End in the face.'

THE ROYAL MEWS

A few hundred yards past the Queen's Gallery is the Royal Mews, where visitors can see the monarch's official cars and carriages, including the Gold State Coach (1762) used for coronations, the Irish State Coach (1851) used for the opening of parliament, the State Landau, used for visiting heads of state, and the romantic Glass Coach (1910) used for the wedding of the Prince and Princess of Wales.

London's Parks:
The Lungs of London

London's parks are one of its special glories and range from ancient common land, like Hampstead Heath, where local people for centuries could graze a cow or gather firewood, to formally sculptured masterpieces like the gardens of Chiswick House (*see p 86*) or Syon Park (*see p 89*). The great royal parks, which enable one to walk from Bayswater to Trafalgar Square through greenery all the way, form the historic core of this legacy. Public parks, as such, date only from the first half of the last century, when a parliamentary committee startled itself with the conclusion that 'the spring to industry which occasional relaxation gives, seems quite as necessary to the poor as to the rich'. It recommended the laying-out of parks in the East End where 'there is not a single place reserved as a Park or Public Walk; yet there is no place in London where such improvements are more imperatively called for.' The earnest hope behind this plea was that not only would the lower orders be afforded opportunity for healthy exercise but that they would also receive spiritual and social benefits from contact with nature and the politer classes and be distracted from their usual recreations – 'drinking houses, dog fights and boxing matches.'

The belated result of this realisation was the establishment of Victoria Park, Battersea Park, Kennington Park, Finsbury Park and Southwark Park, all in the poorer areas of the city. Charitable bequests (e.g. Waterlow Park, Highgate) and municipal foresight have since enlarged the number of Greater London's open spaces of more than one acre to almost 1,700. Particular tribute should be paid to the City Corporation, which saved Epping Forest for Londoners (*see p 152*) and to the London County Council, which initiated a policy of buying up private estates and converting them into public parks.

The first (1892) was at Brockwell, near Brixton, where the LCC's first superintendent of parks, Lt. Col. Sexby, planted the old walled kitchen garden with all the flowers mentioned in Shakespeare's plays. Later acquisitions included Valentines Park, Ilford (1899); Springfield Park, Hackney (1902); Ruskin Park, Camberwell (1907); The Rookery at Streatham (1913) and Danson Park at Bexley (1925).

Hyde Park

When joined with Kensington Gardens *(see p 262)* this huge area is bigger than the entire City of London. The largest of all the royal parks, it began as Henry VIII's personal hunting-ground for hare, partridge, pheasant and heron; it still has almost a hundred species of birds. Charles I opened it to the citizens of London. Cromwell tried to sell it off. Charles II took it back, built a wall round it and re-opened it again. It has since been the site of the Great Exhibition of 1851 *(see p 137)*, the scene of one of London's most turbulent demonstrations *(see p 157)* and the venue for its largest-ever outdoor concerts. Horace Walpole was robbed here by highwaymen. Wilkes *(see p 109)*, Sheridan and Fox *(see p 103)* all fought duels here. Its features include the fashionable riding-path known as Rotten Row *(see p 262)*, the Serpentine, where Shelley's pregnant wife drowned herself, the Italian Water Garden and a pets' cemetery *(see p 284)*. Its statues honour Queen Victoria, the Duke of Wellington *(see p 112)*, Dr Jenner, the pioneer of vaccination, the god Pan and the goddess Diana and Peter Pan. G.F. Watts' dramatic statue *Physical Energy* was originally modelled to adorn the tomb of Cecil Rhodes in South Africa.

Regent's Park

This was also once Henry VIII's private preserve for the hunt. Cromwell leased it off to smallholders after felling most of its 16,000 trees to build ships for the navy. The park, laid out by Nash *(see p 117)* and surrounded by his superbly flamboyant terraces, now houses London's zoo *(see p 133)*, one of the best rose gardens in Britain, an open-air theatre *(see p 199)* and the official residence of the American ambassador.

Green Park

Once the site of a leper hospice, this was long a favoured duelling-ground and also the location for numerous balloon ascents and firework displays. The mound opposite 119 Piccadilly was once an ice-house where Charles II's summer drinks were chilled.

Holland Park

Parts of seventeenth-century Holland House *(see p 131)* survive as a youth hostel, a restaurant and a gallery. Special features of the park include gardens in the Dutch and Japanese style, exotic yucca plants and even more exotic birds from Africa and South America and the largest area of natural woodland in central London.

Battersea Park

This riverside area was once famed for asparagus, petty criminals and enter-tainments of the most degrading kind. Opened as a park in 1858, it became the favoured venue for early cyclists (*see p 178*) and acquired a novel lay-out of gardens at the time of the 1951 Festival of Britain (*see p 211*). The annual veteran (i.e. 1895–1905) car run to Brighton has started from this park since it began in 1933. There is also a children's zoo, a nature reserve rich in butterflies, a garden specially designed for wheelchair users and London's only peace pagoda, embellished with panels depicting scenes from the life of the Buddha.

Victoria Park

Heretics were once burned here and Bernard Shaw and William Morris addressed political meetings here. During the Second World War Margot Fonteyn presented ballet in the open air. The adornments of the park include a Chinese pagoda which was once the entrance to a Chinese exhibition held in Knightsbridge in 1847 and an elaborate Gothic drinking-fountain which is a memorial to Baroness Burdett-Coutts whose philanthropy to East-Enders won her the first peerage ever awarded to a woman in her own right.

London's parks are very much a living heritage. The glass-houses and band-stands characteristic of the Edwardian era have largely disappeared. The twentieth-century cult of 'active recreation' has led to a proliferation of sports facilities. Contemporary planners now favour 'linear parks' as at Mile End and Burgess Park, Southwark, to provide green corridors through urban wastelands. Ecologists criticise exotic planting and labour-intensive maintenance in favour of native species and the encouragement of wild-life. Another kind of con-servationist demands that parks should not be periodically re-designed but preserved as historic landscapes in their own right.

London Bridge and London's Bridges

The Romans built the first bridge over the Thames. It probably stood about 20 yards downstream (i.e. east) of the present London Bridge, so that people crossing from the south side of the river would carry on up the aptly-named Fish Street Hill to approach the forum and basilica which constituted the focal point of Roman London.

For more than a thousand years London's sole bridge was a wooden one, periodically needing extensive repairs to make good the effects of tides, storms and raiders. In 1014 it was burnt down by King Ethelred of England and King Olaf of Norway to split a besieging force of Danes. (Tooley Street on the south side of London Bridge is a corrupted form of St Olaf's Street. The former St Olave's Grammar School stands at the Tower Bridge end.) Norse poet Ottar Svarte celebrated this dramatic event in verse:

> London Bridge is broken down
> Gold is won and bright renown.

Six centuries later his battle epic resurfaced as a children's rhyme. Between 1176 and 1209 London Bridge was rebuilt in stone under the direction of Peter, chaplain of St Mary Colechurch. The modern office block which stands at the southern end of London Bridge is Colechurch House.

London Bridge became one of the wonders of the medieval world. It had 19 arches and was packed with shops and houses, almost 200 of them by the middle of the fourteenth century. At the northern end was a wooden draw-bridge which could be raised against attackers. At the southern end traitors' heads rotted slowly on pikes over the gateway, a practice begun in 1305 with the display of the head of William Wallace, Scottish patriot, who was executed and dismembered at Smithfield. Other heads to be displayed there included those of peasant rebel Jack Cade (1450), saintly Thomas More (1535) (*see p 51*), and royal hatchet-man Thomas Cromwell (1540). A German visitor in 1598 counted no less than 30 heads on show. If this seems unlikely it should be remembered that they probably represented the accumulation of several years, having been parboiled and tarred before being spiked. The custom was ended after the restoration of the monarchy in 1660.

Among its other attractions London Bridge boasted a chapel dedicated to St Thomas Becket (*see p 33*) (where Peter de Colechurch was buried) and, from 1577, the ornate and imposing Nonsuch House, which had been prefabricated in Holland and shipped over in sections. Another continental innovation was a 'forcier' or pump, erected between the arches at the northern end by Pieter Moritz, a German, and used to raise water from the river to supply nearby houses.

With the commercial expansion of the city, traffic congestion on the bridge, which was effectively only nine-feet wide in parts, became a major problem. It is said that the British convention of driving on the left originated in the attempts of the City Corporation to organise this chaos by inventing the first 'rule of the road'. But the watermen, at least, were not complaining. Congestion on the bridge meant good business for them ferrying the frail or the impatient.

Putney Bridge and Westminster Bridge

London's second bridge, another wooden one, was built, far to the west, at Putney in 1729. Its evident value encouraged the passage of an act of parliament to authorise the building of a bridge at Westminster. This project met fierce opposition from the watermen and the archbishop of Canterbury, who owned the only ferry large enough to carry horses and carts. It operated between Lambeth Palace, the archbishop's London home, and the point on the northern bank where Horseferry Road now meets the river. They were bought off – £25,000 for the watermen and £21,025 for the archbishop. Westminster Bridge, designed by a Swiss engineer, Charles Labelye, opened in 1750 with a style befitting its status – a procession of the chief workmen preceded by trumpets and drums. To keep up the tone local by-laws forbade dogs to cross the bridge and threatened graffiti artists with the death-sentence. Generations of English children have learned by heart Wordsworth's sonnet 'Upon Westminster Bridge' –

> Earth has not anything to show more fair:
> Dull would he be of soul who could pass by
> A sight so touching in its majesty:

Labelye's bridge was replaced by the present iron one in 1854–62.

Blackfriars Bridge

Blackfriars Bridge (1760–9) was designed by Robert Mylne, who had spent much time in Rome with Piranesi and was greatly influenced by him. Officially it was supposed to be named in honour of prime minister William Pitt (the Elder) but the Londoners would have none of it and the name of its location, Blackfriars, stuck instead. The present Blackfriars Bridge was opened in 1869 by Queen Victoria, whose statue stands at the northern end. She was just emerging from seven years of strict mourning for her husband, the beloved Prince Albert. Her absence from public life had been so long that a republican movement had begun to emerge. No doubt to her discomfiture she was loudly hissed – perhaps by the many people whose homes had been demolished to make way for new approaches to the bridge.

Kew, Richmond and Battersea

Four other new bridges were built during the eighteenth century, all upriver – at Kew a wooden bridge (1758–9), followed by a stone one (1783–9), a stone one at Richmond (1774–7) and another wooden one at Battersea (1771–2).

Vauxhall, Waterloo and Southwark

London's first iron bridge, originally known as Regent's Bridge, was built at Vauxhall (1811–16) and replaced by a granite and steel construction (1895–1906), adorned with heroic bronze figures. Vauxhall Bridge was originally begun in masonry by John Rennie until he was dismissed and the cheaper iron version adopted. Rennie, after this setback, went on to great success with three major projects – Waterloo Bridge (1811–17) Southwark Bridge (1815–19) and most important of all, a replacement for London Bridge. Waterloo Bridge, originally to be known as Strand Bridge, was renamed in honour of Wellington's great victory. The Italian sculptor Canova described it as 'the noblest bridge in the world, worth a visit from the remotest corners of the earth.' (The present Waterloo Bridge dates from 1937–42.)

London Bridge

London Bridge was Rennie's masterpiece. In 1758–62 the old bridge had been partially modernised by the removal of its houses and the replacement of the two central arches with a single span to enable larger boats to pass through it. Rennie's replacement (1823–31) was complemented by the construction of King William Street as a new approach road on the northern side. If anything it was too solidly built and its 155,000 tons of granite began to slide slowly into the riverbed. It was replaced in 1967–72 by a concrete version weighing only a third as much. The original was sold for £1,000,000 and re-erected over the Colorado river at Lake Havasu, Arizona where the City Corporation owns an acre of ground and an English pub.

Hammersmith and Hungerford

The nineteenth century saw the construction of new bridges by new means and for new motives. A suspension bridge was built at Hammersmith (1825–7) to encourage building on the south bank of the river and another, Hungerford Bridge (1841–5) to attract trade to the market of the same name, until it was replaced by Charing Cross station 20 years later. Seven railway bridges were also built. In 1877 the Metropolitan Board of Works was empowered to buy all of London's privately-built bridges and abolish their tolls.

Tower Bridge

Tower Bridge (1881–94) was the first bridge to be built downstream from London Bridge. The engineer was John Wolfe-Barry and the architect Sir Horace Jones. It was purposely built in a Gothic style to harmonise with the Tower of London, though in fact this deliberately anachronistic design disguised a superb example of Victorian hi-tech – 'steel skeletons clothed with stone' as the architect himself put it. The high-level footbridge, now mainly used by camera-wielding visitors seeking a panoramic view of the river, was originally incorporated to allow pedestrian traffic to continue uninterrupted whenever the 1,000-ton bascules were raised to admit large ships to the Pool of London. In fact this operation took so little time that the footbridge was closed after a few years and has only recently re-opened, primarily as a tourist attraction.

In 1976 the Tower's original steam-powered, Newcastle-built hydraulic machinery was replaced by an electrical mechanism, though it had never once failed in over 80 years.

Dartford

In 1991 the Queen Elizabeth, the Second bridge was opened further down-stream at Dartford, to relieve the strain on the over-crowded Dartford Tunnel, a key link both for daily commuters and Channel-bound business and holiday traffic. This enabled bridge and tunnel to work in tandem, each operating a one-way system.

Millennium Bridge

The elegant Millennium Bridge, designed by the leading architectural practice of Ove Arup, was opened by the Queen in June 2000 and closed a couple of days later. Intended to provide a pedestrian passage from St Paul's to Tate Modern and the Globe, it exhibited an unanticipated tendency to wobble alarmingly when large numbers of pedestrians actually used it. Although the designers averred that the bridge was actually safe engineers spent over a year fitting damping devices to ensure that it felt safe.

Cathedrals of the Steam Age: London's Railway Termini

In one respect, at least, London's architectural heritage can be said to owe little to foreign models. The British invented railways and the buildings to accommodate their passengers. The 'station' was an entirely novel concept, without precedent and therefore without any set style, so every mode, from Greek to Gothic, Egyptian to Etruscan, might seem equally fitting as the competing railway companies battled to advertise their superiority by erecting ever more fabulous termini in the nation's capital. Because the railways were built by competitive enterprise, rather than according to a single state plan, London has far more large stations than, say, Rome or Vienna. And because they were built so extravagantly well, many more of them survive in use today. This produces a tension between conservation and convenience, between those who would preserve them as pioneering examples of industrial architecture and those who would modernise them in the interests of a smoother journey to work. In between these conflicting parties stands British Rail, which must balance the competing costs and constraints of preservation and operation.

Whatever the style chosen for a station, two functional requirements had originally to be met – case of access for foot and wheeled traffic and a high roof, to allow steam, smoke and smuts to disperse. With the advent of electrification the latter is no longer needed and so British Rail has been able to begin a programme of radical rejuvenation by selling off the 'air-space' above the platforms of the engine-sheds for commercial redevelopment and use the funds thus generated to refurbish the operational areas at ground level. The 'pure' commuter stations, which suffer the pressures of 'peak-loading' most strongly but are almost dead outside rush-hours – Blackfriars, Holborn Viaduct, Cannon Street and Fenchurch Street – have all been incorporated into office complexes.

London's earliest railway termini all ended well short of the city itself. The London and Southampton line got to Nine Elms (1838) before being extended to Waterloo a decade later, while the London, Brighton and South-Eastern terminated at Bricklayer's Arms, just off the Old Kent Road (a site now available to redevelopment). To advance further into the city centre required expensive and usually time-consuming negotiations for the purchase of land.

The demolition of existing properties required to clear the way to a central location is vividly described in Dickens' 'Dombey and Son', which chronicles the passage of the London and Birmingham Railway through Camden Town: 'The first shock of a great earthquake had ... rent the whole neighbourhood to its centre. Traces of its course were visible on every side. Houses were knocked down; streets broken through and stopped; deep pits and trenches dug in the ground; enormous heaps of earth and clay thrown up ... in short the yet unfinished and unopened Railroad was in progress; and, from the very core of all this dire disorder, trailed smoothly away, upon its mighty course of civilisation and improvement.'

London and Greenwich

Central London's earliest passenger railway was the London and Greenwich (1836) which ran a modest four miles south-east from London Bridge on a viaduct of 878 arches. The viaduct was in itself such a novelty and wonder that the promoters fondly hoped to develop a promenade alongside it and fill its arches with shops and homes. Railway arches were, as it turned out, to fill quite different functions by providing premises for grubby workshops and a sordid refuge for the homeless to lay their heads in. But these railway pioneers were literally aiming at the carriage-trade, providing ramps at their stations so that private horse-drawn vehicles could be loaded straight onto wagons for the ride into the metropolis. Even if they were to be disappointed in this respect they should have been satisfied by the flow of ordinary passengers – six million by 1840.

God's Wonderful Railway

London's railways, and therefore stations, performed two roles – to handle local commuter traffic and to serve as the focus for the national railway system. The directors of the technically-advanced and self-regarding Great Western Railway (GWR – 'God's Wonderful Railway') initially thought so little of commuter traffic that the first station out of Paddington was at West Drayton, 13 miles away. In 1846, a Royal Commission, alarmed at the implications of the prevailing 'Railway Mania', decreed that railways should not be allowed to penetrate to the very heart of London itself, which explains why three of the largest termini lie within a few hundred yards of each other along the Euston Road. It was not until 1884 that the major termini were conveniently linked by underground railways. In the interim the horse-drawn carriage trade benefited immensely from ferrying passengers between the major stations when they needed to change lines. The construction of the recent Thameslink line which cuts out the need even to transfer to the Underground when travelling north–south across the metropolis represents the fulfilment of an old dream. A projected east–west link direct from Paddington to Liverpool Street will make a welcome complement. London's major railway termini developed between 1836 and 1876, with the exception of Blackfriars (originally called St Paul's) (1886) and Marylebone (1889) which opened just in time to provide a convenient service for local resident Sherlock Holmes.

Euston

The first main line terminus, at Euston, (1839) provided the gateway from the capital to the heart of Midlands' manufacturing, Birmingham. (Alternative sites had been considered as far apart as Islington and Marble Arch.) Its most daring feature was a handsome Doric arch by Philip Hardwick whose 72-foot columns were, when it opened, the highest in London. It was hailed as the eighth wonder of the world; its demolition in 1962–3 took place in the face of protests so virulent that they probably helped to save the other historic termini from a similar fate. The modern station, built in a style dubbed by Sir John Betjeman as 'faceless efficient', at least retains on its forecourt a statue of railway pioneer Robert Stephenson. The memory of the arch is mournfully maintained in the name and sign of a pub on the opposite side of the road. Three decades after its demolition the remains of the arch, which had been 'lost' in the interim, were re-discovered – lining the bed of the River Lea. An appeal has since been launched to fund the re-erection of this lost London landmark.

The Euston Arch

King's Cross

Within a few hundred yards of Euston stand two other major termini, both of which rank as Grade I listed buildings.

King's Cross, named in honour of an unlikely monument to commemorate the unloved George IV, stands on the site of the former London Smallpox Hospital. Designed by Lewis Cubitt (1851–2) London's fifth terminus was, when it opened, the largest station in England. Its twin train sheds were originally intended to cater for arrivals and departures respectively. The idea that traffic might be so frequent as to require trains to 'turn around' within a few minutes of their arrival did not apparently occur to the designer who justified his unornamented construction in terms of 'its fitness for its purpose and its characteristic expression of that purpose.' Modern taste accepts this functionalist argument and finds the plain façade of London brick severe but handsome. The central tower fittingly holds a clock made for the Great Exhibition of 1851, which stimulated the first great surge of excursion passengers to use the station.

The 125-acre site behind King's Cross is scheduled for redevelopment in the 1990s, probably in conjunction with a passenger rail link to the Channel Tunnel. Any approved scheme will have to take account of the presence of existing historic buildings (including a group of gasometers) and the Regent's Canal, which transects the site. One proposal envisages complementing the financially essential mixture of homes and offices with a theatre, leisure complex, 25-acre park, a lake and a nature reserve. Whatever the outcome it should prove an interesting counter-poise to the dynamic development of docklands to the east.

St Pancras

Nearby St Pancras station, described by Professor David Piper as a 'great Gothic phantasmagoria' provides a complete contrast to King's Cross. It stands on the site of Agar Town, a shanty settlement so wretched that Dickens called it '. . . an English suburban Connemara . . . The stench of a rainy morning is enough to knock down a bullock.' The station's 689-foot glass and iron train shed was a triumph of Victorian engineering, incorporating what were then the largest single-span arches in the world. To enable trains to cross the Regent's Canal which blocked off the station approach, the platforms were raised 20 feet above the level of the surrounding streets. The resulting space provided cellars for the brewers of Burton-on-Trent to store barrels of beer before they were distributed to London pubs.

Between the St Pancras train shed and the Euston Road stands the fantastic 250-bedroom Midland Grand Hotel (1868–72), shoe-horned into an awkward triangular site. Designed by Sir George Gilbert Scott, it is often said to have incorporated some of his rejected plans for a new Foreign Office building in

Whitehall. in his memoirs the architect observed somewhat immodestly: 'It is often spoken of to me as the finest building in London; my own belief is that it is possibly too good for its purpose.' The hotel's special features included a huge curved dining-room, a palatial staircase and the first ladies smoking-room in London. It was converted to offices in 1935 but is now in process of reconversion – and its striking silhouette endures, uncompromised.

Paddington

Paddington (1850–4), also a Grade I listed building, was designed by Isambard Kingdom Brunel, the foremost engineer of the day and complete creator of the GWR. His elegant iron train shed was inspired by Paxton's Crystal Palace but is thought to surpass its model in sophistication, although it follows the same basic plan of a broad central aisle and two side-aisles. It provides the setting for W.P. Frith's famous narrative painting *The Railway Station*. A statue of Brunel, seated and nonchalantly nursing his famous stove-pipe hat now admires his handiwork and the delicate ornamentation devised by his collaborator, M.D. Wyatt.

Paddington's complementary 100-bedroom hotel, The Great Western, by Philip Hardwick, was, when it opened, the largest in England. The king of Saxony's physician was struck by how that station 'has called into life a completely new and continually increasing district of the town in its immediate neighbourhood.' Unfortunately the very grandeur of the station hotel meant that few passengers could actually afford to patronise it. Cheap lodging-houses proliferated nearby to meet their needs, giving the vicinity a rather seedy aura. Other termini were to suffer a similar fate for the same reason.

Liverpool Street

Liverpool Street station, on the site of Bethlehem Hospital, medieval London's mad-house, has always been the capital's busiest terminus in terms of daily passenger traffic. It incorporates Charles Barry's Great Eastern Hotel (1884), for long the only hotel within the precincts of the City proper. Among the hotel's unusual features were two Masonic temples and sea-water baths topped up daily by fresh supplies brought from the coast. Liverpool Street, like Victoria and Charing Cross but on a far grander scale, has recently benefited from a brilliant programme of refurbishment, blending ultra-modern elements with a pastiche of the original late-Victorian buildings.

Waterloo and Victoria

Waterloo and Victoria stations, which connect with the Channel ports, have less architectural interest, though the entrance to the former is in the form of a grandiose war memorial and the latter retains the associated Grosvenor Hotel

(1860–1) in more or less its original state. These stations are particularly associated with the ceremonial welcoming of visiting heads of state and, more grimly, the transport of troops and casualties to and from France in time of war.

Marylebone

Marylebone scarcely ranks with the great termini and therein lies its historical interest. Built as the terminus of the Great Central, the last main line to reach London, it incorporated a continental loading gauge to enable it to handle traffic from a projected Channel Tunnel. Such glory failed to materialise and it remains a pretty backwater, handling suburban and commuter services to the Chilterns.

The London Underground

The London Underground is the world's oldest subway system. It is also, with New York and Tokyo, one of the world's three largest. Of its more than 250 miles of track some 100 actually run underground, including a 17-mile stretch of the Northern line which is, in effect, the world's longest tunnel. On an average day about 2,500,000 passengers use the Underground, making roughly 750,000,000 per year.

Early Beginnings

The first person to envisage the advantages of an underground railway was Charles Pearson, solicitor to the City Corporation, who proposed a link between King's Cross (now the system's busiest single station) and Farringdon. His proposals would have had the dual advantages of clearing slums in Clerkenwell and creating a new thoroughfare, under which the railway would run, down the valley of the River Fleet. That was in the 1830s, only a year or so after the inauguration of the very first overground railway. But it was not until some 20 years later, when London had acquired major railway termini, that a scheme finally went ahead, linking Paddington with Farringdon via King's Cross. The dogged Pearson was still in on it, however, and persuaded the City Corporation to put up £200,000 towards the required £1,000,000 budget. Sadly he died just four months before the project was completed and opened to traffic.

THE FIRST LINE

Most of this first underground line was constructed under the then 'New Road' (since 1857 known as the Marylebone, Euston and Pentonville Roads), a route which saved the time and expense involved in buying up and demolishing existing properties. The Brunels had pioneered the use of a tunnelling-shield in driving through their Thames Tunnel a generation before (*see p 146*) but there were still no tunnel-boring machines as such, so the 'cut and cover' method was used instead. This involved digging a trench down to the level required for the

278

road-bed, then roofing it over with bricks and replacing the road-surface above that. The King's Cross–Farringdon section ran through an open cutting which is still in use and visible to Circle and Metropolitan line passengers. The best way to see what the stations were like is to get out at platform 6 at Baker Street, which has been restored to more or less its original condition. The opening ceremony for the new railway took place on 9 January 1863. During its first six months it carried an average of 25,000 passengers a day. Trains ran from 6 a.m. to 12 p.m. at intervals varying from 10 to 20 minutes with a two-hour 'church break' on Sunday mornings.

EXTENSIONS

Within a few years this 'Metropolitan' line had been extended westwards to Hammersmith and eastwards to Moorgate, with spur lines to St Pancras and Smithfield meat market. This system was then further extended to make most of what is now the Circle line, linking existing termini with new ones bringing passengers from south of the river to Victoria (1860), Charing Cross (1864) and Cannon Street (1866). Over the next 20 years much of what is now the western section of the District line was built, joining the affluent suburbs of Richmond (1877), Ealing (1879), Putney (1880) and Wimbledon (1889) to the main network. By 1880 another line had been thrust north as far as Harrow and by 1884 the Circle had been completed and Whitechapel linked into it. Another line, completed in 1876, connected New Cross, south of the river, with what is now Liverpool Street, via the Brunels' commercially unsuccessful but technically sound Thames tunnel.

Technical Advances

The next major phase in the development of the system was made possible by two basic technical advances – the perfection of deep-tunnelling techniques and the invention of electric traction. The result was the first real tube, then known as the City and South London Railway, which from 1891 ran from Stockwell to King William Street at the northern end of London Bridge. By 1907 it ran from Clapham Common to Euston.

The Central line, opened in 1900, was the first to be equipped with electric lighting and lifts and the first to link the City with the shopping and theatre districts of the West End. By 1912 it ran from Liverpool Street to Wood Green, just beyond Shepherd's Bush.

The decade before the Great War saw the Metropolitan and District switch over to electrification. Lots Road power station, Chelsea, was built 1903–5 to supply the electricity and when it was completed it was the largest generating station in Europe. On its 'long-distance' route (i.e. out beyond Rickmansworth) the Metropolitan offered a Pullman car service complete with armchairs and a bar. This was all largely the work of a slightly shady American entrepreneur, Charles Tyson Yerkes, who also built the 'Bakerloo' (i.e. Baker Street to Waterloo), the Piccadilly and the western branch of the Northern line. After these were completed in 1906–7 no further underground lines were to be built for another 60 years.

Frank Pick

In 1908 the managers of what was still a network of interconnecting but separate lines agreed to publicise their railways jointly under the umbrella title of 'Underground' and to distribute free maps of the system, a practice continued ever since. Publicity was placed in the hands of Frank Pick, who proved to be a brilliant patron of first-class design in every field from posters to graphics to station architecture. Another significant development was the introduction of the first 'moving staircases' at Earl's Court. Escalators proved so much more efficient than lifts that after 1912 deep-level stations were built with escalators only. During the Great War labour shortages obliged the Underground to take on female staff for the first time. Maida Vale, opened in 1915 as part of a Bakerloo extension, had the unique distinction of an all-female complement. The first Zeppelin raids set a precedent for the blitz, driving panic-stricken civilians to seek safety 'down the tube'.

OUTER SUBURBS

The main development of the network during the inter-war period was the building of further extensions to the system to penetrate the outer suburbs at Edgware, Stanmore, Watford, Finchley and Cockfosters to the north, Morden to the south and Upminster far to the east. Showpiece architectural ventures included the reconstruction of Piccadilly Circus station, Charles Holden's 'Broadway House' headquarters building (*see p 197*) above St James's Park station and Chiltern Court, above Baker Street, which, when it was completed in 1929, was the largest block of flats in Europe and attracted among its first tenants the novelists H.G. Wells and Arnold Bennett. The major organisational change of the period was the establishment in 1933 of the London Passenger Transport Board to bring the entire system under unified control and integrate it with the bus, tram and trolley services. Frank Pick was appointed chief executive. One of his first achievements was to commission the ingenious diagrammatic map of the system which is still in use.

During the Second World War, apart from providing Londoners with shelter from the bombing (*see p 206*) the Underground provided a headquarters for Anti-Aircraft Command at Brompton Road and at its new depot at Aldenham helped to build 700 Halifax bombers. The immediate post-war period saw the extension of the Central line eastwards via Stratford into rural Essex. During the 1950s new aluminium alloy rolling-stock was introduced throughout the system, reducing both energy and maintenance costs because it was lighter, resistant to corrosion and needed no painting.

Victoria Line

Two major new lines have been constructed since 1945. What is now the Victoria line was planned as far back as 1949 to improve travel within the central area and between four of the main termini. By 1971 it not only did this but extended as far as Brixton and Walthamstow, thus linking previously unserved suburban areas into the system as a whole.

Heathrow Extension

In 1977 the Piccadilly line extension to Heathrow was opened, making London the first capital in the world with a direct underground railway link between city and airport. That was also the year of the Queen's jubilee celebrations – by the time the Fleet Line, then under construction between Charing Cross and Stanmore, was opened in 1979 it had been re-named the jubilee line to mark this event.

Docklands Light Railway

Since then the most important route development has been the construction of the Docklands Light Railway which opened in 1987. In 1991 this was extended to link with the Central line at Bank. The network has since been extended eastwards as far as Beckton to embrace newly-built estates and shopping facilities.

Jubilee Line Extension

The construction of the Millennium Dome at Greenwich prompted the construction of a major extension of the Jubilee line, sweeping through south-east London to cross the Thames back to link up with the Central Line at Stratford. Together with the cost of eleven new stations the project absorbed some four billion pounds. Architecturally, at least, it was judged to be money well spent.

Cities of the Dead

By the seventeenth century London had become so densely populated that the small yards around its hundred-odd parish churches were too full to take more burials. Parishes therefore began to establish separate burial grounds around what was then the edge of the built-up area. They remained in use until they, too, became full and a health hazard by the nineteenth century. In many cases the practice of piling one burial on top of another eventually raised the area immediately around churches several feet above the level of nearby streets. Good examples can be seen at St Olave's, Hart Street in the City and St Giles-in-the-Fields, just off the north end of Charing Cross Road. Many graveyards have been built over but others survive as gardens or recreation areas, providing oases of open space in otherwise densely built-up areas. Examples can be found in Benjamin Street, Clerkenwell; Aldermanbury Square, behind Guildhall; Lambeth High Street; 'Postman's Park' by St Botolph's, Aldersgate; Brunswick Square and Tooley Street.

Religions Groups

Some burial grounds were exclusive to particular religious groups. At East Hill in Wandsworth was one for Huguenots; at Queen's Elm, Fulham Road, one for Jews; and at Long Lane, SE1, one for Quakers. The Moravian Brethren had an acre off the King's Road, Chelsea, laid out in the form of a cross, the four quarters being reserved respectively for married men, married women, single men and single women.

The most famous of these sectarian burial grounds is at Bunhill (originally Bonehill) Fields, opposite Wesley's chapel in the City Road. it was first of all used as a repository for bones from the charnel house at St Paul's and pressed into service during the Great Plague of 1665 when it was enclosed with a brick wall and gates. As it was unconsecrated ground, Dissenters were able to bury their dead without using the form of service prescribed in the Book of Common Prayer and it therefore became the Valhalla of nonconformity. Handsome plane trees now shade the remains of John Bunyan, author of The

Pilgrim's Progress, of Wesley's mother, the redoubtable Susannah, of Daniel Defoe, author of *Robinson Crusoe*, of the poet-engraver William Blake (*see p 128*) and of 120,000 others.

CHOLERA EPIDEMIC

The cholera epidemic of 1832 brought a chronic situation to crisis point and pushed parliament to authorise the establishment of large new cemeteries which, like their seventeenth- and eighteenth-century forerunners, were to be outside the then built-up areas of London. It was required that they should be not only enclosed (with full security against grave-robbers) but also landscaped and properly drained.

New Cemeteries

The first of the new cemeteries was at Kensal Green (1833). it boasted a Doric arch entrance (housing the management offices), gravelled roads, a chapel in the 'Greek Revival' style and 800 specially planted trees. The burials of the Duke of Sussex and of Princess Sophia, both offspring of George III, confirmed the social acceptability of these 'gardens for the – deceased'. Other distinguished burials here include those of the Brunels, father and son (*see p 146*), of Leigh Hunt (*see p 129*) and of the novelists Thackeray, Trollope and Wilkie Collins.

WEST NORWOOD

West Norwood Cemetery, SE27 was also laid out as an English landscaped garden, with chapels in Perpendicular Gothic set at the top of sloping lawns and a special section, with a Greek Revival chapel, reserved for the Greek community. The occupants include Mrs Beeton, author of the classic *Book of Household Management*, Dr William Marsden, founder of the Royal Free Hospital, and Sir Henry Tate, sugar magnate and donor of the gallery which bears his name.

HIGHGATE

Highgate Cemetery was hugely successful – and a tourist attraction – from the start. Luxuriantly planted around an existing cedar of Lebanon, with catacombs in the Egyptian manner, it also incorporated such hi-tech features as hydraulic lifts and a tunnel connecting its eastern and western sections. Highgate's famous dead are nothing if not diverse – bare-knuckle pugilist Tom Sayers, scientist Michael Faraday, novelist George Eliot, poet Christina Rossetti, dog-show founder Charles Cruft, bookseller William Foyle and storekeeper Peter Robinson. The lowering monument of Karl Marx was for decades an object of pilgrimage for communists.

BROMPTON

Brompton Cemetery, SW10 was a private enterprise venture which foundered and was bought out by the General Board of Health in 1852 to become the first London cemetery under municipal control. it was soon full.

MANOR PARK

The largest municipal cemetery in Europe is the one opened by the City Corporation at Manor Park E12 in 1856. It has nine miles of roads and has accepted over half-a-million interments, including those whose remains were reburied when the churchyards of such City churches as St Mary, Aldermanbury and St Mary, Somerset were cleared during the Victorian period and hundreds were removed from beneath St Mary Woolnoth to make way for the booking-hall of Bank Underground station.

GOLDERS GREEN

By the end of the nineteenth century cremation had become socially acceptable enough to warrant the opening of a specialised crematorium at Golders Green in 1902. Among the quarter-of-a-million who have since been cremated there are Sir Henry Irving (*see p 177*), W.S. Gilbert, ballerina Anna Pavlova, Rudyard Kipling, Sigmund Freud, Stanley Baldwin, George Bernard Shaw, Sir Alexander Fleming (*see p 198*) and T.S. Eliot (*see p 7*).

Jewish Community

At Pound Lane, Willesden NW10 a special cemetery was set aside for London's Jewish community. Buried here are members of the de Rothschild family, the financier Charles Clore and Sir Jack Cohen, founder of the Tesco supermarket chain.

Pets Cemetery

London's most unusual cemetery lies in a garden behind Victoria Lodge in the north-east corner of Kensington Gardens. In 1880 the Duke of Cambridge's pet dog was run over in the road nearby and buried here. Since then over 200 other pets have joined it.

London Museums and Galleries[1]

A member of Roman London's élite might have found the idea of a public museum slightly bizarre, but he would have been quite familiar with the idea that over his lifetime a gentleman of wealth and taste might accumulate a personal collection of antiquities, *objets d'art*, natural specimens and intriguing curios to be enjoyed through contemplation, display or discussion with cultured friends. It was just such a collection, that of royal physician Sir Hans Sloane (1660–1753) which formed the nucleus of the first museum in London to be founded as such – the British Museum.

Sloane's long career included travel to the tropics, the society of learned men and professional success at the highest level. After his death his will offered parliament the chance to buy his unique collection of 80,000 objects at a fraction of its true value, the purchase sum going to provide an income for his daughters. The projected museum opened in Montagu House, Bloomsbury (bought and refurbished from the profits of a public lottery) but 'opened' in only a limited sense because visitors had to make prior application in writing and were admitted in groups of not more than five. Not until 1879 was unrestricted access to the galleries permitted, by which time the number of exhibits had been vastly enlarged by gifts from distinguished individuals such as Captain Cook, David Garrick, Sir Joseph Banks and Sir Stamford Raffles and by donations of entire collections from institutions like the Bank of England, the Royal Society and the East India Company.

The expansion of the museum's holdings necessitated the demolition of Montagu House and its replacement by an imposing neo-classical building (1823–47) whose courtyard was subsequently covered by a huge dome to make a reading room which would be used by Carlyle, Marx, Shaw and Lenin.

Now covering over 13 acres, the 'BM' employs some 1,200 staff and receives over six million visitors a year, making it Britain's top indoor attraction. The treasures of the current collection (four million objects, excluding prints and

[1] For addresses, telephone numbers and opening times see *The London Guide* published annually by Time Out/Penguin.

drawings) include Egyptian mummies, the Parthenon (Elgin) marbles, the Rosetta Stone and the blue and white blown-glass Portland Vase. Twentieth-century acquisitions include the Sutton Hoo burial regalia of a Saxon king, the Mildenhall hoard of Roman silver and the naturally mummified remains of a noble victim of Celtic ritual sacrifice, known as Lindow Man. Sloane's weatherbeaten statue (by Rysbrack) now stands just inside the entrance to the museum; a resin copy has replaced it in its original location, the Chelsea Physic Garden.

The BM's natural history collection has formed a separate museum in its own right at the **Natural History Museum**, South Kensington since 1881 in a remarkable Romanesque building by Alfred Waterhouse. The Department of Printed Books and Manuscripts became part of the **British Library** in 1973 and has moved to its new building beside St Pancras station. As the collection grows by enough to fill two miles of shelves a year such a move could scarcely be avoided.

The V & A

The only rival to the British Museum in scale is the Victoria and Albert Museum, which houses the largest decorative arts collection in the world. Founded with profits from the Great Exhibition of 1851, it was intended by its first director, Sir Henry Cole (1808–82) 'to assemble a splendid collection of objects representing the application of Fine Art to manufactures'; but the 'applied' objects were soon joined by purely 'fine' ones, like the bequest of Yorkshire businessman, John Sheepshanks, whose gift included paintings by Etty, Landseer and Constable. The museum soon became, in the words of former director, Sir Roy Strong, 'an extremely capacious handbag.'

The present V&A building (by Sir Aston Webb 1899–1909) now houses in its 145 galleries major collections of British paintings, sculptures, portrait miniatures, historic costumes, musical instruments, wallpaper and English furniture. It also claims to have the most comprehensive collection of jewellery in the world and the best exhibition of Indian art outside India itself. Individual objects range from the gorgeously embroidered thirteenth-century Syon Cope, to a mechanical tiger, the solid jade drinking-cup of the builder of the Taj Mahal and the Great Bed of Ware, a Tudor tourist attraction mentioned in *Twelfth Night* and said to have been capable of accommodating 26 butchers and their wives at once.

Out-stations of the V&A include the **Theatre Museum** in Covent Garden, the **Bethnal Green Museum of Childhood**, with its special collections of dolls, toys and games and, in west London, **Ham House**, with its perfectly-preserved seventeenth-century furnishings and **Osterley Park**, with its superb Adam interiors. The V&A also originally housed the contents of its neighbour, the **Science Museum**, which became a separate entity in 1909. 'Pure' history, in which the raw materials are considered more significant than any specific theme or event might be regarded as the province of the **Public Record Office Museum** in Chancery Lane.

London has more than two hundred other museums to entice and inform the visitor:

WARFARE

The brilliantly refurbished **Imperial War Museum** (Lambeth Rd, SE1) is housed in the former Bethlehem Royal Hospital, a mental asylum completed in 1815. Its unromantic treatment of twentieth-century warfare gives full measure to the civilian side of conflict. Apart from a skilful utilisation of audio-visual presentations it also houses the second largest collection of twentieth-century British art in London, as well as such individual items as the 1945 German instrument of surrender, Lawrence of Arabia's rifle, the engine from the 'Red Baron's' fighter and the smallest boat to have taken part in the 1940 evacuation from Dunkirk. The Imperial War Museum is also responsible for HMS *Belfast*, a 10,500-ton cruiser which saw action during the Arctic convoys, on D-Day and in Korea. Its guns could, from its present mooring opposite the Tower, bombard Hampton Court Palace, 14 miles upstream.

The focus of the **National Army Museum** (Royal Hospital Road, Chelsea) is more restricted in scope but covers a longer time-scale, from Tudor times to the Gulf War. It is particularly strong on military uniforms, medals and hand-held weapons. Regimental museums include those of the **Guards Division** (Wellington Barracks, Birdcage Walk, SW1) and of London's own regiment, the **Royal Fusiliers** (Tower of London). **The Royal Air Force Museum** is housed at Hendon in north-west London, while much naval history is encompassed by the **National Maritime Museum** (Greenwich), though its overall scope is broader.

ART

The major galleries in London are the **National Gallery** (Trafalgar Square) which is primarily of European art from Giotto to the twentieth century; around the corner is the **National Portrait Gallery** showing likenesses of the great and the good. By the river on Millbank is the **Tate Gallery** housing British art and, in particular, **The Turner Collection**. Downstream **Tate Modern**, housed in Sir Giles Gilbert Scott's former (1963) Bankside Power Station, focuses on the modern (since 1900) and contemporary scene. **The Wallace Collection** (Manchester Sq. W1) has a world-class display of eighteenth-century French furniture and objets d'art and European armour, as well as paintings by Rubens, Rembrandt, Titian and Watteau, though its best-known exhibit is probably Franz Hals' *Laughing Cavalier*. The **Courtauld Institute** (Somerset House, Strand) is renowned for its Italian and Dutch Old Masters and French Impressionists. The **Percival David Foundation of**

The huge halls of the Tate Modern

Chinese Art (53 Gordon Sq., WC1) houses 1,500 Chinese ceramics which any emperor would have been proud to own. **Fenton House** (Hampstead Grove, NW3) and **Ranger's House** (Greenwich Park) both hold important collections of historic musical instruments as well as paintings and furniture. Other worthwhile collections are to be seen at beautiful **Kenwood House** (Hampstead Lane NW3), **Sir John Soane's House** (Lincoln's Inn Fields, WC1), the **Thomas Coram Foundation** (40 Brunswick Sq, WC1) and the **Dulwich Picture Gallery** in south-east London.

TECHNOLOGY

There is no technology museum as such, though the **Science Museum's** brief does include industry and medicine and other aspects are dealt with by its neighbour, the **Geological Museum**. Others that could be considered to fall broadly within this category include the new **Design Museum** (Butler's Wharf, SE1), the **Museum of the Moving Image** (i.e. cinema and television) at the South Bank Arts Centre, the **Heritage Motor Museum** (Syon Park, Middx), the **Guildhall Clock Museum**, the **Kew Bridge Steam Museum** (Brentford, Middx), the **Vintage Wireless Museum** (23 Rosendale Rd, SE21) and the **London Transport Museum** in Covent Garden. For real steam trains one must go on a Sunday to the **London Toy and Model Museum** (21/3 Craven Hill Rd W2) which also houses Europe's best collection of model trains.

INDIVIDUALS

Literature provides the largest category of museums devoted to individuals. The house in which **Dr Samuel Johnson** compiled his famous dictionary can still be visited (Gough Sq. off Fleet St.), as can the house in whose garden **John Keats** composed his 'Ode to a Nightingale' (Keats Grove, Hampstead NW3). **Thomas**

Carlyle's house (24 Cheyne Row, Chelsea) is very much as he left it, with his hat still hanging on its peg, while **Dickens'** house (48 Doughty St. WC1) has a basement fitted out like the kitchen at Dingley Dell in *Pickwick Papers*. Memorabilia relating to the diarist **Samuel Pepys** can be seen in Prince Henry's Room (17 Fleet St.) the oldest (1610) surviving domestic dwelling in the City, with an original timbered façade and exuberant plasterwork ceiling. The **Soseki Museum** at Clapham records the London sojourn of Japan's foremost modern novelist, while the **William Morris Gallery** at Walthamstow, E17 celebrates a major designer who was in his own day even more famed as a poet.

Other museums devoted to individuals include those relating to **Sigmund Freud** (20 Maresfield Gardens NW3), the **Duke of Wellington** (Apsley House, Hyde Park Corner), **Baden-Powell**, founder of the Boy Scout movement (Queen's Gate, SW7), **Florence Nightingale** (St Thomas's Hospital, SE1), **Charles Darwin** (Orpington, Kent) and **Linley Sambourne House** (18 Stafford Tee, W8) the well-furnished mid-Victorian (1868–74) home of a well-to-do political cartoonist.

SPECIALIST

Museums with a special focus include the **Bank of England Museum** (money and banking) at Bank junction, the **Museum of Garden History**, by Lambeth Palace gateway, the **National Postal Museum** in King Edward St EC1, the **Geffrye Museum** (domestic interiors) at Kingsland Rd E2, the **Fan Museum** (10–12 Crooms Hill, Greenwich), the **Jewish Museum** (129/131 Albert St), the **Museum of Methodism** (49 City Road, EC1) and **Freemason's Hall** in Great Queen St, WC2.

LONDON

The story of the capital as a whole is the special concern of the **Museum of London** (London Wall EC2). There are museums dealing with the local history of particular districts throughout the suburbs, such as the **Bruce Castle Museum** (Lordship Lane N17), **Church Farm House Museum** (Greyhound Hill NW4), **Forty Hall Museum** (Enfield) **Gunnersbury Park Museum**, W3 and the **Passmore Edwards' Museum** at Stratford.

The London Year

January (last Sunday)	Commemoration of Charles I, Charing Cross
	International Boat Show
	January sales
February/March	Chinese New Year
March/April	Oxford v Cambridge University Boat Race
	Ideal Home Exhibition, Earl's Court
April	London Marathon
Easter Sunday	Easter Parade, Battersea Park
May	Punch & Judy Festival, Covent Garden (also Sept/Oct)
	Chelsea Flower Show
	Beating the Bounds, All Hallows by the Tower
	Lilies & Roses Ceremony, Tower of London
	Oak Apple Day, Royal Hospital, Chelsea
June	Greenwich Festival
June (second Saturday)	Trooping the Colour, Horse Guards Parade
June/July	Wimbledon
June/August	Royal Academy Summer Exhibition
July	City of London Festival
	Doggett's Coat and Badge Rowing race, London Bridge – Chelsea
	Royal Tournament, Earl's Court
July/September	Promenade Concerts, Albert Hall
August	Notting Hill Carnival
	International Street Performers Festival, Covent Garden
October (first Sunday)	Pearly Kings & Queens Harvest Festival Service St Martin-in-the-Fields
November	London to Brighton Veteran Car run
	Lord Mayor's Show, Mansion House (second Saturday)
	Remembrance Sunday, Cenotaph (second Sunday)

December

State Opening of Parliament
Christmas lights, Regent Street
Christmas tree, Trafalgar Square
Royal Smithfield Show
World Travel Market
National Cat Club Show
New Year's Eve, Trafalgar Square

DOMINE DIRIGE NOS

Further Reading

Reference and General

P. ACKROYD – *London: The Biography* (Chatto & Windus 2000)

P. BAILEY – *The Oxford Book of London* (Oxford University Press 1995)

F.R. BANKS – *The New Penguin Guide to London* (Penguin 1958 & later eds.)

F. BARKER & P. JACKSON – *The History of London in Maps* (Barrie & Jenkins 1990)

F. BARKER & P. JACKSON – *London: 2000 Years of a City & its People* (Papermac 1983)

G. BEBBINGTON – *Street Names of London* (Batsford 1972)

M. BILLINGS – *London: A Companion to its History and Archaeology* (Kyle Cathie 1994)

J. BLACKWOOD – *London's Immortals: The Complete Outdoor Commemorative Statues* (Savoy Press 1989)

A. BYRON – *London's Statues* (Constable 1981)

R. CLAYTON – *Portrait of London* (Hale 1980)

H. CLOUT – *The Times London History Atlas* (Times/Harper Collins 1991, 1997)

J. FIELD – *Place-Names of Greater London* (Batsford 1980)

ED GLINERT – *A Literary Guide to London* (Penguin 2000)

R. GRAY – *A History of London* (Hutchinson 1978)

C. HIBBERT – *London: The Biography of a City* (Longmans 1969)

S. INWOOD – *A History of London* (Macmillan 1998)

W.E. JACKSON – *Achievement: A Short History of the LCC* (Longmans 1965)

A.D. KING – *Global Cities: post-imperialism and the internationalisation of London* (Routledge 1990)

M. LEAPMAN (ed.) – *The Book of London* (Weidenfeld & Nicolson 1989)

M. LEAPMAN – *London's River: A History of the Thames* (Pavilion 1991)

A. MITFORD – *Lord Mayors of London* (Comerford & Miller 1989)

P. MURPHY – *The Guinness Guide to Superlative London* (Guinness Books 1989)

L. NICHOLSON – *London: Louise Nicholson's Definitive Guide* (Bodley Head 1988)

R. PORTER – *London: A Social History* (Hamish Hamilton 1994)

J. RICHARDSON – *London and Its People* (Barrie and Jenkins 1995)

A. Saint and G. Darley – *The Chronicles of London* (Weidenfeld and Nicholson 1994)

F. Sheppard – *London: A History* (OUP 2000)

G. Weightman – *London River: The Thames Story* (Collins & Brown 1990)

B. Weinreb & C. Hibbert – *The London Encyclopaedia* (Macmillan 1983)

A.N. Wilson – *The Faber Book of London* (Faber & Faber 1993)

Architecture & Environment

K. Allinson and V. Thornton – *A Guide to London's Contemporary Architecture* (Butterworth 1993)

C. Amery – *Wren's London* (Lennard 1988)

F. Barker & R. Hyde – *London as it might have been* (John Murray 1982)

T.C. Barker & L.M. Robbins – *A History of London Transport* (Allen & Unwin 1975–6)

J. Betjeman – *London's Historic Railway Stations* (John Murray 1972)

M. Blatch – *A Guide to London's Churches* (Constable 2nd ed. 1995)

P. Brimblecombe – *The Big Smoke: A history of air pollution in London since medieval times* (Methuen 1987)

A. Clayton – *Subterranean City* (Phillimore 2000)

A. Crowe – *The Parks & Woodlands of London* (Fourth Estate 1987)

W.R. Dalzell – *The Shell Guide to the History of London* (Michael Joseph 1981)

R.S.R. Fitter – *London's Natural History* (Collins 1945/Bloomsbury 1990)

D. Friend – *Wheels of London: Four Centuries of Commuter Travel* (Comerford & Miller 1989)

M. Galinou – *London's Pride: The Glorious History of the Capital's Gardens* (Anaya Publishing 1990)

O.E. Green – *The London Underground: An Illustrated History* (Ian Allan 1987)

E. Harwood and A. Saint – *Exploring England's Heritage: London* (English Heritage/HMSO 1991)

R. Hawkins – *Green London: A Handbook* (Sidgwick & Jackson 1987)

M. Jenner – *London Heritage: The Changing Style of a City* (Michael Joseph 1988)

D.J. Olsen – *Town Planning in London: The 18th & 19th Centuries* (2nd ed. Yale U.P. 1982)

N. Pevsner – *The Buildings of England: London I. The Cities of London & Westminster London 2: Except the Cities of London & Westminster* (Penguin 3rd ed. 1973)

A. Saunders – *The Art & Architecture of London: An Illustrated Guide* (Phaidon/Oxford 2nd ed. 1988)

A. Service – *The Architects of London & their buildings from 1066 to the present day* (The Architectural Press 1979)

R. Trench & E. Hillman – *London under London: a subterranean guide* (John Murray 1984)

C. Turner – *London Churches Step by Step* (Faber & Faber 1987)
M. Warner – *The Image of London: Views by Travellers & Emigrés* 1550–1920
   (Trefoil Publications/Barbican Art Gallery 1987)
J.T. White – *Country London* (Routledge & Kegan Paul 1984)
S. Williams – *Docklands* (Phaidon 1996)
E. & W. Young – *London's Churches* (Grafton Books 1986)

Periods

A.L. Beier & R. Finlay (eds.) – *London 1500:1700 The Making of the Metropolis*
   (Longman 1986)
C. Brooke & G. Keir – *London 800–1216: the shaping of a city* (Secker &
   Warburg 1975)
J. Clark – *Saxon & Norman London* (HMSO 1975)
W.J. Fishman – *East End 1888* (Duckworth 1988)
C. Fitzgibbon – *The Blitz* (Macdonald 1970)
P. Glanville – *Tudor London* (Museum of London 1979)
I. Grant & N. Maddren – *The City at War* (Jupiter 1975)
B. Hobley – *Roman & Saxon London: A Reappraisal* (Museum of London
   1986)
J. Hall & R. Merrifield – *Roman London* (Museum of London 1986)
S. Humphries & J. Taylor – *The Making of Modern London 1945–85* (Sidgwick
   & Jackson 1986)
N. Johnson – *Eighteenth Century London* (Museum of London 1991)
J. Mack & S. Humphries – *The Making of Modern London 1939–45: London at
   War* (Sidgwick & Jackson 1985)
G. Milne – *The Great Fire of London* (Historical Publications 1986)
J. Morris – *Londinium* (Phoenix Press 1999)
D.J. Olsen – *The Growth of Victorian London* (Batsford 1976)
L. Picard – *Restoration London* (Phoenix Press 1998)
L. Picard – *Dr Johnson's London* (Weidenfeld 2000)
G. Rude – *Hanovarian London 1714–1808* (Secker & Warburg 1971)
J. Schneer – *London 1900* (Yale U.P. 2001)
F. Sheppard – *London 1808–1870: the infernal wen* (Secker & Warburg 1971)
J. Summerson – *Georgian London* (Penguin 1978)
A. Vince – *Saxon London: an archaeological investigation* (Batsford 1990)
M. Waller – *1700: Scenes from London Life* (Sceptre 2001)
G. Weightman & S. Humphries – *The Making of Modern London 1914–39*
   (Sidgwick & Jackson 1984)
G. Weightman & S. Humphries – *The Making of Modern London 1815–1914*
   (Sidgwick & Jackson 1983)
J. White – *Rothschild Buildings: life in an East End tenement block 1887–1920*
   (Routledge & Kegan Paul 1980)

Places

F. ATKINSON – *St Paul's & the City* – (Michael Joseph 1985)

N. BAILEY – *Fitzrovia* (Historical Publications 1981)

P. BEAVER – *The Crystal Palace* (Phillimore 1986)

M.C. BORER – *The Story of Covent Garden* (Hale 1984)

R. BOSTON – *The Essential Fleet St.: Its History & Influence* (Blandford 1990)

A. BRIGGS & A. MACARTNEY – *Toynbee Hall* (Routledge & Kegan Paul 1984)

S. BROWNHILL – *Developing London's Docklands* (Paul Chapman 1990)

E. CARPENTER & D. GENTLEMAN – *Westminster Abbey* (Weidenfeld & Nicolson 1987)

R. CHAMBERLIN – *The Tower of London: An Illustrated History* (Webb & Bower/ Michael Joseph 1989)

J. CHARLTON (ed.) – *The Tower of London: its Buildings & Institutions* (HMSO 1978)

RICHARD CHURCH – *London's Royal Parks: An Appreciation* (HMSO 1993)

A. FIDDES – *The City of London: The Historic Square Mile* (Pevensey Press 1984)

W.J. FISHMAN, N. BREACH & J.M. HALL – *East End & the Docklands* (Duckworth 1990)

D. FORREST – *St James's Square* (Quiller Press 1986)

A. FORSHAW & T. BERGSTROM – *Smithfield: past and present* (Hale 1990)

J. GLASHEEN – *St James's* (Phillimore 1987)

H. GODFREY – *Tower Bridge* (John Murray 1988)

W. GRYNBERG – *The Square Mile: The City of London in Historic Postcards* (Windrush Press 1995)

H. HOBHOUSE – *A History of Regent Street* (Macdonald & Janes 1975)

M. HUNTER & R. THORNE – *Change at King's Cross* (Historical Publications 1990)

C. KERRIGAN – *A History of Tower Hamlets* (London Borough of Tower Hamlets 1982)

C. MANTON & J. EDWARDS – *Bygone Billingsgate* (Phillimore 1989)

S.K. Al NAIB – *London's Dockland: past, present and future* (Thames & Hudson 1990)

G. O'NEILL – *My East End: Memories of Life in Cockney London* (Penguin 1999)

A. PALMER – *The East End* (John Murray 2000)

PAT PIERCE – *London's Royal Parks Souvenir Guide* (The Royal Parks 1993)

J. PUDNEY – *London's Docks* (Thames & Hudson 1975)

J. RICHARDSON – *Covent Garden* (Historical Publications 1979)

A. SAUNDERS – *Regent's Park* (David & Charles 1969)

J. SUMMERS – *Soho: A History of London's Most Colourful Neighbourhood* (Bloomsbury 1989)

R. TAMES – *Bloomsbury Past* (Historical Publications 1993)

R. TAMES – *Clerkenwell and Finsbury Past* (Historical Publications 1999)

R. TAMES – *Earl's Court and Brompton Past* (Historical Publications 2000)

R. TAMES – *Southwark Past* (Historical Publications 2001)

R. TAMES – *The City of London Past* (Historical Publications 1995)

R. TAMES – *Soho Past* (Historical Publications 1994)

R. TAMES – *Dulwich and Camberwell Past* (Historical Publications 1997)

R. TAMES – *St. John's Wood and Maida Vale Past* (Historical Publications 1998)

LUCY TRENCH – *Buildings and Monuments in the Royal Parks* (The Royal Parks 1997)

F.M.L. THOMPSON – *Hampstead: building a borough 1650–1964* (Routledge & Kegan Paul 1974)

A. WALKER – *Kensington & Chelsea: a social & architectural history* (John Murray 1987)

G. WEIGHTMAN – *London River: The Thames Story* (Collins & Brown 1990)

People

P. ACKROYD – *Dickens's London: an imaginative vision* (Headline 1987)

F. BARKER & D. SILVESTER-CARR – *The Black Plaque Guide to London* (Constable 1987)

K. CARTER – *London & the Famous* (F. Muller 1982)

J. CLARKE – *In Our Grandmother's Footsteps* (Virago Press 1984)

A. DAVIES – *Literary London* (Macmillan 1988)

C. FOX – *Londoners* (Thames & Hudson 1987)

P. GIBSON – *The Capital Companion: A Street-by-Street Guide to London & its Inhabitants* (Webb & Bower/Michael Joseph 1988)

M. HALL – *The Blue Plaque Guide to London Homes* (Queen Anne Press 1976)

P. KITCHEN – *Poets' London* (Longman 1980)

Y. MARKINO – *A Japanese Artist in London* (In Print 1991)

L.M. PALIS – *The Blue Plaques of London* (Equation 1989)

F.M.L. THOMPSON (ed.) – *The University of London & the World of Learning 1836–1986* (Hambledon Press 1990)

M. WYNN JONES – *George Cruikshank: His Life & London* (Macmillan 1978)

Walks

P. BEGG – *City Walks of London* (Robson Books 1990)

T. DANEFF – *London Walks: 40 Walks in and around the city* (Michael Joseph 1989)

T.T. DANIELL – *London on Thames: An English Heritage. Upstream – from Westminster to Windsor* (Third Millennium Leisure Ltd 1988)

A. DUNCAN – *Walking London* (New Holland 1991)

A. DUNCAN – *Secret London* (New Holland 1995)

B. FAIRFAX – *Walking London's Waterways* (David & Charles 1985)

K. FLUDE & P. HERBERT – *Citisights Guide to London: Ten Walks Through London's Past* (Virgin 1990)

G. FLETCHER – *London: A Private View* (Cassell 1990)

G. FLETCHER – *The London Nobody Knows* (Hutchinson 1962)

F. HAZELTON – *London's American Past: A Guided Tour* (Papermac 1991)

R. HUDSON – *Bloomsbury & Soho* (The London Guides: Haggerston Press 1996)

R. HUDSON – *Fleet St., Holborn & the Inns of Court* (The London Guides: Haggerston Press 1995)

J. KIEK – *Everybody's Historic London: A History & Guide* (Quiller Press 1984)

M. MASON AND M. SANDERS – *The City Companion* (Robert Hale 1994)

B. MORSE – *Square Mile Walks: Six Walks in the City of London* (Historical Publications 1989)

I. NORRIE & D. BOHM – *Walks Around London: A Celebration of the Capital* (André Deutsch 1984)

JAMES PAGE-ROBERTS – *Dockland Buildings Old and New: A personal anecdotal and historical guide* (The Mudlark Press 1998)

C. PEPPER – *Walks in Oscar Wilde's London* (Gibbs Smith 1992)

D. PIPER – *London: An Illustrated Companion Guide* (Collins 1964–1980)

RICHARD TAMES – *American Walks in London* (Windrush Press 1997)

G. WILLIAMS – *Guide to Literary London* (Batsford 1973)

J. WITTICH – *Explorer's London* (Morning Mist Publications 1995)

Themes

R. BERKELEY – *A Spy's London* (Leo Cooper 1994)

E. HALLGARTEN AND L. COLLISTER – *The Gourmet's Guide to London* (Vermilion 1992)

HANDBOOK GUIDE – *Rock & Pop London* (Handbook Publishing 1991)

B. LANE – *The Murder Club Guide to London* (Harrap 1988)

E. LEE – *Musical London* (Omnibus Press 1995)

J. LINFORD – *Food Lovers' London* (Metro Publications 1995)

K. MANN – *London: The German Connection* (KT Publishing 1993)

I. MCAULEY – *Guide to Ethnic London* (Immel Publishing 1993)

N. MERRIMAN (ed.) – *The Peopling of London* (Museum of London 1993)

D. AND S. ROSEN – *London Science* (Prion 1994)

P. SCHREUDERS, M. LEWISOHN, A. SMITH – *Beatles' London* (Hamlyn 1994)

G. WEIGHTMAN – *Bright Lights, Big City: London Entertained 1830–1950* (Collins & Brown 1992)

Index